THE SOCIALIST NOVEL IN BRITAIN

The Socialist Novel in Britain:

Towards the Recovery of a Tradition

Edited by

H. Gustav Klaus

Senior Lecturer in English,
University of Osnabrück

THE HARVESTER PRESS

First published in Great Britain in 1982 by
THE HARVESTER PRESS LIMITED
Publisher: John Spiers
16 Ship Street, Brighton, Sussex

© The Harvester Press, 1982

British Library Cataloguing in Publication Data
The socialist novel in Britain.
  1. English fiction—19th century—History
and criticism
  2. English fiction—20th century—History
and criticism
  3. Socialism in Literature
  I. Klaus, H. Gustav
  823′.8   PR830.S6

  ISBN 0-7108-0340-0

Typeset in 10/11pt Times Roman by
Rowland Phototypesetting Limited, Bury St Edmunds, Suffolk.
Printed in Great Britain by
Mansell Limited, Witham, Essex.

CONTENTS

CONTRIBUTORS

John Goode is Reader in English at the University of Warwick. He has written numerous articles on late nineteenth-century fiction and lately published *George Gissing: Fiction and Ideology* (1978).

H. Gustav Klaus taught at the Universities of Marburg and Warwick. Since 1977 he has held (untenured) the Chair of English Literature at the University of Osnabrück. He is an editor of *Gulliver—German-English Yearbook* and author of *Caudwell im Kontext* (1978).

Ramón López Ortega is Professor of English at the University of Extremadura (Cáceres). His publications include *Movimiento obrero y novela inglesa* (1976) and *English Literature and the Working Class* (co-editor, 1980).

Jack Mitchell is Senior Lecturer in English at the Humboldt University of Berlin (GDR). He is the author of *Robert Tressell and The Ragged Trousered Philanthropists* (1969) and of several articles on socialist literature.

J. M. Rignall studied at the Universities of Cambridge and Sussex. After teaching for two years at the University of Bonn, he has been since 1971 a lecturer in the Department of English and Comparative Literary Studies at the University of Warwick.

Ingrid von Rosenberg was for seven years an assistant lecturer at the Free University of Berlin and the Technical University of Braunschweig. She is now in the English Language Department at the University of Duisburg. Her study *Der Weg nach oben: Englische Arbeiterromane 1945–78* was published in 1980.

Kiernan Ryan has taught at Cambridge and at the universities of Geneva and Oxford and is now Fellow and Lecturer in English at New Hall, Cambridge. He is currently completing a book on *Literature and Folly: The Renaissance and the Literary Revolution.*

Martha Vicinus is Associate Professor in the Department of English, Indiana University (Bloomington). She is the editor of *Victorian Studies* and author of *The Industrial Muse* (1974).

Raymond Williams is Professor of Drama and Fellow of Jesus College, Cambridge. His most recent publications are *Problems in Materialism and Culture* (1980) and *Culture* (1981).

INTRODUCTION

A difficulty in writing this introduction arises from my position as a student of English literature and culture in a central European institution, which at once permits and obliges me to bear several kinds of readers in mind: those with a purely academic interest in the subject and those who are actively engaged in political work; those who only have access to socialist fiction in the English language and those who bring in knowledge of other socialist literatures; those who live and teach in the countries of Eastern Europe and those who fight for socialism in the West, and indeed the various rival factions within this latter spectrum.

It is partly, then, an acquaintance with too many different discourses which prompts me to cut short what is really a long and twisted terminological debate around that triad of terms: 'proletarian', 'working class', 'socialist'. Of these the once current 'proletarian' is, internationally, on the retreat, while the competing concepts of 'working class' and 'socialist' continue to command about equal adherence. Their co-habitation, both in the general discussion and in this book, seems to me less a matter of confusion than an indication of the ambivalent and multi-layered character of much of the material itself.

If 'working-class novel' can be said to denote the fiction produced by worker-writers (authors still in the production process) or writers with a working-class background, depicting the life of their class, this basic definition yields two criteria: social class and subject-matter. Both are relevant but insufficient, because such a definition still leaves us uninformed about the intention and perspetive of the works in question. There may be novels fulfilling both requirements, that is, being written *by* working men or women and *about* the living and working conditions of their community, and yet such works may actually endorse the subordinated condition of the working class. Therefore in addition to the sociological and thematic criteria we need an ideological correlate which is of primary importance. It is this aspect of works which the term 'socialist' seeks to comprehend. A socialist novel, by being written in the historical interests of the working class, reveals a standpoint consistent with that of the class-conscious sections of this class.[1] The latter definition leaves room for the work of socialist intellectuals, irrespective of subject-matter, to be considered here (see, for instance, chapter 9 by Kiernan Ryan).

A major purpose of the present book is to question and rectify existing notions about the socialist novel. Amidst the general haziness of these notions there is one that recurs with singular stubbornness. It is, briefly, the assumption that, because the novel is genetically tied to the rise and history of the middle class, it remains once and for all a thoroughly bourgeois genre pervaded by a liberal ideology which it can never hope to expunge. 'Thank God', the liberal-minded critic will be inclined to add; 'unfortunately', one condescending species of left-wing critic will comment. That a fair number of Marxist-influenced critics have joined in the chorus which decries the socialist novel as stillborn is a fact, but one which only goes to show how firmly they have remained within the mould of the dominant critical ideology.

One way of countering this objection is to point to recent findings in the field of cultural studies, which draw a distinction between the given material and the cultural practice through which the former is appropriated, re-worked, re-cycled. The meaning of this cultural practice is very unlikely to be identical with the meaning attached to the material by its original producers or practitioners. Transposed to the novel form, or individual elements of it, the implications are not dissimilar. A form available at any given historical moment, and what an author with his or her individual project makes of it, can be two quite different things. In saying this I am not denying the ideological 'contamination' of specific structural components of a genre nor overlooking the possibility that the meaning of such a structural element may outlive its original period. Form, whether as narrative mode or technical device is doubtless a carrier of ideology. However, form is not the only (ideological) constituent of a text, and it is, above all, not some kind of cosmic, transhistorical category immune to change. Hence to accord an ultimate determinant effect, or even priority, to inherited forms is an abstract and constricting conception leading to formalism in the denigratory sense of the term.

In any case, an actual reading of socialist novels will show that it was not the concern of writers merely to pump revolutionary content into conventional or even outworn literary forms, though at an early stage this may have been a necessary and significant intervention. To give but one example, Wheeler's creation of a working-class hero who was a Chartist *and* a sympathetic figure, flying in the face of the contemporaneous middle-class treatment of politicised working-class figures as murderers or demagogues, must be given credit as a pioneering effort (see chapter 1 by Martha

Vicinus). At a later stage and more mature level, however, it became also a question of which devices or elements to take over, adapt, reject, or search for, if the available ones were indeed unsuitable. What we observe in *The Ragged Trousered Philanthropists*, for instance, cannot be explained adequately in terms of the replacement of a middle-class hero by just another central figure, this time taken from the working class; rather the concept of the hero itself is extended to the point of exploding it altogether. In sum, what was at stake was not whether to retain or write off the novel form, but how the genre could be *umfunktioniert*, functionally re-oriented that is, so as best to serve its overriding purpose, an imaginative grasp of reality, but now for the historical interests of the working class. As Brecht, who quarrelled with Lukács over the question of models, once put it: 'The people take as little and as much interest in the novel form as they do in the form of the state. They are not concerned with the question of conservation. For the people there is nothing holy about carrying on a tradition; it may often well be carried on in an unholy manner.'[2]

If the preceding remarks are not rejected out of hand they can be seen to have a bearing on the politics of English Studies, in particular on the construction of Literature as an established canon of works. This construction might be questioned on several accounts. First, it has hardly ever been laid down on which (theoretical) premise it rests. Hence the direction of attack of the reforming side in the recent controversy over the Oxford English Course, when it queried why Burke is being studied but not Bentham, why Macaulay but not Marx.[3] Second, it is a construction heavily biased in favour of the dominant aristocratic and bourgeois tradition, suppressing an entire lineage which is the literature of and in the historical interest of the working class. In terms of the abovementioned debate it might thus be asked why Brontë is being studied but not Bamford, why Conrad but not Carnie, why Woolf but not Welsh.

Though it would be pointless to lament this bias, it can serve as a salutary reminder of the workings of the selective tradition. The way in which whole movements like Chartism have been efficiently elided from the map of English literary history is at once remarkable and disconcerting; and if this has happened to an entire school of writers, how will this process have affected less powerful strands, episodes or individuals?

The genesis and existence, however discontinuous and fragmentary, of a literary culture which embodies values diametrically opposed to the dominant ones, and propagates a fundamentally different idea of itself as literature, is not unique to the British context. In fact there is not a single 'modern' national literature which does not contain pockets of literary culture of a working-class and socialist cast. Socialist literature develops in the womb of the total national culture as elements of the socialist society of the future grow out of, yet in opposition to, bourgeois society. Despite its embryonic shape this literature represents a potential source of threat to the dominant literary culture. Hence the effective dominant mode in its characteristic voracity will strive to absorb and incorporate these emergent literary elements within its reach, or else marginalise and stifle them.

The place which socialist literature occupies within the dominant cultural structure is difficult to determine. Attempts have been made to define it by way of negative delimitation: 'While working-class literature is not an autonomous entity in the total national culture, neither is it an appendage, nor does it follow a completely parallel course.'[4] Perhaps not much more can be advanced at this stage, for it is precisely the lack of coherent knowledge on the subject, the absence of a full-scale history of working-class and socialist literature, of which at present little more than the rough contours are known, that limits our understanding and prevents certain theoretical questions from being adequately formulated, let alone solved. This situation obviously reflects, too, on the presentation of the contributions to this book, which to some extent are necessarily descriptive and documentative.

Without wanting to belittle the advances made over the last years, I would maintain that we are still a long way from safe ground on which to start thinking fruitfully, rather than speculating, about developmental laws of socialist literature. Such generalisations as 'it is only during moments of social crisis that any significant number of English novelists have attempted to write fiction centred upon working-class life'[5] have all been proved wrong, as has the contentious assertion, made primarily (though not exclusively) about the German situation, that 'working-class literature is absent at the height of revolutionary struggles and equally absent at times of stagnation of the labour movement'.[6] Even on the strength of the present survey, confined as it is to one genre, it would be pretty hazardous to proceed to any such conclusions.

It should have become clear by now that *The Socialist Novel in Britain* is intended more as a beginning than as the last word on the subject. I do not hesitate to admit that what is offered here even on the nineteenth century cannot lay any claim to comprehensiveness. No study or bibliography of that period has as yet revealed the real scope of what has survived as novel-writing by working men and women and socialists. A more reent and reliable estimate than the frequently quoted overview by Keating speaks of some sixty works of which hardly a fifth have ever been the object of criticism. There remain then tremendous opportunities for research, not all of which will of necessity entail a 'rescue operation', but which will have to be carried out if the course of the genre is to be constructed. In this long overdue discussion, which the present volume will hopefully stimulate, every serious intervention is welcome—a measure of its seriousness will be how seriously it takes its subject.

The process of sifting and assessing is thus still before us. But, as Raymond Williams reminds us in his contribution, work in this field ought not to exhaust itself in the opening of yet another academic sub-discipline. Much as the foundation of lecturerships devoted to the study of socialist literature is to be wished, their legitimation cannot be that of a director of archives. What we need, and what the public has a right to demand, are editions of the works themselves, which will enable the socialist as well as the general reader to form an opinion. Here is a challenge for enterprising publishers to make this heritage available. It has to be recalled that whole areas, like the Chartist novel, have to this day never been published in book format.

Of course, there are signs of progress. *The Ragged Trousered Philanthropists*, *A Scots Quair* and *Love on the Dole* have now been almost continually in print in paperback editions for a decade. And with the recent interest in the 1930s some more works, by Lewis Jones and Jack Common among others, have been reprinted. So has Macdougall Hay's *Gillespie*, given prominent treatment here (see chapter 4 by Jack Mitchell). But these have been largely individual efforts, without a sense of general purpose or the prospect of continuity, without circumspection and, in most cases, critical introduction. What is required is a systematic move to facilitate this process of recirculation and reception, ideally some kind of Library of Socialist Classics.

Yet there is a further reason for insisting on having the more important of these works in print. The history of the socialist novel reveals again and again, as late as the 1950s, how aspiring worker-writers set out not only against all the odds but also largely unaware of the struggles and results of their literary ancestors. Cut off from their very own tradition, every group or generation invariably felt anew that it was starting from scratch, without the benefit of much inherited literary experience, without the knowledge of previous achievements and experiments; in fact, quite conversely, all too often overloaded with the 'ballast' of the dominant tradition. This is no doubt one of the reasons for the qualitative setbacks the tradition has suffered. For such a state of things is as material an impediment to the development of a socialist literature as the absence of a publishing house, a chain of bookstores or a bookclub, an understanding reviewing press, and an 'informed' public—by which is meant one appreciating the *sui generis* quality of socialist literature—have been in the past. Where would the labour movement stand today without the full range of the strategies and lessons, victories and defeats of the past? The literary heritage of the working class is, potentially, part and parcel of the same accumulated reservoir of knowledge and experience, meaning and values. It is the job of socialist critics to contribute to its activation here and now.

NOTES

1 For a more historically grounded entry into the terminological discussion see my articles 'Socialist Fiction in the 1930s: Some Preliminary Observations', in John Lucas (ed.), *The 1930s. A Challenge to Orthodoxy* (Hassocks, 1978), p. 14; and 'Socialist Novels of 1936', in Francis Barker *et al.* (eds), *1936—The Sociology of Literature*, vol. 2 (Essex, 1979), pp. 143–4.
2 Bertolt Brecht, 'Über den Realismus', in *Werke*, vol. 19 (Frankfurt, 1975), p. 333 (my translation—HGK).
3 See, for instance, Terry Eagleton, in *The Times Higher Education Supplement*, 21 March 1980.
4 P. M. Ashraf, *Introduction to Working-Class Literature in Great Britain, Part I: Poetry* (Berlin, 1978), p. 17.
5 P. J. Keating, *The Working Classes in Victorian Fiction* (London, 1979), p. 124.
6 Redaktionskollektiv Alternative, 'Thesen zur Arbeiterliteratur', *alternative* 90 (1973), p. 129 (my translation—HGK).

Chapter 1

CHARTIST FICTION AND THE DEVELOPMENT OF A CLASS-BASED LITERATURE

Martha Vicinus

The Chartist movement (1837–53) was the most significant attempt by nineteenth-century working people to take control of their lives. Politically Chartists wanted to transform England into a representative democracy where the working-class voice would be heard.[1] Culturally Chartist writers sought to create a class-based literature, expressive of the hopes and fears of the people. The years of the movement saw an outpouring of speeches, essays, prison letters, dialogues, short stories, novels, songs, lyrical poems, epics and, later in the century, autobiographies.[2] As with so many political movements, the richest literary period came when the movement was declining and its political goals seemed more remote than ever. Most Chartist fiction dates from after 1848. Those interested in revitalising political activity wrote fiction that combined the romantic, forward-looking fervour of Chartist songs and poems with the exciting plots and characterisation of the popular novel. Political and didactic ends were grafted upon a popular genre to create the first sustained working-class fiction in England. The results were necessarily mixed, not so much because of the political failures of the time, as the literary limitations of the authors and their forms. Depite the flowering of realistic fiction in the late 1840s, with the publication of works by Dickens, Charlotte Brontë, Thackeray and Mrs Gaskell, the major influence on Chartist writers was the longer standing romantic tradition embodied in the popular fiction of the day. The melodramatic and romantic seemed to be closer to the world view of these writers, and more appropriate to their goal of infusing political beliefs with fiction. This essay is an examination of the parameters of Chartist fiction and an analysis of why Chartist writers chose melodrama over realism as more expressive of their lives and aspirations.

I

Working-class fiction is rare in nineteenth-century English literature, and serious criticism of it even rarer. Although the poor and criminal classes had long been incorporated into English fiction, the working class as a class had not been. In the 1840s the dominance of realism in the novel was still new. The industrial novelists of the period—middle-class authors writing for the middle class—backed away from portraying positively any political activity among working people, and labelled it dangerous and/or useless. Mrs Gaskell, for example, lovingly described the daily life of the Bartons in *Mary Barton* (1848), but John Barton's political work is called 'widely-erring judgment'. Disraeli in *Coningsby* (1844) and *Sybil* (1845) seems to draw upon a combination of Blue Books and the Newgate adventure novels in his descriptions of political activity, rather than actual working-class experience. Working-class characters were permitted a very narrow range of experience, with political action consistently treated as suspect.[3] It was not until the end of the nineteenth century that writers could draw upon the traditions of French naturalism to write realistic political fiction. The best alternative for Chartist writers appeared to be the contemporary popular novel, with its combination of romanticism and melodrama.

Chartists were most influenced by the enormously popular Chartist supporter, G. W. M. Reynolds.[4] Although Reynolds never wrote directly political fiction, he did pioneer the presentation of a politically sympathetic hero embroiled in romantic and financial misadventures. *The Mysteries of London* (1846–50) includes many political episodes along with bitter polemics against the rich. 'The Seamstress' (1850), which appeared in *Reynolds's Miscellany*, contains a detailed account of the exploitation of seamstresses. But Reynolds's attacks on the rich are kept apart from specific political action, and the focus is on dramatic events, sensual scenes and complicated plots, all characteristic of popular fiction of the time. Realistic descriptions jostled with romantic posturing. This style of fiction had to be adapted for more directly political and class-oriented ends by Chartist writers, but the melodramatic perspective was kept.

The central difficulty for political writers was to combine a realistic portrayal of the plight of the working class with a message of hope and the possibility of future change. Chartist fiction always described society as desperately corrupt; the aristocracy is invariably brutal and dissolute, the middle class selfish and materialistic, and the working class downtrodden and miserable. Yet somehow the innate nobility of mankind must shine through this abomination. The result was often what William Empson has called the 'realistic pastoral', in which the focus upon human waste and social injustice yields in the reader a fuller conception of the possibilities of life.[5] Many of the most 'realistic' scenes in Chartist writings, such as the family sitting by the hearthside, seem idealised and pastoral; the edge of realism is blunted by the author's effort to present a sense of completion and fullness. Chartist novelists also expressed a hope for a better future which is close to a pastoral world where conflicts could be reconciled and the simple, natural human sentiments could reign unchallenged. In judging the contrast between what is—human waste—with what should and could be—human fulfilment—an author will soften at least some of the elements of class conflict in order to present the means of changing the old into the new. If he does not do so, the difficulties of affecting change seem insurmountable, and the reader will not believe in the promise of fulfilment. Moreover, if the potential conflict appears too destructive, the reader may consider the price of change, even when it brings improvement for himself, to be too high. Sympathisers from all classes are needed to bring about a people's revolution. At the same time the hope for a new society involves a simplification of the complex—a process which concentrates and makes more forceful the wrongs suffered by the people, and thereby heightens the sense of class conflict.

Although few writers managed successfully to combine strong class divisions with the dream of future reconciliation, the choice of popular fiction as a model for political fiction proved to be the best possible solution available. Popular fiction's melodramatic plotting, characterisation and action were sufficiently commodious to permit the inclusion of propaganda without completely damaging the work's appeal. But more importantly, melodrama itself seemed like a psychologically accurate reflection of working-class life. Melodrama's character typing, with the clear struggle between good and evil, was attractive at a time when traditional values were being undermined; moreover, it provided a vehicle for the full expression of sentiment and emotion, without concern for character motivation or development. Melodrama appeals to those who feel that they have no control over their lives, but are prey to larger social forces; tragedy appeals to those who feel, however erroneously, that they can control their own lives. After a decade of political agitation, many Chartists came to feel that they could not seize control of the political and economic direction of their lives, and that all forms of social change had been blocked. Catastrophic and uncontrollable change marked the early stages of industrialisation, and melodrama provided an explanatory model for why the good and just must suffer while the rich and powerful prosper. It consistently sided with the powerless against the powerful, so political writers had only to take its conventions and accentuate them to drive home their political message: the good but powerless worker eventually triumphs over the villainous and powerful rich man. This happy ending was not seen as a realistic portrayal of actual events, but rather as a longed-for condition. The form of melodrama made possible the realisation of a better future; it promised a pastoral reconciliation of class conflict. Despite its basically conservative nature, melodrama could thus be altered to fit the revolutionary needs of political fiction.

Chartist novelists borrowed readily from the conventions of popular fiction: the heroine was a passive victim; the villain was brought to justice by fortuitous events; the hero was manly, idealistic and honest; the aristocracy was selfish and cruel, but had its heartaches. Vague democratic principles rather than particular Chartist demands made up most of the speeches and actions, so as not to alienate particular sections of the movement. Emotionally charged situations carried the political burden; class conflict was justified through the villainy perpetrated by a careless and selfish member of the ruling class. Seduction of an innocent servant girl, dismissal of a faithful retainer, or a more personal cruelty pinpointed his perfidy, which was then declared to be typical of his class. A tortuous plot frequently led up to a confrontation between the hero and the villain; a fair damsel was the reward. If the villain won her, it was implied that such a personal defeat notwithstanding the forces of democracy would eventually triumph, and so the brave hero continued his political work despite a heavy heart. In this way melodrama's happy endings, with justice to all, could be adapted to fit the more open-ended state of Chartism.

Chartist fiction combined many realistic details about working life with stereotyped characterisation and plotting. Authors broke away from the character development and unified action found in the bourgeois novel in order to emphasise the political implications of a situation. Readers were expected to identify with the hero as a typical honest-hearted working man who embodied their best characteristics. A great many events befall the hero in order to document as fully as possible the oppression of the working class. Characters frequently die not simply as a convenient way to end a story, but also to bring home the conclusion that death is inevitable if oppression is left unchanged. The courage of the hero combined with his many misfortunes focuses the anger of the reader against those in power. Since the characters and events are familiar to the reader, he is not waylaid by a consideration of motivations or other alternatives. Psychological analysis gives way to political analysis of why good people are trodden down by circumstances. This fiction, and here it differs from popular fiction, ideally quickens the reader's existing anger, and then channels it toward a political outlet. Social tension is increased, rather than dissipated.

Unable to control much of their own situation, working people found emotional satisfaction in the conventions of popular fiction. They could identify more readily with the hero or heroine who was largely a victim of circumstances; such a character showed how misfortune was not a reflection of one's own personal worth, but rather a testing of pre-existing virtue. Change is brought about not so much from the actions of the good, as from a change of heart in the evil, who come to recognise the value of goodness. All characters in melodramatic popular fiction share the same moral values, only the villain has prospered in the past by flaunting them. The good are rewarded, as they had suffered, by a change in outward circumstances. A favourite device, frequently turned to by Chartist writers, was the rewarding of the poor but virtuous through an unexpected inheritance or the benevolence of a wealthy outsider. The better writers, however, hated this solution, and argued that it violated the Chartist belief in the working-class's ability to change conditions. As the late Chartist leader, Ernest Jones (1819–69), insisted,

It is folly to say 'we can't help it', 'we are the creatures of circumstances' —'we are what society makes us'. We *can* help it—we can *create circumstances*—we can make *society*—or whence the efforts to redress and reform—moral, social, political, religious.[6]

The problem was how to graft a sense of instrumentality upon a melodramatic plot. The less skilful sacrificed their political message to the exigencies of romance. The machinations of the upper-class villain gave the opportunity to pillory those in power, but the emotional interest centred on the young lovers. The overall impression is of thwarted love, with political principles often reduced to a hatred of the upper classes. The more sophisticated writers tried to alter conventions in order to show men working together, creating circumstances. A disaster, such as the burning down of a factory, was used to show men organising for a better tomorrow. The superior knowledge and good charac-ter of the hero occasionally enabled him to influence the course of

events. The constraints of plot, however, were most frequently
broken by authorial interruption calling for united political action
on the part of the working class.

The habit of breaking into a political speech in the midst of an
emotional scene had the effect of distancing and denying the
intrinsic power of the scene. Intrusive propaganda characterises
much of Chartist fiction. Even when most descriptive, authors
seldom resist pointing to a moral. Readers were frequently
reminded that when the characters were happy, it could not last,
and when they were unhappy, the blame rested with the rich, who
themselves were unhappy but powerful. The appropriate balance
between realistic description and political message was difficult to
find, but the best narratives did include effective scenes combining
action and analysis. Jones, in *De Brassier*, for example, describes
the motivations and satisfactions of a mob plundering a banker's
home; at the same time he analyses the moral dilemma faced by
the hero. If he defends the banker, he will lose all credibility with
the men, but if he permits them to continue, he knows that the
general public will turn against the cause of democracy. Jones does
not evade the implications of political leadership, nor does he
flinch from portraying the weaknesses of the people. When the
hero's conflicts are effectively shown, as in this scene, rather than
told, the reader can sympathise and gain understanding of the
political process. In such situations, Chartist writers were forced to
move away from the stereotypes of popular fiction, but ordinarily
it proved to be exceptionally difficult to graft political analysis
upon a romantic plot without alienating the reader. Chartist
writers had chosen the popular novel as a form because it supplied
the most accurate psychological interpretation of their lives, but
then they were trapped in its conventions, which left little room for
political change.

II

Although all Chartist fiction uses melodramatic forms, the short
stories and sketches tended to move toward becoming moral
fables, while the novels were more clearly a combination of
political didacticism and popular conventions. The moral fables
emphasised a straightforward portrayal of the people's injustices;
the novels stressed action and the possibilities of change arising
out of extreme plot complications. Fable-like short stories can be
found in many Chartist periodicals from the beginnings of
Chartism, but most date from the later period. Realistic descriptions of working conditions are combined with representative

characters who are punished or rewarded according to the rules of melodrama. Honest Age, Corrupt Parson, Faithful Child and Venial Aristocrat were some of the most popular figures. Educational Chartists found this form especially congenial as a means of presenting their case for gradual reform and sensible behaviour on everyone's part. But the more militant found sketches to be opportunities for describing the utter corruption of the wealthy and the total virtue of the poor. Although limited in literary technique, these writings are interesting examples of efforts to personalise both friends and enemies of the Chartist cause. The social criticism is always open and obvious but solutions are less clear, leaving the necessary actions to the reader.

A particularly lurid example of the Chartist fable is Jones's 'The London Door-Step' (1848),[7] which describes the death of an honourable woman picked up for vagrancy when she rested momentarily on the door step of a mansion in Grosvenor Square. The 'proud aristocrat' within, who earns £15,000 annually and has two country homes and a government sinecure, orders his 'powdered lackey' to expel 'that drunken woman'. The woman's husband had left Leicester some weeks previous in search of work. Attempting to stop a policeman from beating a woman after a Chartist meeting, he was struck with a truncheon and killed. His wife had come to London to find him, and after weeks of fruitless searching, sinks onto the door step under the burden of hunger, fear and exhaustion. Jones anathematises the aristocrat as 'A SOCIAL MURDERER' for his unwillingness to share 'a trifle with that wretched victim'. The piteous and helpless state of the woman is emphasised over any possibility of change, but the anger and virulence of the prose conveys a message of militant action. Jones's story simply confirms what his readers already know; he does not need to tell them how necessary it is to change the contemporary social situation. His tale is simply meant to arouse and reinforce their already existing anger.

Educational Chartists usually had an equally obvious, albeit different, moral to draw in their fiction. Mutual improvement, self-help, steady work habits and 'laying by' for the future are all portrayed in a variety of sketches that appeared in late Chartist periodicals.[8] The Leicestershire Chartist leader, Thomas Cooper (1805–92), was an important exponent of self-help and gradualism. Inordinately proud of his own learning, gained under difficult circumstances, he veers between advocating education as a panacea for working-class ills and appealing to the better-off to recognise their obligations to the respectable poor. The difficulties of combining realism and instruction can be seen in 'Seth Thompson, the Stockinger', written while Cooper was in jail for leading the Leicester Chartists in 1842. After years of semi-starvation in the slums of Leicester, Seth and his family are saved by the opportune arrival of a long-lost uncle:

'Are the working people of Leicestershire usually so uncomfortably situated as you appear to be?' asked the stranger in a tone of deep commiseration which he appeared to be unable to control.
Seth Thompson and his wife looked uneasily at each other, and then fixed their gaze on the floor.
'Why, sir,' replied Seth, blushing more deeply than before, 'we married very betime, and our family, you see, has grown very fast; we hope things will mend a little with us when some o' the children are old enough to earn a little. We've only been badly off as yet, but you'd find a many not much better off, sir, I can assure you, in Hinckley and elsewhere.'
The stranger paused again, and the working of his features manifested strong inward feeling.
'I see nothing but potatoes,' he resumed; 'I hope your meal is unusually poor to-day, and that you and your family generally have a little meat at dinner.'
'Meat, sir!' exclaimed Seth; 'we have not known what it is to set a bit of meat before our children more than three times since the first was born; we usually had a little for our Sunday dinner when we were first married, but we can't afford it now!'
'Great God!' cried the stranger, with a look that demonstrated his agony of grief and indignation, 'is this England—the happy England, that I have heard the blacks in the West Indies talk of as a Paradise?'⁹

Seth is given £50 and a half-yearly remittance, with which he sets up his own shop, employing his fellow stockingers at a fair rate. But business reversals force him into bankruptcy, and he leaves England for his uncle's West Indian plantation. It is as if Cooper knew that a single rich uncle could not solve England's economic problems, so that he takes away even Seth's good fortune, and pushes him out as a disillusioned emigrant. The ostensible message is to work hard and be honest, and you will be rewarded, while the actual conclusion argues that a virtuous individual will still be trapped by economic circumstances beyond his control.
The confused political message and stiff predictable dialogue of 'Seth Thompson' compare poorly with a similar situation described in Cooper's autobiography (1872). As a newly arrived journalist, he had attended a Chartist meeting in Leicester, and on the way home around eleven o'clock, he overheard stockingers at work:

'And what may be the average earnings of a stocking weaver?' I asked,
—'I mean when a man is fully employed.'

'About four and sixpence,' was the reply.

That was the exact answer, but I had no right conception of its
meaning. I remembered that my own earnings as a handicraft had been
low, because I was not allowed to work for the best shops. And I knew
that working men in full employ, in the towns of Lincolnshire, were
understood to be paid tolerably well. I had never, till now, had any
experience of the condition of a great part of the manufacturing population of England, and so my rejoinder was natural. The reply it evoked
was the first utterance that revealed to me the real state of suffering in
which thousands in England were living.

'Four and sixpence,' I said, 'Well, six fours are twenty-four, and six
sixpences are three shillings; that's seven-and-twenty shillings a week.
The wages are not so bad when you are in work.'

'What are you talking about?' said they. 'You mean four and sixpence a
day; but we mean four and sixpence a week.'

'Four and sixpence a week!' I exclaimed, 'You don't mean that men
have to work in those stocking frames that I hear going now, a whole
week for four and sixpence. How can they maintain their wives and
children?'

'Ay, you may well ask that,' said one of them, sadly.[10]

Cooper has vividly recreated his personal shock, leaving the
reader to draw his own conclusions. Unfortunately he was never
able to dramatise the difficulties of working-class life as well as this
in his fiction. The obvious conclusion to his experience in Leicester
was to organise the stockingers for better pay and protection; this
is precisely what he did at the time. The obvious conclusion of
'Seth Thompson' is that one man cannot overturn the economic
system, and so should work with others—yet Cooper did not draw
that conclusion openly, but rather sent Seth to the West Indies,
and in his other stories advocated sturdy individualism. Indeed,
Cooper has Seth utter the conventional Malthusian wisdom of the
time by apologising for marrying 'betime'. Moreover, he does
nothing to save himself, but relies entirely upon his uncle. In this
he violated not only Chartist precepts, but also Cooper's own
ambitions for self-improvement.

However weak Cooper's fiction may be, he does point up the
difficulty of creating viable, active working-class characters. The
alternative models drawn from the industrial novels seemed too
limited, too confining, to portray the working man as he ought to
be—or could be. The question was how to include the struggle for
human justice and dignity along with a prophetic sense of a better
future. The rousing of the powerless against the powerful found its

most effective expression in two novels by Ernest Jones and
Thomas Martin Wheeler (1811–62).[11] Jones, a latecomer to the
movement, came from a wealthy family and was well educated; he
was one of the leading poets and journalists of Chartism, and
devoted his life to the workers' cause. Wheeler, a long-time
activist, had been a baker, gardener, schoolteacher and organiser.
He served as secretary to the Chartist Land Company and was a
successful participant in the settlement at O'Connorsville. Both
men were convinced that the events in which they had participated
would interest readers if described fictionally. They argued that
there was no better way to review the immediate past and to learn
from it. As Wheeler explained, 'the opponents of our principles
have been allowed to wield the power of the imagination over the
youth of our party, without any effort on our part to occupy this
wide and fruitful plain.'[12] Fiction would be the means of both
educating readers about political work and of galvanising them for
future action.

   Both Jones's *De Brassier: A Democratic Romance* (1850–1) and
Wheeler's *Sunshine and Shadow* (1849–50) examine the basis of a
class-divided society, even to the detriment of the plots. The
behaviour of individuals is placed in a social and political context,
so that hatred of the ruling class is shown to arise out of a class
analysis. Both authors include scenes of crime. They do not excuse
the criminals, but argue that great poverty and great wealth cannot
exist together in a healthy State. Hatred and violence are the
inevitable result of England's condition. Until a just society exists,
class solidarity is the workers' only protection against the economic, social and political power of the wealthy. This perspective
differs sharply from that found in the middle-class industrial
novels. Mrs Gaskell, Disraeli and Dickens all sought a solution to
social problems through better understanding between the classes.
In their works conflict is reduced to a failure of communication or
to the weaknesses of individuals within each class. Unions,
Chartism and any other form of organised class solidarity are
treated with fear and distortion; indeed, these middle-class writers
were unable to believe that the working class as a class was capable
of organising itself for social betterment. Christian fellow feeling
and gradual amelioration are their solutions to social problems.
Jones and Wheeler, as champions of class conflict, followed a new
course in presenting the social system from the perspective of the
politically aware working man.

   The purpose of *De Brassier* was to examine 'why democracy has
so often been foiled', or as Jones explained more explicitly, 'The

object of "De Brassier" is to show the People how they have but too often been deceived and betrayed by their own presumed friends. Deceived and betrayed, not by an individual selling them to the government, but by the individual *selling them to himself.*'[13] Although he insisted that the novel contained no portrayals of Chartists, the heroes Edward and Latimer espouse Jones's opinions, and the demogogic, self-seeking De Brassier is clearly Feargus O'Connor. In the novel Jones shows every possible weakness of the movement and gives every possible strength to the government and the forces of oppression. He saw his work as a warning to his readers not to repeat either the errors of the past or the worst evils described in the novel.

The plot of *De Brassier* is exceptionally complicated, with many subplots designed to drive home particular political points. The action centres on the well-known aristocrat, Simon De Brassier, who tempestuously leads the people forward in massive marches, appeals to parliament and other activities similar to the Chartist movement of 1838–9. De Brassier successfully blackens the reputations of upright and committed leaders, such as Latimer and Edward. As social tensions come to a head, he temporises and the democratic cause loses the initiative; the government easily defeats a divided and dispirited people. The oppressive treatment of tenants and farm workers by De Brassier's older brother forms an important subplot, as does an attack on the banking and factory interests. Jones did not finish the novel; it ends with the successful destruction of the people's movement by the government and the sentencing of every leader except De Brassier, who escapes into parliament, where he can mismanage government funds with impunity.

The novel repeatedly contrasts the lack of foresight of the people with the well-developed sense of cause and effect of the rich. De Brassier invests in stock when the market falls as a result of his agitation; he sells at a great profit when his failures in leadership steady the market. The factory owner insures his property for twice its value, hoping the workmen will burn it down and save him the cost of buying new equipment and making necessary repairs. The aristocracy may fear the people on occasion, but it always has plenty of toadies and spies to keep it informed of the divisions and weaknesses within the people's movement. Jones gave the upper classes so much power in order to warn working people against underestimating their enemies. In the past fiery Chartist speechmakers had told their followers that firmness of purpose and moral superiority would bring down the government. These simplicities angered Jones, who hoped to encourage a more analytic and considered political position among his readers. Unfortunately the extreme self-confidence and even omnipotence of the ruling class is both unbelievable and discouraging; political action seems neither feasible nor sensible, given the power of the establishment.

The workers compound their powerlessness by a love of drama, style and blood. Much of De Brassier's initial appeal comes from his dashing aristocratic manner and well-known connections. His 'fitful, selfish, and uncertain guidance' enchants them, so that despite repeated lies and prevarications, as long as he appears noble, they forget the past and obey his rulings. Even when his thundering rhetoric on behalf of arrested men yields more severe sentences the prisoners are proud of his speech and their own self-importance; they give no thought to the years away from home, but yield to the drama of the moment. Latimer and Edward, in contrast to De Brassier's success, must suffer mockery, accusations of spying, poverty and general disrespect for their efforts. Speaking from bitter personal experience, Jones describes the reluctance of the people to support their own leaders, particularly when their advice is unpopular; the ordinary organiser or editor is expected to live by his wits while the people fight for a fair day's wage. Yet in spite of all of his criticism of the working class, Jones—unlike the middle-class novelists of the times—never presented working people as children in need of instruction. Whatever their faults, from ignorance or delusion, they were adults who must be responsible for their mistakes.

Jones also included a love interest, but only of the most conventional sort; the main focus was his attack on false leadership and his efforts to educate his readers as to their true goals. He used melodrama as the most effective means of showing the relationship between the powerful and the powerless. But its emphasis upon pre-existing passive virtue ran counter to the main point Jones wished to drive home, namely the potential of the working class to change its own conditions. Moreover, he himself encouraged a feeling of hopelessness by endowing the ruling class with so much power. So too the act of presenting actual Chartist events as fictional drama—the very thing he attacked De Brassier for doing—undercut his didactic purposes. Jones was caught in a literary dilemma. Melodrama was the best means of presenting the connections between good and evil because his readers felt themselves to be in the grip of uncontrollable evil forces. But it also offered no logical way for them actively to seek change. Thus,

Jones was forced to alter some of melodrama's conventions and to find some means of injecting a sense of agency—but by and large his hatred of O'Connor, represented by De Brassier, led him to paint an even blacker picture of the possibilities of change than he might otherwise have done.[14] Even in his other, less ambitious fiction, such as 'The London Door-Step', Jones heightened the contrast between the powerful rich and the powerless poor at the price of showing the possibilities of change. His fiction functions to arouse anger in the reader, but not to show the way to actual political and social change.

Thomas Martin Wheeler's *Sunshine and Shadow* is in some ways more successful than *De Brassier*. Published in thirty-seven parts in the *Northern Star*, it too is a recounting of the early days of the Chartist movement, relived through the eyes of a single, model working man. Wheeler wrote his novel because 'Our novelists—even the most liberal—are unable to draw a democrat save in war-paint.' *Sunshine and Shadow* would:

prove that Chartism is not allied with base and vicious feelings, but that it is the offspring of high and generous inspirations—that it looks not to self but to mankind: that whilst working for the Present, it holds the future in its grasp, that it is founded upon justice and true to nature, and, therefore must ultimately prevail.[15]

Throughout the novel Wheeler emphasises the high idealism that impels men to join the Chartist cause; the truly degraded are the unprincipled, who are guided solely by selfish desires. He repeatedly turns to Nature as a touchstone for the good and just. The present state of society is unnatural, but Chartism, and especially its Land Plan, will restore Nature's plan and justice will then reign. Until that time life will be only a 'shadow' for working men, with gleams of 'sunshine' in the distant future.

The novel goes from the beginning of Chartism until 1850. The difficulties of dealing with a subject all his readers knew are overcome by avoiding most of the major controversies and by leaving the hero's actual political activities vague. The plot revolves around Arthur Morton, an idealistic working man who is drawn into the Chartist movement at an early age. Forced to flee England in 1839 he meets and falls in love with the sister of his boyhood friend who is on her way to join her husband, the dastardly Sir Jasper, governor of a West Indies island. Soon after Julia's premature death, Arthur returns to England and again throws himself into Chartism. He then happily marries a young

woman who shares his principles, but misfortune dogs him. After
months of unemployment, Arthur succumbs to temptation, and
robs a drunken merchant—his former schoolfriend. 'His pure
feelings of morality' have been 'broken and disturbed', but he is
able to pay his bills and find work. Arthur bitterly returns once
again to politics, determined to remove the evils besetting his own
class 'with the iron weapons of reality' and 'the demonstrative
power of practical experiment'. He becomes a leader in the Land
Plan, but once again government oppression drives him into exile.
The novel ends with his wife and daughter faithfully waiting his
return, hopeful of the future.

The novel falls into two parts: in the first Arthur undergoes a
series of romantic adventures in the manner of G. W. M.
Reynolds, but in the second half his career becomes a paradigm of
the idealistic working man beaten down by economic circumstances. Unlike Jones, Wheeler did not have any close knowledge
of the upper classes, and he is at his weakest in attempting to
dramatise their lives. Julia's forced marriage to Sir Jasper is the
result of an unbelievable deception practised by her brother,
contrived by Wheeler less out of hatred for the ruling class than
from an effort to keep Julia perfect. Arthur and Julia's love
comes straight from the popular novels of the day, with Wheeler
justifying it by declaring, 'Love in her was no crime, albeit she was
the bride of another,—it was the result of feelings as pure as nature
ever implanted in human breast.'[16] After several panting scenes,
the lovers part, for Julia chooses 'wealth and respect, but a
blighted heart and an early grave' and 'the world's wisdom hallows
her choice'. As a final gesture toward his reader's vicarious sexual
satisfaction, Julia is placed in quarters resembling a harem, where
she pines away in spite of numerous blacks catering to her every
whim.

Fortunately Arthur is made of sterner stuff, and the novel
returns to its political objectives. Jones's work is most interesting
when he is dealing with the dilemmas of leadership; Wheeler is
most interesting when he explores the problem of poverty and the
respectable worker. Months of unemployment reduce Arthur to
'apathetic dullness', dividing him from the rest of humanity, whose
relative success only deepens the shadow of his own misery.
Wheeler does not pretend that love is strengthened under ad-
versity. Although Arthur and his wife do not cease to love each
other, they no longer find the same perfect congeniality in each
other's company. Arthur torments himself watching Mary eke out
a living he feels to be his duty to earn, while she must suffer from

his moody bitterness. Only after he is again in work does Arthur have the energy to look about him and rejoin the Chartist movement. Wheeler's language is plain and harsh when he describes Arthur's descent into 'outcast humanity', with none of the falsely heightened tone he felt necessary for important occasions. It is a stark and moving account of a life many readers must have recognised.

After Arthur robs his old schoolfriend, Wheeler muses upon the effects of conscience on those 'driven by stern necessity' to thievery. While Arthur may suffer inwardly, he is not so overcome with remorse as to throw himself into the arms of bourgeois justice. The overwhelming guilt that seems to grip most Victorian heroes and heroines when they have transgressed society's laws, no matter what the circumstances, is seen as artificial and wrong by Wheeler. He does not excuse Arthur, but points to 'the laws of nature', which lead him to take the only recourse open for survival. Attacking conventional morality, Wheeler explains, '[B]ut better far to our ideas of religion and morality is the victim to one great and solitary crime, than the man of the world,—the respectable villain, whose whole life is a series of meanness and hypocrisy, unrelieved by magnanimity of any description. . . .'[16] Arthur's wasted talents, idealism and leadership are but a single example of the price working people pay for society's injustices. The triumph of the democratic movement will bring a return to a natural state where man's impulses for goodness and happiness will flourish.

Sunshine and Shadow and *Dr Brassier* differ from the other stories written by Chartists in several ways. In these two novels Wheeler and Jones have kept political issues to the fore, and have not given easy solutions to the problems raised. Emigration, heaven or an inheritance are not available; love is difficult and lovers do not live happily ever after. These authors attempted to recast the conservative plotting and characterisation of the popular novel in order to create a new radical novel. Wheeler and Jones believed in the eventual triumph of revolutionary forces, but since change had not yet come and did not appear imminent, they left their novels open-ended. The only possible ending was revolution. Arthur's 'fate is still enveloped in darkness, what the mighty womb of time may bring forth we know not.' Edward and Latimer languish in jail. Unlike Cooper's fables, there is no personal solution for these three heroes because their lives are entwined with the fate of Chartism.

Can new fiction be written in traditional form

yes

III

These novels, however, raise the question of whether it is possible to write revolutionary fiction using a traditional form. The English bourgeois novel has been about a hero or heroine who tries and fails to surpass an objectively limited destiny; he becomes chastened and usually adjusts to his fate within a faulty society. In *Sunshine and Shadow* and *De Brassier* the virtuous heroes attempt to change society rather than themselves. They are held back by conditions which the authors consider temporary—the ignorance and selfishness of men, or the power of their oppressors. Once these conditions change, society must necessarily change. But oppression and ignorance are so powerful in the novels that the reader is uncertain about the possibility of revolution. When the processes of change are shown, such as rioting and burning, they are fearsome and destructive of the people's cause. Melodramatic interventions beyong the control of the heroes only reinforce the hegemony of the ruling class. In both novels the possibility of a more perfect future is ever-present, but the process of class struggle takes its toll on the heroes. Since they must be left still believing in the cause, and unadjusted to a faulty society, the novels must be left unfinished.

A major problem faced by all Chartist writers was their distance from both the working class and their material. While seeing themselves as representative of the working class, their education and ambition separated them from it. Even Wheeler, who remained the most closely linked with working people, held a variety of jobs that freed him to do full-time political organising instead of the more confining bakery work for which he had trained. He, like Jones, Cooper and others who wrote for fellow Chartists, were leaders of the movement, and wrote necessarily as leaders. Didacticism dominated their fiction almost by definition. Moreover, each author had particular political biases that influenced his writing. Cooper, who longed for literary acclaim from the middle class, found it difficult to sustain the role of a representative of working-class politics; he moved readily into writing a fiction of self-help and individual perseverance in a manner antithetical to Chartism. Jones, stung by his sense of being spurned by the workers, focused on the evils of the class he had left and the weaknesses of the working class. Wheeler, who questioned the ideology of Chartism the least, found it difficult to reconcile the actual position of working people with that of his fictional characters; Arthur happy and effective is far less believable than Arthur miserable and politically impotent. At the same time the limitations of melodrama as a vehicle for political action accentuated the distance between the author and his audience. The result necessarily was a less successful literature.

Jack Mitchell has argued that one of the reasons why the working-class novel did not flourish in England until the early twentieth century was the failure of writers to accept the validity and permanence of the industrial proletariat.[17] Assuming that industrialisation, and more specifically, the condition of the working class itself, must be temporary, the writers looked to the future, hoping for and advocating radical change. This insistence upon a better future, rather than exploring and validating the here and now, no matter how grimy and degraded, prevented authors from treating seriously contemporary working-class life and from developing character and conflict within the existing world. It is in this sense that Empson is correct in labelling all proletarian fiction as pastoral—in actuality it is better described as visionary melodrama. Not content with the existing world, Wheeler, Jones, Cooper and their lesser peers, wrote first political statements and then literature; they started with their political objectives and built their characters and action around them. Politics does not mingle with fancy, but the two are served up in separate batches. In their anxiety to present the possibilities or desirability of a better future, these writers described only the evils of daily life—unrelieved poverty, irrational actions and oppressive conditions alternate with the political message and brief interludes of fantasy-pleasures. The combination of an inadequate literary form and a future-oriented historical perspective limited the literary potential of Chartist fiction.

Yet even later in the century, a new generation of working-class writers did not successfully portray the nature of working-class life and its aspirations. The thread of working-class fiction *by* working men remained slight throughout the nineteenth century in England; sketches and poetry abound, but full-length novels were more difficult. The lack of appropriate literary models had led both Wheeler and Jones to adapt the popular novel of the day. This had provided useful conventions and had touched a familiar chord in readers by means of the melodramatic style and characterization, but the form was too rigid and innately conservative to be effective for the heavy weight of politics imposed by the Chartists. But Wheeler and Jones did establish the right of future working men to write a fiction of class solidarity. The importance of political struggle as a part of literature was often forgotten by

self-educated writers who were anxious to write about the familiar
or the ideal, and not the realities of political life. The loss of
struggle and conflict in their works can be linked with the fate of
the Chartist movement. By 1850 Jones was a solitary voice calling
for a popular insurrection. Far more workers, like Cooper, were
making new alliances and seeking co-operation and power within a
more limited sphere than that promised by the six points of the
Charter. The single-minded emphasis upon class struggle combined with stereotypes drawn from popular fiction was not a
successful literary venture. The Chartist novel remained an
isolated example of an effort to combine political aspiration with
realistic descriptions of actual working conditions. Rather than
complaining about its weaknesses, however, it is better to see
Chartist fiction as a valiant pioneering effort. Had Cooper, Jones,
Wheeler and others not persisted in their writings, we would have
had a poorer record of working-class concerns and hopes during its
formative years.

NOTES

1 The goals of Chartism were embodied in its famous 'Six Points':
universal adult male suffrage, voting by ballot, equal electoral con-
stituencies, annual parliament, no property qualification to sit in
parliament and the payment of parliamentary members. The literature on Chartism is enormous, but see Mark Hovell, *The Chartist
Movement* (Manchester, 1925) and David Jones, *Chartism and the
Chartists* (London, 1975), who provide excellent overviews of the
movement.

2 For a fuller discussion of Chartist literary culture see Martha Vicinus,
*The Industrial Muse: A Study of Nineteenth-Century British Working-
Class Literature* (London, 1974), pp. 94–139, and Martha Vicinus,
' "To Live Free or Die": The Rhetoric and Style of Chartist Speeches,
1838–39', *Style*, 10 (1976), pp. 481–503.

3 For an extended discussion of the middle-class treatment of working-
class characters, see P. J. Keating, *The Working Classes in Victorian
Fiction* (London, 1971), pp. 3–28.

4 Reynolds was one of the most prolific and best-selling authors of the
nineteenth century. In the late 1840s *Reynolds's Miscellany* was
selling 30,000 current numbers weekly and 10,000 back numbers;
The Mysteries of London sold 40,000 copies a week. See Louis James,
Fiction for the Working Man (London, 1963) pp. 40–3 and Margaret
Dalziel, *Popular Fiction 100 Years go* (London, 1957), pp. 35–45.

5 William Empson, *Some Versions of Pastoral* (London, 1935), pp. 17–20.
6 Introduction to *Women's Wrongs*, Book IV, *Notes to the People*, II (1851–2), pp. 913–14. Italics in the original.
7 First published in *The Labourer*, III (1848), pp. 228–32. Reprinted in *Notes to the People*, I (1851–2), pp. 207–9.
8 See especially *Eliza Cook's Journal* (1849–54), *Howitt's Journal of Literature* (1849–51), *The Family Economist* (1848–60) and *The Family Friend* (1849–1921).
9 *Wise Saws and Modern Instances* (London, 1845), I, pp. 222–3.
10 *Life* (London, 1872), pp. 138–9.
11 See William Stevens, *A Memoir of Thomas Martin Wheeler* (London, 1862) and John Saville, *Ernest Jones, Chartist: Selections from the Writings and Speeches* (London, 1952). See also the recent brief comments of Ray Faherty, 'The Memoir of T. M. W., Owenite and Chartist', *Bulletin of the Society for the Study of Labour History*, 30 (Spring 1975), pp. 11–13.
12 Thomas Martin Wheeler, *Northern Star*, 31 March 1849.
13 Ernest Jones, *Notes to the People*, II (1851–2), p. 833. Italics in the original. *De Brassier* appeared regularly throughout volume I, and was started again midway through volume II. It was unfinished when the periodical died, and Jones appears never to have finished it.
14 In this interpretation I disagree with John Saville, who argues that 'by no stretch of imagination can O'Connor be identified with the character of Simon De Brassier' (*Ernest Jones*, London, 1952, p. 253).
15 Chapter 12, *Northern Star*, 23 June 1849.
16 Chapter 33, *Northern Star*, 1 December 1849.
17 'Aesthetic Problems of the Development of the Proletarian-Revolutionary Novel in Nineteenth-Century Britain', in David Craig (ed.) *Marxists on Literature* (Harmondsworth, 1975), p. 248. See also Dipendu Chakrabarti, 'The Case for a Serious Study of Chartist Literature', *Essays Presented to Professor Amalendu Bose* (Calcutta, 1973), pp. 100–10.

Chapter 2

BETWEEN CHARTISM AND THE 1880s:
J. W. OVERTON AND E. LYNN LINTON

J. M. Rignall

The Chartist novelists seem to have left no direct heirs, for in the years between the demise of Chartism and the re-emergence of socialism in the 1880s there are no novels with the political conviction and polemical vigour of Wheeler's *Sunshine and Shadow* and Jones' *De Brassier*. What little fiction there is by working-class writers tends to have gained in literary sophistication and imaginative grasp of the reality of working-class life, but at the expense of political awareness and socio-critical ambition. There are signs of an accommodation both with the existing state of society and with the conventions of the respectable bourgeois novel. Thus when Thomas Wright turns from his documentary writings as the 'Journeyman Engineer' to present to his middle-class audience the life of his own class in the form of a novel, he revealingly describes his work, *The Bane of a Life* (1870), as 'a quiet story, illustrative of some of the phases of social life and modes of thought existing among the middle working class.'[1] The contiguity of 'middle' and 'working' suggests his particular perspective: working-class individuals are shown living through experiences that are the conventional stuff of the Victorian novel; an unwise marriage, financial extravagance, debt, desertion and death-bed reconciliation. And although the central character also suffers misfortunes more specific to his class—imprisonment for embezzling a small sum of money to pay his wife's debts to the talleyman, and subsequent unemployment and penury in the East End—he is held to be personally responsible for all this rather than the victim of an inequitable social and economic system. He himself, it is stressed, is the bane of his own life, bringing suffering on himself and his family by his self-willed choice of an unsuitable wife. Wright's novel is a competent but pedestrian exercise in a conventional mode, and although it is formally a more accomplished work than the Chartist novels, it lacks their energy and political commitment. It is 'quiet' to the point of political quietism; what has disappeared is an urgent sense of the need for, and possibility of, radical social change.

As an informed and intelligent commentator on working-class

life Wright was certainly neither ignorant of working-class political activities and aspirations, nor necessarily out of sympathy with them—so much is clear from his journalistic writings.[2] But his consciousness of addressing a middle-class audience proves to be more inhibiting in his fiction than in his journalism, leading him to reproduce the idiom and the limited perspective of the least critical and most narrowly bourgeois novel. It seems that he has been unable to use the novel form without adopting at the same time the values and viewpoint of the class with whose hegemony it is historically associated.

However, if in *The Bane of a Life* the proletariat has simply become an enfranchised inhabitant of the world of bourgeois fiction, there are other novels of this period where it inhabits the world less comfortably. Another working-class writer, John W. Overton, in his two novels *Harry Hartley: or, Social Science for the Workers* (1859) and *Saul of Mitre Court* (1879), begins rather like Wright by narrating the emotional trials and personal fortunes and misfortunes of an artisan, but he is clearly concerned with issues which go beyond the private and domestic sphere, and in his second novel he comes to envisage the regeneration of society along Positivist lines. And in a work inspired by the Paris Commune, *The True History of Joshua Davidson, Christian and Communist* (1872), Eliza Lynn Linton recaptures something of the polemical energy of the Chartists, at a higher level of sophistication, in telling the story of a Christ-like Communist carpenter who suffers not on his own account, but as a martyr to his political and religious faith. None of these works could be called a particularly successful novel, but their weaknesses are in some ways instructive of the difficulties involved in writing within certain literary conventions without at the same time reproducing a conventional bourgeois view of experience and society. The conventions are more often those of the mediocre popular fiction of the day than those of the main realist tradition,[3] but in either case there is evidence of a strained relationship between form and ideology, as both novelists attempt to reach beyond prevailing values and modes of consciousness, seeking alternatives to capitalism and the ethos of individualism associated with it. Neither writer is strictly speaking a socialist, and only Overton is working class, but both come to see working-class action as the means by which a just and equitable society can be created, and in this respect they belong to the intellectual and cultural matrix which was to produce the socialist movement of the 1880s.

All that is known about John W. Overton is to be found in a brief obituary sketch of his life and character by E. S. Beesley in *The*

Positivist Review of 1893, which honours him as 'one of the most
remarkable men who have been attracted by Positivism in this
country'.[4] He died in 1890 at about the age of fifty-seven, having
worked all his life as a coppersmith. After trying more than one
religious sect and preaching for a while in a Nonconformist chapel,
he became a convinced Positivist in about 1869 and remained so
until his death. On the evidence of his novels he was a Londoner by
birth and upbringing, and a self-educated working-class intellectual
who fully deserved Beesley's description of him as a man of
'extensive reading' and 'strong literary tastes and faculties'.[5]
Whether he could have made a living as a writer, as Beesley
claims, it is impossible now to say, but the important fact for an
understanding of his novels is that he chose not to try, that 'he
took a fierce pride in remaining a workman'. It is his loyalty to his
own class, his suspicion of 'workmen who raised themselves in the
world', and his conviction that 'workmen could only be led out of
intellectual and industrial bondage by men of their own class' that
inform and shape his novels.

In both works, as their titles suggest, he focuses on an individual
life, yet at the same time he is concerned not to privilege that life,
not to allow the central character finally to rise above the working-
class world of his origins. Thus one common trajectory of the
nineteenth-century bourgeois novel is at first intimated, but then
resisted by a commitment to values other than those of individualism. *Harry Hartley* is, then, the story of a workman who
does try to raise himself in the world, only to find in the end that
his true role lies bck where he began. His taste for the penny
theatre, and the example of a fellow workman who has become a
successful actor, induce him to attempt a career on the stage. In
doing so he renounces not only his job but also his respectable
fiancée, and then takes a stage-struck and impressionable girl as a
mistress. Soon achieving some success in the melodramas of the
penny theatre, he resolves to study for serious dramatic roles,
returns to his old job as a metal-worker and abandons his mistress
in her turn. At this point he comes across the Young Men's
Christian Association and gets to know a Mr Wilson, who urges
him to take the Gospel to his fellow workmen as a lay-preacher.
The same man introduces him to the young, beautiful, rich and
philanthropic Isabel Clinton, who falls in love with him and urges
him to become a clergyman, so that there should be no class
obstacle to the marriage which they both desire. This he refuses to
do, ostensibly on the grounds of independence, but secretly
because he fears that it would involve revealing the truth about his

dishonourable relationship with his mistress. However, his past behaviour catches up with him nonetheless: the former mistress, ravaged by gin and (it is suggested) prostitution, summons him to her deathbed and reveals that she has borne him a child, who has already died. Plagued by guilt, he takes to drink is rescued by Wilson and nursed back to health by his long-suffering and still faithful fiancée. In the end he marries her and resolves to remain a workman, and at the same time to assist in Wilson's scheme of social improvement by spreading the Christian faith among members of his own class.

There are crudely conventional and melodramatic elements in all this, as Overton himself seems to be rather uncomfortably aware. On the one hand he makes fun of the absurd melodramas served up at the penny theatre, describing them in a tone which varies between the fastidiously disapproving and the condescendingly facetious, while on the other he falls frequently into a similar mode in his own narrative. There is, for instance, a self-conscious and exaggerated theatricality about Harry Hartley's final reconciliation with his faithful fiancée and his conversion to Christian proselytism, and the episode is actually introduced by a trite stage-direction: 'Scene—a chamber darkened, a sick man lying on a couch, a lovely maiden and her elderly friend standing near him discovered.'[6] The way in which Overton alternates between the use of a popular, romantic and melodramatic mode and lofty expressions of superiority to it suggests the uncertain narrative technique of a novice writer, and in particular one who is not sure of the level on which he should address his middle-class readers. But it also indicates that the aspect of his novel which most seriously concerns him is not the plot, with its hackneyed romantic complications and its conventional dramatic dénouement of deathbed, cathartic sickness and happy ending at the altar. 'As for the story itself,' he writes in the preface, 'while it must be always looked upon as the medium by which I have sought to convey a true representation of the real state of affairs among the artisans, at the same time must be understood to be founded on facts; every character therein being drawn from the life. . . .'[7] The real life of the artisans and the truth of the characters constitute the serious ground of the novel, not the rather perfunctory way in which they are brought into dramatic relation with each other.

A contemporary reviewer denied that Overton had achieved what he had set out to, claiming that there was 'no evidence of insight into the social tastes and habits of the cultivated, well-read artizan', and that Harry Hartley was 'not a type of the working man of England'.[8] But this is to be distracted by incidentals, by the peculiar theatrical bent of the character's ambitions and the melodramatic nature of the narrative. At a deeper level there lies the serious, and typical, predicament of the intelligent artisan who seeks a social role which is commensurate with his abilities but which does not involve breaking with his own class. It is an issue which George Eliot is to deal with a few years later in *Felix Holt, the Radical*, although Felix consciously resists the temptation of entering the middle class which Harry Hartley falls prey to. Overton's character never articulates his dilemma, nor is the charge of class-betrayal ever explicitly made by anyone else, but behind the conventional mechanics of the plot there is an implied debate between two principles; self-advancement and loyalty to the life of one's own class.

Set against the central character, and the ultimate failure of his ambition, there is the boiler-maker Ned Webb, who has become a successful actor and who, in a chapter significantly entitled 'Social Science', tells the story of his life and reveals the nature of his opinions. The story is one of successful careerism and the opinions are those of a cynical and unashamed individualist. Contemptuous of the restrictions of matrimony, he accepts prostitution as a convenient means of satisfying his appetites; dismissive of education for the working class as a whole, he is eloquent in praise of intellectual culture as its own reward in the context of his own life. Proud of his grasp of natural science and political economy, he regards himself as having risen above the life of the masses and aligns himself with the interests of capitalism: 'I look upon skilled labour and raw material as the stones, and upon unskilled labour as the concrete of the road, over which speculation drives the car of capital to Belgravia or Basinghall Street.'[9] Where success is identified with views such as these, failure assumes a certain air of probity, and the figure of Webb throws into relief the morally positive consequences of Harry Hartley's defeated ambition. The fact that he is reconciled to life as an artisan and marries a girl of his own class, leaving the wealthy Isabel to marry her military cousin, is not simply a defeat which subserviently confirms the existing order of society, since it involves at the same time a rejection of the dominant values of that society—material acquisitiveness and individual ambition. Moreover, in assisting Wilson in the propagation of the Gospel to the working class, he finds a role and a faith which make sense of his life, not in terms of Webb's cynical individualism but rather in terms of Christian brotherhood and 'the companionship of those who labour'.[10] There is, then, an undercurrent of critical dissent in what, on the surface, appears to be a thoroughly conventional ending where problems are resolved, characters are reconciled and the social order is left intact.

There are echoes of *Alton Locke* in this conclusion and in other aspects of Overton's novel, but the differences are marked and significant. There is nothing explicitly Socialist about the Christian teaching here, and what it has to compete with and supersede is not the political gospel of Chartism but the temptation of personal ambition. This defines the historical distance between the late 1840s and the late 1850s: there is no longer a political movement to demand the attention of an artisan like Overton or his fictional characters, and the appeal of Christianity is not, as it seems to be for Kingsley in *Alton Locke*, that it presents a means of diverting revolutionary energy, but that it offers an alternative to self-seeking individualism. Overton is not exercised by Kingsley's fear of revolution, nor does his commitment to Christianity have any of the emotional intensity of Kingsley's. Indeed, there is something rather perfunctory about its role in *Harry Hartley*, as though it represents simply the best available, rather than the definitive, solution to the problem of values and beliefs which the novel poses. The need for a faith or an ideology by which the intelligent artisan may live is clearly revealed, but it does not appear to be finally satisfied.

Overton's second novel underlines the fact that this conventional Christian ending only marks a temporary solution as far as his own development is concerned. It shows that the search for a faith continues and leads him to discover in Comte's altruism another alternative to individualism, in Positivism a true 'Social Science for the Workers', and in the Religion of Humanity a spiritual home which is not mortgaged to middle-class philanthropy.

Saul of Mitre Court: Being Extracts from the Papers of Mr Gadshill (1879) is less formally coherent than the first novel, but far more original and more secure in its ideology. There is none of the uncertainty of attitude that is discernible in *Harry Hartley*, particularly in the preface, where obsequious deference to middle-class readers, who are asked 'to regard this book as the work of one who has availed himself of some of the many privileges which they have conferred upon the workers', coexists uneasily with expressions of sturdy independence: 'I have ever held that workers must elevate themselves.'[11] Overton has now found a faith which is not associated with middle-class hegemony, and the point is emphasised by the first epigraph of the new novel, a passage from *Alton Locke* in which Mackaye condemns the exclusiveness of

Christianity: '"I'm thinking ye'll no find the workmen believe in't till somebody can fin' the plan o' making it the sign o' universal comprehension."' Comte has provided such a plan, although not for Christianity, and the Religion of Humanity offers Overton both a faith which is universally comprehensible and an ideological standpoint from which he can look upon life without subservience.

However, he appears to remain uncertain about one thing; his role as a writer. There may be intimations of self-doubt in the fact that *Saul of Mitre Court* was printed at his own expense and, instead of being offered for sale, was simply given away to his friends. Certainly the opening chapter of the novel explicitly raises questions about literary aptitude and the value of producing yet another literary work. It takes the form of a meditation by the editor, ostensibly Overton himself, on his undertaking, interspersed with letters from the Mr Gadshill of the title, the man whose autobiographical writings he has solicited and is now attempting to edit. The two men clearly represent different aspects of the same self, as though Overton is seeking to dramatise different possibilities in his own existence. Saul Gadshill is for the editor 'a bodily presentment of that other and ideal self which . . . accompanies every man through life';[12] he is his 'genius' in the flesh. And both versions of the self express doubts about writing, the editor lamenting his lack of literary skill and Saul maintaining that there are already enough books in existence, since 'to a man who believes with Pascal that the entire succession of men through the whole course of ages must be regarded as one man always living and incessantly learning, all books will seem mostly repetitions and expansions of a few ideas.'[13] Significantly, what overcomes these doubts and objections is a desire to serve and enlighten other members of the same class, in the belief 'that the only way to make high philosophical principles interesting to workmen was to show them their immediate bearing on their lives, to show them that no life, however lowly, was beyond the reach of high principles and that it could be made to set forth the highest social truths'.[14] The proselytising ambition that was the final refuge of the hero of the first novel thus becomes the motive-force of the second, with the difference that the gospel to be preached is Comte's rather than Christ's.

Overton's didactic intention casts a different light on the weaknesses of this second work. Whereas the uncertainties of *Harry Hartley* are often those of a working-class writer trying nervously to prove himself worthy of the attention of his readers, the incoherences of *Saul of Mitre Court* stem partly from an effort to make Positivist doctrine dramatically interesting and persuasive. The novel is an ungainly composite of utopian fiction, spiritual autobiography, social satire and romantic melodrama; and of these the latter element is the one which most obviously seeks to emulate the appeal of popular fiction and which is the most obvious literary failure. Overton has the sense to abandon it well before the end but without thereby solving his formal problem—the problem of presenting the story of an exemplary life, a critical view of society and a new view of its possible transformation within the conventional framework of a novel. It is hardly surprising that he does not fully succeed and that, while the work is assured in its ideology and original in its ambition, it remains curiously hesitant in its form, changing from one mode to another without finally committing itself to any.

The utopian mode predominates in the opening chapters, which describe how the editor first encounters Saul Gadshill. Walking in the country one Sunday he comes across by accident a newly built township whose inhabitants present a perplexing combination of 'home-spun, country costumes' and 'town-sharpened faces',[15] and speak in accents which suggest that they are drawn from every county in England. It transpires that Thorncum, as the place is called, is an experimental venture, a community established and run according to Positivist principles. Built on the estate of an enlightened aristocrat named Bethune, a representative of 'moralized capital', it consists of 'brick-built, not unpicturesque, one storeyed, detached houses'[16] grouped around four small public buildings; Theatre, Exchange, School-house and Temple. The latter is a glass dome supported by columns, above the capitals of which are busts of the thirteen great men who give their names to the months of the Positivist calendar, and it is administered by Saul Gadshill, now known as Father Saul, the secular priest of the township. Impressed by Saul's intellectual and moral stature, the editor tries to get to know him more closely and asks for an account of his life. The rest of the novel is the story of that life, supposedly put together from various autobiographical writings, and narrated in the first person.

In many respects it represents a re-working of the substance of the first novel: an intelligent artisan, metal-worker by trade, who clings in his youth 'to the gates of the poor man's university—the theatre',[17] seeks, and at last finds, a faith by which he can live. However, this time Overton not only reaches beyond Christianity at the end, but also begins by reaching back farther into the past to encompass the experiences of childhood and adolescence. He traces the way in which an ugly but imaginative boy, who plays the role of storyteller and scribe to other working-class children, develops through the experiences of unreturned love, hard labour in the workshop and self-education, into the Positivist priest and near saint of Thorncum. This development is narrated without the detailed physical description of the working-class world that might have been expected from a novel so clearly written in the shadow of *Alton Locke*.[18] This is, no doubt, partly because Overton knows it too well to respond with Kingsley's combination of intense horror and compassion—the reaction of an outsider—and there is a cool dignity in the laconic way in which he describes the 'hell' of the metal-workshop. But it is also because he yields too far to the conventions of popular fiction. Indeed, the first half of the story is dominated by a fancifully romantic and melodramatic plot, involving a triangular relationship between Saul, his handsome and unprincipled younger brother, and the beautiful Helen Graham, whose father turns out to be a successful coiner. Although infatuated with the younger brother, Helen is finally moved by the moral example of Saul, the honest workman, to ask him to destroy the machine with which her father produces their wealth in the form of counterfeit banknotes. This he does, in a passage in which melodrama move into allegory as he gradually dismantles 'the most extraordinary piece of human ingenuity it has been my lot to see'.[19] The plot is then brought to a conclusion with merciful speed: the brother, now penniless, enlists as a soldier after first marrying Helen, and is killed in the Crimea, leaving her with a child. She soon sickens and dies in her turn, entrusting the care of her daughter to the faithful Saul.

The summary despatch of this strand of the novel suggests that Overton is, in the end, concerned less with the emotional life of his central character than with his intellectual development, and, indeed, concerned less with that character for his own sake than with the regeneration of society as a whole which he comes to work for. In the latter part of the novel the scope of the narrative widens and its focus becomes predominantly social, as though Overton sees a need to resist the bias of the novel form, and the first-person narrative in particular, towards the experience of a central individual. He anticipates Tressell's later and finer achievement along the same lines as he extends his cast of characters with portraits either sympathetic or satirical. In the first category there are figures such as Clough Berne, the stalwart son of a Northumbrian miner, who finally becomes the blacksmith of Thorncum: an

atheist, socialist and Republican, it is he who first persaudes Saul
Gadshill to assume the role of intellectual leader and spiritual
guide to working people, and his inclusion in the utopian community shows how Overton shares Comte's and Beesley's mistaken
view that socialism would prepare men for Positivism, rather than
the reverse.[20] In the second category there are sharply satirical
sketches of social types: Bestall, an unregenerate capitalist; Mac
Spanner, a self-made man, about whom 'there was quite a halo of
romance for those who go in for the deification of greed';[21] and
Mr Long Canvass, a middle-class opinion-monger and amateur
saviour of society, 'a cockey, little, sniffing, yellow man going to
seed', who has latched onto the Positivist movement for his own
advantage and who seems 'like unto an organ perpetually supplied
with wind from an invisible bellows touched by a spirit hand'.[22] It
is against the backdrop of this gallery of rogues that the attempt is
made to create a new form of society at Thorncum, and the final
chapter of the novel returns to the utopian setting of the opening.

The strongest and most interesting aspects of *Saul of Mitre
Court* are these two, the satirical and the utopian, but they cohabit
uncomfortably in the same work and there is inevitably a hiatus
between them. In trying to bridge the gap Overton exposes not so
much a deficiency on his own part as a writer, as a weakness in the
theory on which his work is based. Although his ideal community
is more modestly and realistically conceived, and more firmly
rooted in nineteenth-century circumstances than, for instance,
Morris' slightly later vision of a socialist future in *News from
Nowhere*, it still involves one crucial element of wishful thinking.
The moralisation of capital is one constituent of Positivist theory
that seems peculiarly fanciful in historical retrospect, and here it
has to play a decisive role in the process of social regeneration.
Without the enlightened Bethune there would be no Thorncum,
and it is his fortuitous combination of wealth and benevolence that
forms the only, and inadequate, link between the satirically and
critically observed world of mid-Victorian London and the utopian
vision of a new community. The hiatus remains, and in this case
the rift in the formal texture of the work mirrors a flaw in the
theory which, in other respects, is the novel's strength and
inspiration. Thus, ironically, a novel whose originality lies in its
firm commitment to Positivism as a radical programme for social
change, bears in its Positivist conclusion a resemblance to a
conventional form of ending in Victorian novels, where, under the
wise and benevolent auspices of a Jarndyce or a Brownlow, a few
select characters are brought together in 'a little society, whose

condition approached as nearly to one of perfect happiness as can ever be known in this changing world.'[23] The attempt to imagine a new society is a bold one, but it does not finally succeed in distinguishing itself clearly enough from the more limited re- demption which is the only consolation that Dickens can offer.

E. Lynn Linton in *The True History of Joshua Davidson, Christian and Communist* (1872) entertains no such illusions about capital and is openly critical of Comtean theory on this point: 'To wait for the free gift of the capitalist, through his recognition of human duties, as some among the Comtists urge, would be to wait for the millenium.'[24] Where *Saul of Mitre Court* starts from and returns to a reconciliation of the actual and the ideal, *Joshua Davidson* makes a polemical case by showing the ideal to be repeatedly defeated by existing social and political circumstances. Like Overton, Lynn Linton takes a working-class character, an intellectual artisan, and tells the story of his life, but this turns out to involve not the development of a Positivist priest, but the creation of a Communist martyr. Unlike Overton, who is coolly matter-of-fact about the hardships of working-class life and con- fident about the future, seeing society as entering its last and permanent form in Comte's evolutionary process, she displays controlled anger at oppression and hypocrisy, a sympathetic onlooker's compassion for the sufferings of the poor, an urgent belief that society must be changed, but no firm conviction that it will be. Inspired by accounts of the Paris Commune, *Joshua Davidson* is the culminating expression of the social and political principles that had sustained a middle-class writer from the days of her radical youth, although it was written at a time when, in other respects, she was already showing signs of retreating into the unremarkable conservatism of her later years.

Eliza Lynn Linton was already well established as a journalist and minor novelist when she published *Joshua Davidson* at the age of fifty. She had behind her an unsuccessful marriage to the wood- engraver and writer William James Linton, a Chartist and Republican; a number of not very distinguished novels; and considerable experience of writing for newspapers and periodicals. In one of these, *The Saturday Review*, she had caused a stir in 1868 with a series of articles, of which 'The Girl of the Period' was the most notorious, attacking what she saw to be the excesses of the campaign for female emancipation. This crusade in defence of the duties of wifehood and motherhood came curiously from the pen of a woman who had herself made a career in a profession dominated by men, becoming the first woman newspaper-writer to draw a fixed salary, and who had previously been in the forefront of the struggle for women's rights. The contradiction was, however, characteristic, manifesting her capacity for holding opinions with passionate intensity rather than consistency.[25] It was also a contradiction that went unperceived by the public at large, since the conventions of *The Saturday Review* ensured that her articles remained anonymous.

It was behind the same cloak of anonymity that the first edition of *Joshua Davidson* was published in 1872, perhaps because her experience with *The Saturday Review* had convinced her that this was the appropriate form for polemical writing, or simply because, as a well-known figure in the literary society of London, she was concerned about the possible repercussions of such a spirited attack on religious and political orthodoxy. In any case she was soon encouraged by the immediate success of the book, which went into a third edition within three months, to acknowledge her authorship, and this she did in the preface to the sixth edition in 1874. *Joshua Davidson* continued to sell and proved to be the most popular of all her works, establishing a permanent reputation for her as a writer.[26]

Joshua Davidson, the son of a Cornish carpenter, is a man of compassion and uncompromising commitment to the truth who seeks to lead a life such as Christ would have led had he been born in the nineteenth century. Convinced that 'the modern Christ would be a politician' who 'would work at the destruction of caste, which is the vice at the root of all our creeds and institutions',[27] he breaks with established Christianity and becomes at first philanthropically active among the London poor, and then, when he realises that private charity can at best prove a temporary palliative, commits himself to political action. He joins the IWMA (International Working Men's Association) as one of its first members, in the belief that only the combined activity of the working class can bring about the necessary re-organization of society, and goes to Paris to help in the cause of humanity as soon as the Commune is declared. He survives and returns to England, only to be beaten to death by a mob at the instigation of a bigoted clergyman after he has attempted to give a lecture on the Communism of Christ and his apostles.

Mounting a powerful attack on the hypocrisy of professing Christians who acquiesce in the injustices of a society governed by the principles of political economy, and defending the Commune for 'supporting the rights of humanity against scientific arrangements', Lynn Linton urges on her readers the necessity of choosing

between Christianity and Communism on the one hand, and on
the other 'the maintenance of the present condition of things as
natural and fitting . . . the right of the strong to hold, and the duty
of the weak to submit'.[28] *Joshua Davidson* is, as a contemporary
reviewer noted, 'a socio-political pamphlet in the guise of a
story',[29] more concerned to make a compelling case than to create
the substantial fictional world of the realist novel. Narrated by a
shadowy friend and disciple of the hero, the story is a distanced,
retrospective, hagiographic account of a life, and it only achieves
dramatic immediacy in the scenes of argument and debate which
punctuate the narrative. It is ideas that are important here, not
individuals, and Lynn Linton works against the tendency of the
novel to create a primary interest in character by making the
Christlike carpenter an exemplary figure, significant not in his own
right but for the views he propounds and the ideal he embodies.
With the exception of historical figures such as Félix Pyat and
Delescluze, who are given approving mention, the characters who
people his world represent social types and prevailing attitudes.
They serve as his opponents in debate, like 'Mr Grand', the overbearing representative of the established church; Lord X, a
shallow and spasmodic philanthropist; and an unnamed MP who
acts as the spokesman of political economy. The creation of
character, as opposed to caricature, is not allowed to get in the
way of the thrust of the argument, even though this leads to certain
imaginative impoverishment of the work as a novel.

The argument is clearly and vigorously made, but the use of the
terms Christianity and Communism to define the alternative to
political economy and 'scientific arrangements' raises certain
questions. It might suggest a typical Christian-Socialist position
where Communism is used, as it often is in this period, as a
synonym of Socialism, were it not for the fact that Lynn Linton
was a confessed agnostic. The role of Christianity here is certainly
not determined by faith, although at the same time it cannot
simply be reduced to a matter of polemical tactics. As the daughter
of a clergyman and granddaughter of a bishop she knew the
established Church well, and real anger at what she considered to
be its hypocrisy and complacency seems to be one of the motivat-
ing impulses of the book, prompting her to turn the Gospel against
its supposed adherents. In this respect, although acting without
any religious fervour or doctrinal interest, she aligns herself with
that tradition of dissent which has always fed the radical stream of
English political life.

However, the position that Joshua Davidson finally adopts goes beyond that of any Nonconformist sect in its emphatic secularity, stressing the humanity of Christ and seeing in Christianity not 'a creed as dogmatized by churches but an organization having politics for its means and the equalization of classes as its end'.[30] It provokes the question of why Lynn Linton still stands by Christianity at all and issues her appeal for radical social change in its name, rather than breaking with it like Overton. This cannot be adequately understood as either the deliberate provocation of a rebellious rationalist, as she has been aptly called,[31] or the considered tactics of the seasoned pamphleteer bent upon present- ing her case in terms most likely to compel the assent of her audience. It seems, rather, that Christianity is a means of mediating between the known and the new, between accepted values and revolutionary ideals, as much for the author herself as for her readers. It enables her to find a sanction in traditional culture for a radical transformation of society, to preserve con- tinuity while urging the need for change, and to contain revol- utionary fervour within a reassuring moral framework. It is a way of rejecting revolutionary violence while appealing for radical change, and it makes *Joshua Davidson*, for all its impassioned defence of the Commune, a very English work.

Communism also requires qualification. Defined in terms of Christian brotherhood and used interchangeably with socialism and Republicanism, it is here the description of an ideal state and not the political programme of a revolutionary party. Lynn Linton certainly gives unequivocal support to the revolution of the Commune, and the narrator expresses the belief that, if successful, it 'meant the emancipation of the working class here, and later on the peaceable establishment of the Republic';[32] but it is viewed retrospectively in the light of its final defeat, so that it has about it more the pathos of a lost cause than the power of a political example. Nor is Joshua, despite his commitment to working-class political action, exactly a revolutionary: his involvement with the International is subject to repeated qualifications, which stress the fair-mindedness and liberalism which set him apart from the other members, and his antipathy to violence: 'Yet the International represented no class enmity with him. He had no dreams of barricades and high places taken by assault. It was to him, as to his other English brethren, an organization to strengthen the hands of the labourer everywhere, but not to plunge society into a bloody war.'[33] In fact he is so unswervingly true to his own principles that the ideal which he represents has an air of uncompromising individualism about it, which is at odds with the idea of collective action. He is, too, so invariably misunderstood, suspected even by many of his political comrades, and in the end reviled by un-enlightened working men as well as bourgeois bigots, that he becomes himself a figure of pathos rather than political hope. His end is a crucifixion without the prospect of a social resurrection, and the work concludes with an almost despairing question: 'And again I ask, Which is true—modern society in its class strife and consequent elimination of its weaker elements, or the brotherhood and communism taught by the Jewish carpenter of Nazareth? Who will answer me?—who will make the dark thing clear?'[34]

In a number of ways, then, Lynn Linton checks the revolution-ary impetus of her argument. Fired by a momentous historical event, she has made the imaginative effort to step outside her own class in creating an artisan hero and envisaging the transformation of society through working-class action, but she has not entirely discarded the values and modes of thinking of the culture to which she belongs. Her alternative to individualism has a distinctly individualist aspect, embodied as it is in an idealised figure so saintly that he is set apart from all sorts and conditions of men. Furthermore, the milieu from which he comes, and in which he works, is never convincingly realised. Nevertheless, she remains resolutely free from the fears and prejudices that afflicted greater writers, for, unlike Dickens, or Gaskell, or George Eliot, she never sees in working-class action simply the uncontrolled move-ments of a mob with a terrifying potential for violence. *Joshua Davidson* has many limitations, but it represents a bold and honest attempt to look beyond a society governed by the principles of political economy and to challenge the naturalness of the existing order.

Eliza Lynn Linton might have been expected to associate herself with the Socialist movement of the following decade, but by then she had moved in the opposite direction, towards a conservative defence of class society.[35] It was left to other novelists to respond to the political developments of the 1880s, and the most common form which that response took was an account of the experiences of a man from the upper or middle class who embraces socialism. Grant Allen in *Philistia* (1884) and Constance Howell in *A More Excellent Way* (1888) both focus on the intellectual development of such individuals and the ostracism they suffer, while the upper-class anti-hero of Shaw's much livelier novel, *An Unsocial Socialist* (1884), raises the temperature in society drawing-rooms with a combination of socialist theory and Shavian wit. In each case a new political awareness brings about estrangement from the

world of birth and upbringing, and although the politics may be
subversive, this pattern of individual rebellion and separation is
readily accommodated by the conventions of the <u>bourgeois novel.</u>
Working-class life need only be observed from the margins and
never imaginatively entered. Even a novel such as Clementina
Black's *An Agitator* (1894), which squarely confronts problems of
trade-union organisation and political corruption, retreats finally
into convention by turning the life of its central character, first a
union branch-secretary and then an aspiring socialist politician,
into a typically Victorian moral pilgrimage. Imprisoned as a result
of the machinations of his political enemies, he comes to learn not
the ways of the political world, but the virtue of humility and the
error of his own past arrogance. Social issues are submerged in
moral sentiment.

There are other novelists who both keep a greater distance
from such conventions and also engage more fully with working-
class life: for instance, Margaret Harkness, who is considered
elsewhere in this volume (see chapter 3 by John Goode); H. J.
Bramsbury, whose *A Working Class Tragedy* (1888–9) marks a
return to the manner, and in particular the melodramatic mode, of
Chartist fiction; and W. E. Tirebuck, whose more accomplished
novel *Miss Grace of All Souls'* (1895) combines the theme of
middle-class conversion to the working-class cause with a detailed
account of a coal-mining community and its experiences during the
great lock-out of 1893.[36] Tirebuck writes in the light of an actual
historical event, and this is an indication of what distinguishes all
these novelists of the 1880s and 1890s from Overton and Lynn
Linton: they are writing at a time when socialism is an active
political force and the Labour movement growing rapidly in
strength and importance. By contrast, what Overton and Lynn
Linton respond to and record are the undercurrents of change in a
period of less overt working-class activity, when the upper stratum
of that class is feeling its way towards a new political awareness
and an understanding of its potential role.

This openness to the possibilities of change is the most distinctive and interesting quality of their novels. In many ways they
appear to be unremarkable minor tributaries of the great mainstream of the English novel, sharing with their contemporaries an
intellectual climate shaped by Comte and Darwin, a belief in the
moral evolution of humanity, and a commitment to the principle
of altruism as a secular version of the Christian injunction. But
what sets them apart from other minor novelists of the period is
their readiness to contemplate a radical reshaping of society, and

yes alternative from capitalism

the intellectual and imaginative effort they made to envisage alternatives to capitalism and individualism within the conventional framework of the novel.

NOTES

1 Thomas Wright, *The Bane of a Life* (London, 1879), p. xi.
2 See, e.g., 'The English Working Classes and the Paris Commune', in Royden Harrison (ed.) *The English Defence of the Commune* (London, 1971), pp. 133–44. Wright's next novel, *Grainger's Thorn* (1872), does come closer to the spirit of his journalism in so far as it focuses on an overbearing entrepreneur and his impact on a community in the Black Country, but it is still predominantly conventional in its values and perspective. Much of the novel is concerned with the financial and emotional affairs of middle-class characters, and the general problem of the relationship between capital and labour, which is raised in a dramatic strike scene, is then submerged in a personal feud between the capitalist Grainger and one particular worker. The result is a melodrama which stresses the demonic singularity of Grainger and the inordinate self-will which is his fatal moral flaw. However, a recent study has managed to make more of the political and socio-critical implications of both these novels: see P. M. Ashraf, *Introduction to Working Class Literature in Great Britain, Part II: Prose* (Berlin, 1979), pp. 87–105. Ashraf also discusses Overton's novels, *ibid*. pp. 114–22.
3 One explanation for this is offered by Jack Mitchell, 'Aesthetic Problems of the Development of the Proletarian-Revolutionary Novel in Nineteenth-Century Britain', in David Craig (ed.) *Marxists on Literature: An Anthology* (Harmondsworth, 1975), pp. 245–66.
4 E. S. Beesley, 'The Worship of the Dead', *The Positivist Review*, I (1893), pp. 141–2. Subsequent quotations in this paragraph are from the same passage.
5 Rather like Hardy, much of whose learning was also independently acquired, he tends to parade his wide reading and considerable erudition in his novels. Kingsley, Dante, Pascal, Sterne, Defoe, Fourier and Plato are all either quoted or knowledgeably referred to within the first six pages of *Saul of Mitre Court*.
6 J. W. Overton, *Harry Hartley: or, Social Science for the Workers* (London, 1859), pp. 289–90.
7 *Ibid.*, p. viii.
8 *Athenaeum*, No. 1678, 24 December 1859, p. 851.
9 *Harry Hartley*, p. 106.
10 *Ibid.*, p. 291.
11 *Ibid.*, pp. v, vii.
12 *Saul of Mitre Court: Being Extracts from the Papers of Mr. Gadshill,*

Edited and arranged [or rather, written] by John W. Overton (London, 1879), p. 3.

13 *Ibid.*, p. 3.
14 *Ibid.*, p. 4.
15 *Ibid.*, p. 9.
16 *Ibid.*, p. 8.
17 *Ibid.*, p. 114.
18 Saul even has, like Alton Locke, a strange evolutionary dream in which he lives through the development of the human species. However, the evolution is seen in Comtean terms, and ends with the vision of a civilised landscape and the building of a national monument which takes the form of the Positivist emblem—a woman holding a male child in her arms.
19 *Saul of Mitre Court*, p. 151.
20 See Royden Harrison, *Before the Socialists: Studies in Labour and Politics 1861–1881* (London, 1965), p. 33.
21 *Saul of Mitre Court*, p. 147.
22 *Ibid.*, pp. 227, 228.
23 *Oliver Twist*, ch. 53.
24 E. Lynn Linton, *The True History of Joshua Davidson, Christian and Communist*, 6th edn (London, 1874), pp. 145–6.
25 W. J. Linton, giving reasons for the failure of their marriage, made the revealing comment: '"It is true . . . that she is enthusiastic about Garibaldi; but then she is just as enthusiastic about Lord Palmerston."' George Somes Layard, *Mrs. Lynn Linton: Her Life, Letters, and Opinions* (London, 1901), p. 104. Layard's is the best account of her life, but there is also a largely autobiographical late novel, *The Autobiography of Christopher Kirkland* (London, 1885), which is particularly informative about the development of her early radical sympathies.
26 See Layard, *op. cit.*, pp. 179–80. It was apparently admired by Frederick Harrison and John Bright, while Charles Bradlaugh bought a thousand copies for distribution. Its sales were so extensive (it was re-issued in Methuen's Shilling series as late as 1916) that it must have had an appeal beyond the intelligentsia, and one can assume that it found working-class as well as middle-class readers.
27 *Joshua Davidson*. pp. 81, 82.
28 *Ibid.* (preface to the sixth edition), pp. vi, viii–ix.
29 *Athenaeum*, No. 2455 14 November, 1874, p. 635.
30 *Joshua Davidson*, p. 83.
31 Jack Lindsay, 'The Commune of Paris and English Literature', *Marxist Quarterly*, I (1954), p. 178.
32 *Joshua Davidson*, p. 230.
33 *Ibid.*, p. 146.
34 *Ibid.*, pp. 278–9.
35 See, e.g., E. Lynn Linton, 'Class Sympathies', *National Review*, XXVI (1895), pp. 400–8.

36 Constance Howell, *A More Excellent Way*, and W. E. Tirebuck,
   Miss Grace of All Souls' are both discussed at some length by P. J.
   Keating, *The Working Classes in Victorian Fiction* (London, 1971),
   pp. 235–42.

Chapter 3

MARGARET HARKNESS AND THE SOCIALIST NOVEL

John Goode

I Socialism and literature in the 1880s

The 1880s is the decade in which the modern Labour movement begins to take shape. On the political level, it begins with the founding of the Democratic Federation, the first political organisation to adopt the principles of revolutionary socialism, and ends with the first conference of the Scottish Labour Party in 1888 with its foreshadowing of the movement resulting in the foundation of the ILP in 1893. On the industrial level, the 'new unionism' sees the mass organisation of urban unskilled workers and reaches a climax in the Dock Strike of 1889. And on a sociological level, it is the decade of 'outcast London' and the visions of urban poverty which finally result in Booth's 'scientific' enquiry *Life and Labour in London* which began to appear in 1889. The triad of concepts which motivate the present Labour movement—the concept of a working-class politics, the concept of trades union power and the concept of welfare—get its first firm start.[1]

The most striking feature of this complex history is that in the interaction of these levels and in their separate developments, all the unsolved problems of the Labour movement are rehearsed in microscopic form. The political organisation was minute (Pelling describes it as a 'stage army'[2]), nevertheless there is an immediate tendency to schism. The Democratic Federation became explicitly socialist in 1883, and the breakaway Socialist League, with its own tensions between Marxists and anarchists and its own later fissures, was formed in 1884. The right wing of the remaining SDF formed the Socialist Union in 1885, and Hyndman's right-hand man, H. H. Champion, broke away finally in 1888 to work towards the ILP, only to find himself deserted by Burns and Mann and their supporters in 1890. This fissuring tendency was related to the essentially middle-class base of the political organisation, and the fact that it drew support from disaffected Conservatives, such as Hyndman, as well as disaffected Liberals, such as Morris. Given its funding from private wealth, such as that of Hyndman,

Champion, Morris and Carpenter, and its relative insignificance
for the working class it served, political issues tended to be highly
abstract on the one hand and highly personal on the other. The
questions of palliatives, parliamentarianism, grass roots organisation were not anchored in a concrete situation and thus play a
freewheeling part in the rhetoric of contending factions. Most
obviously fraught was the relationship with what was the most
solid achievement of the decade—the new unionism, and this too
is fraught with its own problems. The Dock Strike of 1889, for
example, was certainly a triumph for independent working-class
action and a blow for the power of labour against capitalism, but
its resolution was the result of 'non-political' intervention from the
outside (i.e., Cardinal Manning). The vexed history of the 'non-
political' strike is evident here—the new unionism was faced with
an extremely complex mode of incorporation, which can be most
graphically illustrated by the fact that the energies of Tom Mann in
the promotion of the Eight Hour Day are diverted by the need to
establish better wages. And the embroilment of the Fabians with
the positivist sociology of Booth is another barrier, although no
one would want to deny the importance of its implications for
welfare. Every achievement is equally a defeat, which does not
mean that we can simply write it off.

Given this complexity, it is not surprising that the literary
response to the new social reality came more readily from conservative sources. A well-documented theoretical challenge to the
ideology,[3] the sudden realisation of the depth and extent of urban
poverty and the vague rumblings of working-class organisation,
but without a certain relationship between all three, was a reality
most easily construed as threat of 'anarchy' (Gissing, James) or
appeal to complacent benevolence (Besant) depending on whether
the political potential of the situation or the abject misery of the
people who were caught in it struck the writer as predominant.[4] It
is interesting that the two writers of substance who did identify
themselves with socialism, Morris and Shaw, both felt compelled
to work in a different aesthetic frame from that of the realist
novel. On a general level, of course, this merely responds to the
fact that realism is not available to socialist writers in its classic
form because it assumes that reality is merely to be perceived and
not made. But this does not answer the specific question of why
these writers did not make more use of the transformations of
realism already achieved by other writers, most notably Zola, but
also in England in different ways by Meredith, Rutherford, Pater
and indeed Gissing and James themselves. Morris and Shaw

cannot, of course, be bracketed together by the decisions they made, but *A Dream of John Ball*, and *An Unsocial Socialist* can be seen as responses to a common problem. The non-socialist writers I have mentioned respond to the new reality by a relativist displacement. They escape the realist assumption of personal convexity by deepening the personalisation of experience, and hence, in different ways, escalating the determinism of the given: this is true even of Meredith and Rutherford in spite of their consequent insistence on the active role of fiction in exposing the fictionality of that personalisation.[5] When Morris writes of nineteenth-century novels in *News from Nowhere* it is precisely to draw attention to the limits of the individuation of experience,[6] and Sidney Trefusis in his appendix to Shaw's novel points to the same inevitable limitations of the form itself:

I cannot help feeling that, in presenting the facts in the guise of fiction, you have, in spite of yourself, shown them in a false light. Actions described in novels are judged by a romantic system of morals as fictitious as the actions themselves. The traditional parts of this system are, as Cervantes tried to show, for the chief part barbarous and obsolete: the modern additions are largely due to the novel readers and writers of our own century—most of them half-educated women, rebelliously slavish, superstitious, sentimental, full of the intense egotism fostered by their struggle for personal liberty, and, outside their families, with absolutely no social sentiment except love. Meanwhile, man, having fought and won his fight for this personal liberty, only to find himself a more abject slave than before, is turning with loathing from his egotist's dream of independence to the collective interests of society, with the welfare of which he now perceives his own happiness to be inextricably bound up. But man in this phase (would that all had reached it!) has not yet leisure to write or read novels.[7]

The apparent sexism of this is only part of Shaw's irony—the attack on the 'feminine' values of romantic fiction must be taken in the context of a sequence of novels which very clearly indicate the cultural conditioning of women to confine them within the ambience of the personal life. This means that although Trefusis seems to be attacking only sentimental fiction, in doing so he challenges the frontier of fiction itself, for as long as it confines itself to the 'fight for personal liberty' the novel cannot acknowledge the 'collective interests of society' except, as in the cases of Meredith and Rutherford, as a function of that liberty. Radical and important as their novels of the 1880s are, these writers (and I would want to add the author of *Marius the Epicurean*) do not write socialist novels. The implication in this passage and in the practice as well of Morris, is that there can be no such thing.

I am fully aware of the many questions this analysis fails to meet, but I am simply trying to clear a space for the specific tasks of a socialist fiction. Transcending the limits of the personal vision is a condition of socialist writing but it does not constitute socialist writing. It merely brings the writer to the point of retreating into a culturalist sublimation of the opposing self, or of projecting into a corporatist ideology—social Darwinism, pessimism, vitalism and so on.

The most obviously socialist text of the 1880s is *Germinal*, which brings relativism to the service of a revolutionary concept (the title, of course, is naturalistic but it alludes to the revolutionary calendar). Zola's novels were not understood in England as experimental novels which produce reality but as extensions of realism and at best encouraged a 'combative realism'[8] which needs to be socialised by socialist literary history. Nevertheless, there is one writer who was inspired by Zola and who did, I want to argue, produce at least one socialist novel. In a late autobiographical novel, *George Eastmont, Wanderer*, Margaret Harkness writes of her hero in the 1880s: 'A course of Zola would probably have taught him more than Maurice or Kingsley. He had just returned from a visit to the mines in Scotland, and there he found *Germinal* better than any guide book.'[9]

Her first novel, *A City Girl* appeared in 1887, a year or so after *Germinal* and was published by Zola's English publisher, Henry Vizetelly. We know of it because the author sent it to Engels, and although it is not obviously a Zola-esque novel, it provoked Engels' famous elaboration of his preference for Balzac over Zola. She went on to write three more novels in the 1880s and it is the object of this essay to introduce some of them as real attempts to achieve a specifically Socialist fiction building on rather than rejecting the forms of critical realism, by trying to negotiate the three levels of 'socialist' discourse I have mentioned, not as an ideological entity but as the problematic which confronted socialists at the beginning of their history.

II Who was Margaret Harkness?

There is no clear answer to this question because the evidence about her is muddled and confusing.[10] We know that she was a cousin and very close friend of Beatrice Potter who went with her on a trip to Austria in 1884 after the latter's emotional crisis over her relationship with Joseph Chamberlain and who introduced her to Sidney Webb in 1890. Beatrice Webb's diaries give very graphic accounts of her but they are contradictory and clearly subjective, and we know that although she bequeathed her books and pictures to Harkness in 1886, she quarrelled with her definitely in 1891, after a long time of suspecting the novelist of unreliability. We know that she became a close friend of Eleanor Marx who relied on her for information about the London poor, but she attacked Aveling and so lost that friendship. We know that just before and for a short time after the Dock Strike, she worked closely with Tom Mann and John Burns but quarrelled with them as well. We know that she was active in the SDF and later in the moves to create an Independent Labour Party but that by 1891, she was describing socialism as 'foolish' and 'wrong'. We also know that she be-friended Olive Schreiner and Annie Besant, but that she also worked with religious institutions and edited an important series of articles, 'Toilers of London' for the *British Weekly,* a dissenting journal. What we don't know is whether she was a woman of consistent ideas who worked opportunistically in a series of alliances (her own image of herself), a radical feminist converted to socialism in the mid-1880s and disillusioned by it in the early 1890s, or simply a neurotic of wide but volatile sympathies vacillating between seeing herself as a journalist in pursuit of 'cold-blooded copy' and a rejected saviour of the working class. All these images are made possible by the patchy chronicle I have been able to construct.

According to Beatrice Webb, Margaret Harkness was the child of 'clerical and conventional parents' who 'tried to repress her extraordinary activity of mind'.[11] She emancipated herself from them by doing 'literary piecework' and living with the Poole family near the British Museum. Her life in the early 1880s seems to have been very much part of the world evoked in Gissing's *New Grub Street* (which, of course, is set in 1884): 'there you get', says Beatrice Webb, 'real intellectual drudgery'.[12] She wrote several articles on social questions, 'Women as Civil Servants' (1881) and 'Railway Labour' (1882) for the *Nineteenth Century* and two articles on 'The Municipality of London' for the Conservative *National Review* in 1883. At the same time she produced two books on British Museum antiquities for the Religious Tract Society's *Bypaths of Bible Knowledge* series on Assyrian and Egyptian life (the former has no date but precedes the latter which is 1884). None of these forecast the socialist novelist except in so far that a concern for social issues is revealed. The first merely

commends the Post Office decision to employ a small number of
safely middle-class lady clerks, mildly criticising the social exclusiveness and low rate of pay and tentatively aligning itself with a
liberal feminism close to that which emerged from the 1850s:
'Patience is all that is needed and a bond of mutual helpfulness,
binding together all women irrespective of class to meet the
obstacles incident to a changing world'.[13] The phrase 'irrespective
of class' is the nearest we come to any radical perspective in these
articles; those which follow move to a more overtly conservative
position. She recommends the amelioration of the conditions of
the railway workers and even describes the safely past period of
1866–71 as one of 'white slavery', but she explicitly denies the
prospect of independent working-class initiative:

I entirely agree with the men themselves in their conviction that they may
trust implicitly to the railway companies for the ultimate solution of their
difficulties, and for the redress of the grievances and hardships of which
they very justly complain.[14]

and concludes with a classic formulation of the division of labour
'Those who think must govern those who toil'.[15] The articles on
the government of London in the *National Review* are largely a
detailed history but attack current proposals for reform along
orthodox conservative lines, objecting to centralisation (because it
is unEnglish), paid government officials and anything which
enhances democratisation:

Politics would be introduced into municipal elections, for the political
value of municipal power would lead to the exclusion of unobtrusive men
willing to work conscientiously for the welfare of the community in favour
of political demagogues, who might, as in Paris, prove a danger to the
State, or as, for many years, in another capital, misappropriate public
funds.[16]

The problem is how to read this work in connection with her
later commitment. On the one hand, they all have the note of hack
work (especially the history of London which resembles some of
Walter Besant's romanticisation of the past). The two books
written for the Religious Tract Society are overt vulgarisations of
the work of more serious scholars, and in so far as attitudes appear
at all, they seem to have vestiges of a radical position, such as the
insistence on sexual equality among the Assyrians or the praise of
the humanity of the Egyptian legal code which 'is shown by a
clause which protects the labouring man against the exaction of

more than his day's labour'.[17] And at times she seems to admire
the secular tendencies of their religious attitudes. But at the same
time she does praise the superiority of the Hebrew religion
because of its sense of sin and its conception of a Divinity which is
remote but in control of 'the smallest events'.[18] In her diary,
Beatrice Webb says that although, in 1883, Harkness was logically
a rationalist, she believed in a 'personal adoration of Christ',[19] and
though her novels sustain a radical critique of religious institutions
(the Catholic Church in *City Girl*, the Methodists in *Out of Work*,
the Anglicans in *Captain Lobe*) she shows a great respect for
religious people—notably the soldiers of the Salvation Army. She
is even said, by one historian, to have gone to Cardinal Manning to
persuade him to intervene in the Dock Strike,[20] and it may be
indicative that her late novel *George Eastmont, Wanderer* (1905)
was published by Burns and Oates. Was she a Christian radical or a
humanist following in George Eliot's footsteps? The same question
is raised by the development of her political attitudes. For
although the early articles just discussed bear no relation to the
socialist commitment in evidence later, her critique of socialism in
the 1890s, especially in two articles written for the *New Review* in
1891 and 1893, 'A Year of My Life' and 'Children of the
Unemployed' stress patience, evolution, hope against the threat of
violent change. Conservatism was one known starting point of
middle-class members of the SDF. On the other hand, when
Beatrice Webb does identify her cousin as 'a strong socialist' she
adds that she is 'apparently uninterested' in economic facts. 'She
says that when I argue I am unattractively combative'.[21] It suggests
that her involvement with socialism may have been emotive rather
than thought out, and with the usual corollary that sentimental
commitment tends towards opportunistic alliance. 'A Year of
My Life' seems to confirm this to some extent. Writing that she
had wanted to work as 'a member of the English Labour Party' she
goes on to explain the 'brief success of the Socialist Party in
England' as 'due to its advocacy of the cause of the unskilled
worker just before he broke his shell and became a "divine
animal"'.[22]

   On the other hand, it is difficult to believe that a writer as deeply
paternalistic as these early and late essays suggest could have so
fully entered into the consciousness of her working-class protagonists, and there is a possible political explanation for these shifts
of position. It is clear that the man with whom she most closely
worked in the SDF was H. H. Champion. He, of course, was
himself a highly enigmatic figure. Upper class and military in back-

ground, he financed the publication of much socialist material and
was until the late 1880s secretary of the SDF. He was also involved
in the Tory gold scandal of 1885 and left the SDF after Hyndman
had accused him in *Justice* in 1888 of being a tool of the Tory agent
Maltman Barry. There is also some evidence that he used Tory
funds to finance Keir Hardie's Mid Lanark election expenses in
1889. But one way of seeing Champion's position is that he
foresaw the need of an independent Labour party. He certainly
published Tom Mann's pamphlet advocating an eight-hour day.
Like Mann, Burns and others, he saw the need to establish a
political expression of the new unionism. Certainly, as late as 1889,
he was very much in Engels' favour, as seems to have been
Harkness herself until she attacked Aveling in November. Both of
them worked very closely with Mann and Burns both during the
Dock Strike and during the early years of the independent Labour
movement. This is not to exonerate Harkness' apparent unreliability but rather to suggest that it puts her at the point of the
many tensions of the Labour movement at that time. There was a
great deal of poverty and hardship, and the beginnings of an
organisation to combat it. But the politics of that organisation was
a matter of deep controversy. If Champion was devious, wasn't
Hyndman too dogmatic and Morris too pure? Beatrice Webb
complains of Margaret Harkness' treachery and later says that
Tom Mann distrusted her because of her cousin's calumny. But
this might reflect not just on her own instability but the instability
of the Labour movement at this point.

A complete profile of Margaret Harkness would, I believe, be a
fascinating case study of the fraught conjuncture of radical
feminism and socialism, and of the role of the intellectual in the
Labour movement. I cannot complete that profile without much
more evidence. Beatrice Webb wrote in 1899:

She is typical of the emancipated woman who has broken ties and
struggled against the prejudice and oppression of bigoted and conventional relations to gain her freedom but who has never been disciplined by
a Public Opinion which expects a woman to work with the masculine
standard of honour and integrity.[23]

But she has just admitted that she has 'splendid opportunities' for
observation. Perhaps it is precisely because she was required to
live by cold-blooded copy, that she had a complex sympathy for
those who struggle and that like the working class themselves she
was not yet disciplined by public opinion that Harkness produced a

sequence of remarkable novels. For puzzling as she is, she is alive to the puzzle of a new reality and she makes, in my view, a new mode of fiction out of the instability.

As these novels will be unknown to most readers, I propose to write about each of them separately trying to show how she progressively abandons fictional forms as she progressively politicises the 'reality' she evokes.

III *A City Girl* (1887)

Engels praises this first novel because of the 'truthfulness of presentation'[24] by which 'the old, old story of the proletarian girl seduced by a man from the middle class', is made new. This is a very accurate analysis of the first half of the novel. The constituents of the newness form a 'new' reality which is the cause not merely the site of this story. The 'city' is established with great visual accuracy but it is defined in terms of relationships. The opening, for example, is a description of Charlotte's buildings which is the physical embodiment of a rent relationship and the picture is framed by that sense. The heroine's 'real' is defined by these buildings, the sweatshop in which she works and the family for whom her sole value is as a wage earner. The seduction is made inevitable by this 'real', because it responds to a subjectivity that is repressed by it (it is thus at a second level of potential subjection).

This is stressed by the fact that the material base is offered primarily as the provocation of ideological formations. The opening chapter rapidly moves from naturalistic description to the voices which emerge from the picture:

Charlotte's buildings were, at that time, about two years old. They had been built by a company of gentlemen to hold casuals. The greater number of people who lived in them thought that they belonged to a company of ladies.
  Why?
  'Because they are built cheap and nasty' said the men. 'Women don't understand business. Depend upon it, some West End ladies fluked money in them.'
  'Because ladies collect the rents', said the women.[25]

This is followed by the activities of the rent collectors and the comments that follow them, by the Irishwoman's speculations on what the rich think of them, and by the children's myths about the nearby reservoir. This gives way to an indication of the dominant catholicism and the dominant violence of the tenants' lives. It is a total scene into which Nelly is introduced, but one which is less pictorial than choric. Separate conscious articulations of the environment play through the novel, such as George, the good lover's single norm of military stability, or Father O'Hara's wrapping his intellect in a napkin. The East End is not made exotic, as it is in the later cockney school.[26] It is negotiable and determining. It is the source of Nelly's formation.

She is offered as innocent victim, but again Harkness does not, as with other 'realists', offer her as a consciousness which somehow transcends this environment. On the contrary, the seduction is fully portrayed as the effect of her trying to live within the given. She is special only because she is 'the masher', capable of a vitality contradicting her world's oppression in ways which are permitted and shared by her class. Her first concern is with buying a feather for her Sunday hat. The bedroom which centres on the mirror, the market and Petticoat Lane are the site of her own identity. The seduction begins effectively during a day out in Battersea Park. She sees it as 'a picture in a book' as he tries to recall which painting she reminds him of. The park and the palace are artefacts containing the natural and the romantic:

As Nelly sat there eating cake, and listening to the music, she felt in Paradise; work and trouble were forgotten in the joys of the present, sweaters and trousers became things of the past; mother and brother were changed into fond relations; her companions were no longer George, Jack and Mr. Grant, but the handsomest, the best, the kindest men on the face of the earth.[27]

There is nothing patronising about this illusion: it is won out of the relief from oppression meticulously recorded earlier. It needs to be contrasted with the Crystal Palace episode in *The Nether World* which simply sees the 'holiday' as a momentary unleashing of degenerate instincts. Nelly's day out is a day of dreams but the dreams are of the ideology of civilisation—art, the family, chivalry. Parks are constructed to sustain such illusions; they fence in 'nature'. Later, Arthur Grant takes her to a theatre which further compounds the alienated illusion. The play is about a wronged wife and her sorrowing husband. Nelly feels treated 'like a lady'. She dreams what she is supposed to dream and because Grant enables her to do it: 'she saw herself far away from the buildings'.[28] Further meetings are at Kew and Greenwich, the excursion spaces within the city that allow for and enclose what the 'buildings' exclude.

This evolution of a city consciousness—at once one of many voices and articulated in terms of the specially individuated dream—is responded to by the urban consciousness of Arthur Grant. Engels is right to say 'your Mr. Grant is a masterpiece'. In four pages in the centre of the Battersea Park episode, this middle-class radical is shown to be not wicked but highly conditioned, comfortably married and 'playing truant'. Nelly thus appears to him as an object of truancy and it is not accidental that it is in the theatre that she overwhelms him with her beauty:

Her complexion was dazzling by gas-light, and excitement made her eyes sparkle between their long dark lashes. Absolutely unselfconscious, trembling with pleasure, she was a picture worth looking at.[29]

Later she hides her face in red velvet cushions. It is not merely that she is 'a picture', an object, but that, linked with gaslight and red cushions, she is the licensed object of his truancy. Later, we are told that he writes novels which base themselves on psychological studies, but this does not extend to Nelly because it does not extend to her class: 'She was no psychological study, this little Whitechapel girl, only something pretty to look at'.[30] Again, she poses for him: 'she put on her wreath and looked like a wood-nymph.' If the park is for her a licensed day which she takes too far, she is for him a licensed consumable.

This process of voices and image making within the material base of wages and rents governs the novel at least for the first six chapters. The problems arise with the second half. Engels claims that it is not realistic enough because it shows the working class as a mere passive mass. To some extent, and, in fact, in the final instance, this is true, but it is more complex than that. Chapter VI, entitled 'East and West', contains all the radical ironies of the first part. We move into winter, allusions to philanthropic concerts and invitations to wedding breakfasts are juxtaposed against the pregnant Nelly's drudgery while she tries to seek some contact through confession and instead goes to seek Grant in West Kensington, where through the window she sees him shut in by the golden gates of domestic peace and happiness[31] (it is another highly wrought image). This brings her to realise the immense gulf between East and West, and she also is without money to return. She is forced to beg and predictably a policeman suspects her of soliciting. On the edge of this abyss, the man she begs from happens to be a well-known philanthropic lawyer. Then she is beaten up by her brother because she has been sacked and is taken by her good unrequited lover to a Salvation Army captain. All this bears out what Engels is saying. Harkness can neither push her into the abyss of the fallen woman, nor see how, in any way, energies of survival and improvement can come from within Nelly's own class. Except for her lover, George, who is in any case trained outside as a soldier, Nelly is taken out of that abyss by outside help.

But these interventions are strictly limited. The philanthropic lawyer only provides her bus fare back. Captain Lobe only takes her to decent lodgings and gets her more sweated work. More importantly, the rescue enables Nelly to move to a new phase of consciousness which the author of the *Origins of the Family* should have seen. When Father O'Hara asks Nelly whose child she has had, she replies 'mine'. Like Tess later, she is prepared to christen it herself. She maintains this stand in the face of her rejection by the 'supportive' institutions, the sweatshop and her family. But it goes further than this: it actually raises the question of monogamy and sexual equality as a question. George too wants to know the father's name, but Captain Lobe resists the implication of this: '"Well, I don't see myself why women should have only one sweetheart and men half-a-dozen", remarked the Captain. "In the Army we have the same set of rules for both men and women. The general favours neither sex"'.[32] What seems to privatise Nelly's story (the rescue) serves in fact to become the instrument of a sexual political affirmation. The episodes which follow, when the baby becomes ill and she has to face the institutional indifference of hospitals, show her locked in a solitary struggle with the powers that be.

Nevertheless, if she is taken out of passivity by what happens, she is not, of course, taken out of individual isolation. Engels admitted that East End society was the most passive working class he had known. Only the very last years of the decade with the Match Girls' strike and the Dock Strike is there much sense of organised resistance. And, as has often been pointed out, it is significant that it is a women's union that starts the whole process. But *A City Girl*, if it foreshadows that in an indirect way, has a largely rhetorical feminism of protest. Oddly, it is precisely the taking of Nelly out of passivity into the loneliness of single parenthood which contains both the novel's political thrust and writes it back into a recognisable fictional shape. For it the story of the fallen woman is thwarted in order to make a feminist affirmation, the illness and death of the child are the fictional means by which, for the reader, a compensating pathos is generated, and, for

George, the way is made clear to 'forgive' and redeem Nelly. This trite ending, however, does nothing to make up for the radical documentary of the hospital and its alienating attitude. The ending is so muted that the sense of anger generated by the picture of social injustice is unrelieved by moral purgation. The political consciousness is uncontained by the narrative sequence.

IV *Out of Work* (1888)

Harkness' second novel shows many signs of a sophisticated response to Engels's critique. It does not become more Balzacian but rather is beyond Zola's experiment, breaking open the fictional frame to embrace an unfictionalised actuality. It opens, for example, with the Queen's Jubilee visit to Whitechapel and reaches a climax with the Trafalgar Square riots of November 1887, and between these events offers a picture, not, like *A City Girl* of a social *section*, but of a social *situation*, the consequences of unemployment. Its protagonist becomes the register of vividly rendered experiences of the doss house, the dock gates and the casual ward. Its incorporation of documentary in this sense looks forward to the Orwell of the 1930s and to the non-fiction novel of recent years. But the function of the documentary is strictly to gain access to kinds of experience denied by the parameters of hermetic fiction. Harkness makes it obvious from the start that she is concerned not with actuality but versions of it and their ideological role. Thus the opening centres precisely on the crowd around the People's Palace which in itself stands for one version of the critical alienation of the working class. In *All Sorts and Conditions of Men*, Walter Besant had depicted an East End likely to become dangerously political if the diversions of civilisation were not made available. Strangely enough, the novel's recommendation inspired enough fear and complacency to become one of the many programmes of the ruling class to prevent the politicisation of the poor; Harkness is immediately on to the ironies of this—the way in which it supplies reassuring versions of the situation:

Reporters were busy at work concocting stories of the royal progress through the East End for the Monday papers; artists were preparing for the illustrated weekly papers pictures of Whitechapel as it may possibly appear in the Millenium. No one would speak about the hisses which the denizens of the slums had mingled with faint applause as Her Majesty neared her destination; no one would hint that the crowd about the Palace of Delight had had a sullen, ugly look which may a year or so hence prove dangerous. The ladies on their way to the Queen's Hall, who had leant back in their carriages, heedless of ragged men, hungry women and dirty little children, the *blasé* frequenters of Hyde Park and the clubs, who had glanced carelessly at the people as they accompanied their wives and daughters to the People's Palace, would be quoted by philanthropic persons intent on ministering to the poor by the unction of their presence, and represented by the artists as so many unselfish ladies and gentlemen who had given up an afternoon's pleasure-hunting in order to gratify the eyes of under-paid men and over-worked women by their shining hats and charming bonnets.[33]

On one level reporters, artists and philanthropic persons are making the episode into an *event* with its built-in reading. On the level of the situation itself, the ruling classes are looking at the working class who have come to look and comment on them. Later, this image of the crowd is complemented by working-class comments in the Queen. What immediately clinches the irony, however, is that 'Millenium' and 'unction' lead to the comment which follows this, that as it is Sunday the bells are 'calling upon the people to forget earth and think of heaven'. This novel will not forget earth, nor will it allow report, picture and comment to hold the sullen crowd at bay. We move immediately to a Methodist service, disrupted by a down-and-out who asks the minister if he has ever been hungry.

Of course, there is nothing specifically radical about this kind of irony: it simply calls attention to ruling class complacency and that can be and was a rhetoric used both by philanthropists and conservatives. But this is only the prelude to the much more radical fictional strategies: the secularisation of values by the inversion of fictional possibilities and the socialisation of experience by the contextualisation of consciousness as a voice among many anonymous voices. In *A City Girl*, a very conventional story is completed—it has a 'happy' (individual) ending. I have argued that this story is marginalised by the experience Nelly has to go through and the specific form of resistance which she has to develop to withstand it. *Out of Work* goes much further. Again the story is of a young girl caught between two men, but there is no question here of a steady lover able to rescue the trapped female victim. On the contrary, the 'steady' lover is a lugubrious Methodist teacher who uses his influence to gain his own ends, who works in the Mint because his father did before him, who is sexually nauseating to the heroine and whom she chooses in the end simply because: 'I'm going to marry a godly young man with a settled income'.[34] The unemployed hero is thus faced with his own social condition as an ultimate measure of love, and his own comment 'you little hypocrite' and the author's chapter title 'she jilts him' starkly challenge the reader's romantic speculations which have been encouraged by the rendering of the heroine's awareness of her feelings for him and revulsion from the man she will marry. As though to emphasise this by reference to *A City Girl* the steady lover of the earlier novel is an ex-soldier who retains a military integrity, and in this novel, there is an ex-soldier who is merely one of the anonymous victims of the recession, a man with a character reference who, because of that, is rejected by the envious dock gangers and whose presence is ultimately registered by a protesting inscription on the cell wall of the casual ward. Furthermore, the heroine has a wise sceptical Jewish 'uncle' from whom she seeks advice and who has no effect on events whatever. Early in the novel, Harkness offers a social Darwinian perspective which is presented ironically as though the novel will ultimately disprove it: 'it is a law of existence that the weakest must go to the wall, and a dogma, established by experience, that mind rules matter, no matter how strong matter may be'.[35] But the novel enacts this bitter conjunction of Darwinism and idealism. The ex-soldier and the hero, both strong capable men, cannot cope as weaker types can with the work of the casual ward. The deep commitment of the novel as a form to the survival of 'nature' is overturned by a more potent social reality.

This is matched in the life of Jos, the country boy driven by economic necessity into the army of casual labour in the city, by an inverted pastoral. From the beginning, what defines him is his sense that beyond the misery of urban experience lies a solider world of belonging and peace in the village where he has grown up. At the point of greatest misery, he decides to return to his home, but it is only to die, and the death is no release. It is stressed that there is no work in the village, and that Jos' mother and the rector who had shown some concern are both dead. The return is therefore a desperate illusion: 'Now that Polly had jilted him, the "lone" woman's memory was something to fall back upon, and he recalled numberless traits of tenderness, little things he had almost forgotten until that evening'.[36] But the comment on this is:

Human nature *must* have a fetish.

If a man does not worship his own shadow, he falls down before the shadow of someone else. When these things fail to satisfy, he calls out for God Almighty, be it Humanity, Zeus or Justice.[37]

His own death is specific, not reconciling—he dies of starvation. The 'peace', the 'home' he reaches is ironic—a meeting with 'the Absolute', but a burial by a stranger. As though to deepen the sense of anger, Jos does have a strange relationship with a petty thief known only as The Squirrel. Her final act of devotion is suicide. The end of the novel, final as it is, drawing on the rhetoric of catharsis as it does, only stresses the specific injustice which has brought it about. There is no 'so be it'.

This kind of analysis only takes us to a certain point. I have shown elsewhere how Gissing, especially in *The Nether World*, also sets up fictional expectations which are defeated by the specific recalcitrance of the social actuality. This merely brings Harkness into the category of a combative realism. But *Out of Work* is combative in a sense which seems to me to be specifically Socialist. Partly I mean by this that the realism generates as its most coherent gloss a socialist discourse embodied by Jos' docker friend and by a speaker on Mile End Waste at the end of Chapter Four when the ironies of the Jubilee, the chapel and Victoria Park (versions of Sunday release) give way to the unsolved problems of unemployment. The speaker stresses that the misery is caused by the Age of Competition which is really at an end. This theme is picked up again and again, on the level of romance, as I have indicated, by the distortion of social Darwinism and its allegiance with Christian self-righteousness, on the level of industry by the focus on dock labour: 'He began to realise that a job could only be obtained by physical strength, that he had no chance until his leg was well again',[38] and on a general social level by the description of Jos' social place as among 'the great army that goes marching on, heedless of stragglers, whose commander-in-chief is laissez faire.' Jos' way out of this becomes gin, but that is firmly contextualised. He takes to gin when the hunger is so bad he faints at the home of his docker friend who gives him spirits to revive him. Likewise, he is supported through his misery by a petty thief. Crime and drink are not merely seen as the bad consequences of poverty, they are linked with the repressed corporateness which the Socialist on Mile End Waste says will replace competition. Before the fight for work at the dock gates, travelling to the battle, men are able momentarily to show a camaraderie: 'the only good thing that comes of being unemployed is "I help you, and you help me, because we've no place in society".'[39] Socialism is not an imported utopian answer, it emerges as a necessity and a possibility. The novel's finest passage is the build-up to the Trafalgar Square demonstration. The unemployed resort to the Square as a place to sleep. They are watched by the ruling class night after night. It is impossible to convey by quotation how concretely Harkness renders this breaking out of misery and its encampment in the arena of the oppressor. It is as though a truth has broken its bounds, geographically and socially. And given that the alternative to the Square for Jos is the casual ward (again rendered with horrifying concreteness as a personal experience) the reader is projected towards sharing the release of the riot.

The novel goes further than this. It overcomes one of the most obvious problems for the socialist writer. Fiction has as one of its primary values the personalisation of social experience but this is why it remains such a bourgeois form, because Socialism clearly demands the extra-mural sharing of consciousness. Jos' story is highly individualised, but it is not declassed. On the contrary, Harkness carefully inserts what he learns into a context of anonymous voices. The man at the Methodist service is merely a voice challenging one level of coherence. The dock labourer radical is never named. The ex-soldier is represented only by his graffiti. No little community is set up to mark the specialness of the individual case. Jos' story is specific but it is the story of the unemployed—not because that story can be concentrated in that one life, but because it belongs with all the other separate lives which intersect his path. This is the very opposite of the convexity which is the primary aesthetic end of bourgeois realism. Depressing as this novel is, and lonely as the social rejection leaves the hero, all the other versions of defeat and loneliness are brought together as a common pool of experiences and defeats. The novel itself by its form organises this sense of oppression and in doing so secularises it. Jos dreams of 'home', but he does not take his comrade with him. She only knows that he has gone away. Jos perceives the stars as a mocking universe but that indifference is also glossed as the social system. And very briefly the common pool is articulated in Trafalgar Square. This brings us back to the first point—that the documentary in the novel is not of place but of event. Inarticulate as the voice of the unemployed is in the face of the institutions which silence it, royalty, Methodism, casual labour, poor relief, we see it in the process of becoming history. That is why, I think, Harkness thought about and assimilated Engels' criticism. Zola showed that working-class history could not be embodied in the protagonist, but he has to make it, as did in his very different way, Morris, a matter of vision. Harkness goes a long way towards making it the voice of many voices.

V *Captain Lobe* (1889)

After *Out of Work*, *Captain Lobe* is inevitably disappointing but
the reasons why it is so are not simple. The decision to use the
Salvation Army as a focus for a novel about 'darkest London' does
not seem strange if we bear in mind Engels's comment on its
appearance in *A City Girl* when he praises 'your sharp repudiation
of the conception of the self-satisfied philistines, who will learn
from your story, perhaps for the first time, why the Salvation
Army finds such support among the masses of the people.'
General Booth wrote an appreciative preface to the novel, but he
clearly recognises that it is not written by an author who shares his
values. The motive is rather surely that the Army, more than any
socialist organisation, had a structure sited within working-class
London and thus has access to a reality which can otherwise be
seen only hazily. What is more disturbing is the positive use of a
melodramatic plot, a heroine who by virtue of her inheritance is
only an observer and later benefactor of the working-class girls
employed in the factory she owns, and the overall marginalisation
of political readings to two outside voices who present their case
episodically as a single contained discourse. At the same time, it is
a novel whose documentary aim seems to take over—as for
example when space is given to the tattooed man to relate his
'history' at length as though we were simply taken to the entertainment and left to look on.

But this is not to deny the strengths which are quite different
from those of *Out of Work*. The Army, for example, is used in a
brilliantly complex way both to act as a critical organisation and to
be seen as being unable to meet the material case of poverty. The
most striking episode of the book is Ruth's guided tour by two
Army lassies through Seven Dials in the Fifth and Sixth Chapters.
It is preluded by a rare account of the conversion of a stockbroker
who is brought to salvation by a dream of social guilt. Captain
Lobe himself is presented as an ascetic whose concern for the souls
of the poor is underwritten by his awareness of what he terms 'lust
of the spirit' in the rich, and his closest friends are an agnostic lady
who, despite her scepticism about existing socialist organisations,
urges that socialism is in the air, and a doctor who, contemptuous
of his West End colleagues, quotes Engels and reveals an ambition
to be a constitutional socialist. Lobe himself has to keep thanking
God that he has no intellect:

Salvationists do not attempt to reason; they appeal to a man's heart, and think the intellect a little thing that requires wheedling. Consequently, few educated men and women join their ranks, and they cannot point to one scholar in their camp of any importance. But in slums and allies their work is a real force, for the inhabitants of these places recognise their sincerity of purpose, and do not approach them in a critical spirit.[40]

The Army then is not sentimentalised—it is rather a mode of insight, which has to be theorised.

Equally it is a mode which meets continual resistance. The slum sisters meet not merely an unregenerate lumpenproletariat but also an articulate 'materialism' to which they have no answer.

'Are you saved, brother?' they asked a man with a white face and bloodless lips, whose clothes hung loosely on his emaciated body.

'If starving will save me, I ought to have been saved long before this', the man answered.

'You must give up your sins; then God will send you food', was the reply.

The man shook his head, and said 'The Bible calls God a father, and no father would starve his son for sinning. He would give him food first, and speak about his sin afterwards.'[41]

The dialogue continues but the man has the last word—'I'm hungry.' Later Captain Lobe regrets having to consign his people to damnation, and we are told that: 'He had no great affection for the Salvation Army. But he did not know any other organisation that worked so hard'.[42] From the novelist's point of view because it works so hard in darkest London, its very failure to make headway (which is what is stressed) exposes the nature of the problem, and both of Lobe's confidants express an alternative to salvation— socialism makes more sense in terms of what we have seen.

The real limitations of this privilege are precisely that the novel tends to become a series of tableaux, brilliant and angry but static and without much development. This is true as well of the later stages when Ruth is taken to the homes and the places of entertainment of her workpeople by the confused socialist/feminist forewoman, Jane Hardy. Equally, as this suggests, characters tend to become very static. In fact the novel gravitates towards the spectacle of the Penny gaff and although the hop-picking episode has more movement it is still within the terms of a contained sequence.

The reasons for these limitations are not difficult to define. What has given the earlier novels their specific effectivity, the cutting

into the picture of voices which promise the voice of the working
class, has now been abandoned. On the one hand there are radical
versions, *articulate* but from an *outside* middle class. On the other,
the proletarian world itself is only allowed to speak in contained
theatres—the doss house or the police court. Clearly Harkness
wanted to articulate a more specific political programme and
equally clearly she couldn't. Only the ideology of the Army set
against the resistance of the working class (that is the most depressed among them). The melodrama of Captain Lobe rushing
back to marry Ruth displaces any political action, but it is almost
necessary to sidetrack the stalemate between what is effectively
constituted as the ideological organisation of the poor and the
hunger of the poor.

There are many ways in which this might reflect Harkness' own
political confusion as the arguments of the late 1880s come to a
head. But it also reflects on the difficulty of following *Out of Work*
with a novel which could build on its positivity without being
utopian. By seeing the truth through the alien utopia of the
Salvation Army, Margaret Harkness seems to wish to correct the
possible vagueness of her own political perspective. She succeeds
almost too well, and produces an endless documentary within the
confines of a terminated story. But what I insist on is that like *A
City Girl* and *Out of Work*, *Captain Lobe* ought to be read by
anyone concerned with the implications for the literary production
of the socialist movement.

NOTES

1 The historical details in this paper derive largely from Henry Pelling,
   The Origins of the Labour Party 1880–1900 (London, 1954), but I
   have also found E. P. Thompson, *William Morris, Romantic to
   Revolutionary* (London, 1955), Chushichi Tsuzuki, *H. M. Hyndman
   and British Socialism* (Oxford, 1961), Dona Torr, *Tom Mann and His
   Times* (London, 1956) useful in forming a general perspective. The
   synthesis offered here makes no claims to originality, but it is my own
   and I am only too aware of its eclecticism and simplification.
2 Pelling, *op. cit.*, p. 48.
3 Pelling *op. cit.*: 'The fact was that, although it was to the interest of
   the working class that the Socialists appealed, there was a very high
   proportion of middle-class people among the converts of this period,
   and what the societies lacked in numbers they made up in the comparative energy, ability and financial generosity of their members.

This alone can account for the flood of Socialist periodicals and pamphlets which already poured from the presses.'

4 See my 'Gissing, Morris and English Socialism', *Victorian Studies*, XII, 1968, pp. 432–40, and John Lucas, 'Conservatism and Revolution in the 1880's'', in John Lucas (ed.), *Literature and Politics in the Nineteenth Century* (London, 1971), pp. 173–219.

5 I don't wish to underestimate the quite remarkable achievements of Meredith and Rutherford, nor indeed to suggest that in more than this strictly limited local context they can be bracketed together. See John Lucas, *The Literature of Change* (Hassocks, 1977), Chapter II for Rutherford.

6 In Chapter XVI. See my essay on Morris in Lucas, *Literature and Politics*, p. 232.

7 Bernhard Shaw, *An Unsocial Socialist* (London, 1914), pp. 324–5.

8 The term is Gissing's. See my *George Gissing: Fiction and Ideology* (London, 1978), Chapter 1.

9 John Law (i.e. Margaret Harkness), *George Eastmont, Wanderer* (London, 1905), p. 125. All of Margaret Harkness' novels were published under the pseudonym of John Law.

10 The main source of this section is the unpublished diary of Beatrice Webb. I have also found Norman Mackenzie (ed.), *The Letters of Sidney and Beatrice Webb* (London, 1978), vol. I useful. For her relationship with Eleanor Marx see Yvonne Kapp, *The Crowded Years* (London, 1976).

11 Unpublished diary, entry of 24 March 1883.

12 *Ibid.*, 13 February 1882.

13 'Women as Civil Servants', *Nineteenth Century*, X (1880), p. 381.

14 'Railway Labour', *Nineteenth Century*, XII (1882), p. 721.

15 *Ibid.*, p. 732.

16 'The Municipality of London', *National Review*, n.s., 2 (1883), p. 105.

17 *Egyptian Life and History* (London, 1884), p. 54.

18 *Ibid.*, p. 68.

19 Unpublished diary, entry of 24 March 1883.

20 Ann Stafford, *A Match to Fire the Thames* (London, 1961), p. 155.

21 Unpublished diary, entry of 18 October 1887.

22 'A Year of My Life', *New Review*, 5 (1893), p. 376.

23 Unpublished diary, entry of 13 November 1889.

24 Karl Marx and Frederick Engels, *Literature and Art* (Bombay, 1956), pp. 35–8.

25 John Law, *A City Girl* (London, 1887), p. 9.

26 See Adrian Poole, *Gissing in Context* (London, 1975), for a discussion of this group of writers.

27 *A City Girl, op. cit.*, p. 47.

28 *Ibid.*, p. 70.

29 *Ibid.*, pp. 66–7.

30 *Ibid.*, p. 76.

31 *Ibid.*, p. 100.

32 *Ibid.*, p. 126.
33 John Law, *Out of Work* (London, 1888), p. 2.
34 *Ibid.*, p. 221.
35 *Ibid.*, pp. 18–19.
36 *Ibid.*, p. 240.
37 *Ibid.*, p. 241.
38 *Ibid.*, p. 163.
39 *Ibid.*, p. 129.
40 John Law, *Captain Lobe* (London, 1889), pp. 33–4.
41 *Ibid.*, p. 50.
42 *Ibid.*, p. 226.

Chapter 4

EARLY HARVEST: THREE ANTI-CAPITALIST NOVELS PUBLISHED IN 1914

Jack Mitchell

1914 is something of an *annus mirabilis* in the publishing history of the British proletarian and revolutionary-democratic novel. At the high point of that first modern rank-and-filers' counter-attack against monopoly capital, known as the Great Unrest, three works appeared through which that same spirit barged into the mainstream of the English novel. In Robert Tressell's *The Ragged Trousered Philanthropists* and in Patrick MacGill's *Children of the Dead End* it expresses itself directly; in John Macdougall Hay's *Gillespie* more indirectly. All three helped, to a varying degree, to lay the foundations for a new departure in realism. In formulating the following remarks I have assumed that the reader is better acquainted with Tressell's classic than with the other two works.

I

The Ragged Trousered Philanthropists and *Children of the Dead End* must be seen as part of the world-wide breakthrough of proletarian and socialist-realist imaginative prose which took place almost immediately upon capitalism's transition to its imperialist and decadent stage in 1900. In the few years between the 1905 revolution in Russia and the outbreak of World War I, were written, apart from those mentioned: Upton Sinclair's *The Jungle*, Jack London's *The Iron Heel*, Martin Andersen Nexø's *Pelle Erobreren* and Maxim Gorky's *Mother*.

Conquest of the longer imaginative prose genres is part and parcel of the general coming of age of the working class. Of course the class could not and did not wait until entering upon its maturity to produce a complex and effective body of literature, particularly in the field of poetry and the 'operative' genres. But that universal, insatiable, positive curiosity about every detail of their living and their society, which is a *sine qua non* for the mastery of the *strategic* realist prose form,[1] is only reached after the class has 'convinced itself' through a long history of achievement that not only has it something to offer in human terms but that it is coextensive with humanity as such, humanity in its dynamic essence. Both the cumulative *practice* of the international proletariat and the development and dissemination of its scientific *theory* had established the basis for such a view of itself by 1900.

The achievement of aesthetic-literary maturity was therefore not only a matter of the vanguard grasping in theoretical-scientific terms the historical role of their class, but of the ripening of proletarianised senses, a proletarianised sensuality, a new quality of sensibility, a proletarianised imagination. More stumbling-blocks on the way to this adequate subject-object relationship had to be overcome by the proletariat than by the bourgeoisie in their day. As Engels wrote, 'In European countries, it took the working class years and years before they fully realised the fact that they formed a distinct and, under the existing social conditions, a permanent class of modern society.'[2] They had to learn that their class was not a historical aberration but a human category already giving birth to new and exemplary forms of human-social relationships and behaviour, forms which would not be negated through the revolution but freed by it to become the social norm.

The proletariat's total objective politico-cultural activity and achievement (trades unions, educational institutions, political parties, campaigns and strikes, international solidarity, etc.) lay the foundation for their cultural-aesthetic maturity in the narrower sense. Despite all unevenness of historical development in the various sectors of advancing capitalism, by the turn of the century the 'latecomers' among the international proletariat in the industrialised areas had caught up with those sections of longer standing and entered their maturity more or less simultaneously with them.

Tressell's *The Ragged Trousered Philanthropists* (known as *RTP*) is the most profound and universal incarnation in our literature of this new self-assurance, new Humanism, new sensibility, new aesthetic. He was not without immediate forerunners however—above all in the prose and verse of Tom Maguire and in Charles Clarke's novels.

Tressell's novel is the story of a group of downtrodden 'Mugsborough' housepainters and their relations to their pastors and masters, and to their workmate Frank Owen, who tries desperately to drive his socialist message into their confused minds. It was written between 1905 and 1910 and published in a severely truncated form in 1914. The author, whose real name was Robert Noonan, was born in Dublin in 1871 and died of poverty and tuberculosis in 1911. Noonan-Tressell worked in the building trade as a housepainter. *RTP* became *the* 'underground classic' of the British working class, even in its mutilated form. The full text was finally published in 1955.

One of the most immediately striking features of Tressell's method is the fierce *satire* which he levels at his own class (see the book's title). In the uncompromising honesty and courage of the criticism levelled at the illusions hampering his class in fulfilling its historical responsibility Tressell is in line with contemporaries and immediate successors like Gorky (*Lower Depths*), Lu Hsun (*A Madman's Diary*, etc.), O'Casey (the Dublin Plays) and others. This approach demonstrates that the exploited workers are strategically no longer on the moral defensive, no longer feel obliged to gloss over their weaknesses and 'justify' their class and cause at some abstract court of appeal against the slanders of their enemies. They are now in dialogue with themselves only. This radical self-criticism conducted by the class through its writers is historically an essential part of the stripping for the coming fight. In this way young proletarian socialist realism develops the constructive critical content and *function* of realism beyond anything achieved by bourgeois critical realism. The rising proletariat injects fresh blood into realism as such.

Tressell, like O'Casey, goes unerringly to the heart of the matter. This, in modern Britain, is the mental manacles clapped on the workers' minds by the imperialist manipulators—the main guarantee of their continued hegemony. In *RTP* Tressell gives the classic close-up study of this newly 'matured' chauvinist corruption, this mental fifth column, contrasting their illusory picture of themselves with their actual condition. Concurrently with this runs Owen's and Barrington's practical demonstration of the Marxist analysis of exploitation and the socialist alternative. Thus the duel between false and true (class) consciousness, which remains the basic daily battlefield for the small army of dedicated socialists in a country like Britain, forms the crux of the novel—a dramatic, unfinished public debate and conflict which never fails to fascinate because in its positive outcome lies the key to so much, and never fails to inspire because of the undaunted and incorruptible perseverance with which it is waged in the teeth of seemingly overwhelming odds.

The *satirical* tone has, it seems to me, contradictory sources. Mockery of the elements of slavishness in the working masses had been a tradition in English democratic literature going back at least to Shelley's *Song to the Men of England*. It was also the tone of much of the propaganda of the socialist groups in the 1880s and

1890s. This reflected their isolation from the organised class struggle and certain immaturities in their theory of the revolutionary process. Tressell was not free from these weaknesses and the somewhat carping and repetitive sarcasm which increasingly affects the book reflects an element of pessimism caused by the failure of the purely 'evangelising' approach. Yet basically the satire is a unique strength of the novel. Satire based on paradox is an eminently fitting method of opening up imperialist reality, which is itself the epitome of paradox, a world stood on its head. Many of our post-Tressell working-class and socialist writers have fought shy of applying it to working-class character and situation. One source of this once again seems to have been the relative isolation and smallness of the revolutionary party (here the Communist Party). There has been a sort of defensive 'diplomacy', an avoidance of anything that might be construed as a libel on the working class. Militant workers have, however, much preferred the undiplomatic tone of *RTP*, a fact that surely reveals a deep self-confidence and optimism in both readers and author.

Tressell can criticise his fellow workers in this way because his vision of them, being totally from the inside, is, unlike that of the Gissing-type 'satirist', simultaneously poetic, affirmative. The book is addressed exclusively to them, as the exclusive representatives of Humanity. This is seen in its most subtle form in the author's inability to hold his satirical distance, even in scenes which are conceived as basically burlesque. He becomes fascinated by the workers' activity 'for its own sake'. In this process their spontaneously combative, re-creative relationship to the enemy environment emerges. Situations which are set up by the exploiters as tools against the workers are temporarily and partially wrested from their control and transformed into vehicles for expressing the specific humanising quality of working-class living. This occurs at all levels. Capitalist alienation in its imperialist stage forces its way into every 'refuge' (one of the pressures driving Tressell to social universality!)—even into the Englishman's home, supposedly his castle. Tressell shows it to be, as Marx says, 'an alien habitation'.[3] The shoddy articles in the Easton flat, produced by the workers' hands, are 'for him an *alien*, hostile, powerful object independent of him'.[4] But the point is that for long periods Ruth Easton succeeds in transforming them into more than the semblance of a home. In 'The Filling of the Tank,' the pub, that legendary cultural centre of the Englishman, is revealed as a centre of stupification. Yet, during the game of hooks-and-rings, it too becomes momentarily *their* institution through which they express a kind of victory over degrading 'circumstance'. The same happens on a larger scale in the struggle for control of the annual Beano outing. During their work, that is at the point of production (the genesis-point of all alienation) the best workers fight to preserve a human relationship to their labour. This reaches its highest expression in Owen's partially successful struggle to decorate the Moorish Drawing Room on *his* terms. The 'instinctive', all-pervading, grass-roots fight-back of the workers in defence of culture and man's human essence—a theme eminently suited to artistic treatment—has rarely been so brilliantly conveyed. It is one of Tressell's most important contributions to the renewal of realism.

What emerges from this is not only the thing being fought against, but what has to be fought *for*. We recognise, through the degradation, new human relations, a new way of living, in embryo, hemmed in, crippled and denied as yet, in the womb of the old. If we do not experience the class struggle at its highest and most organised level (and this of course is a serious gap in the book's universality) we do learn to appreciate what this struggle is finally about. The task is to liberate these potentials, and, by establishing their social hegemony, to transform and 'purify' them. Here lies the perspective *implicit* in Tressell's apparently static picture.

The centre of attention has become the rank-and-file workers' group, of which, despite all differences, the individual hero Frank Owen is merely the quintessence. They are no longer just a chorus or undifferentiated background to the massively portrayed bourgeois or artisan hero. Another part of Tressell's realist 'innovation' lies in articulating this monolith into a gallery of unforgettable individuals who at the same time never become detached from the group-organism whose characteristics they all have in common. Behind this new dialectical grasp of the relationship between working-class individuality and the collective lie the exploits of the rank-and-file masses and their leaders since the late 1880s, when they began to take over the historical initiative.

This necessitated radical innovations in the structure and organisation of the novel. Tressell replaced the old plot-in-length with a new-type plot-in-breadth. In this way he could tell the story of the broad mass and at the same time indicate the universal and systematic nature of capitalist exploitation much more effectively than through the life-story of a single central hero. The bio-graphical path of the worker from the cradle to the grave is divided up among the characters so that its different phases run parallel to each other. In this way the possibility of chance and exceptional circumstances being perhaps responsible for the fate of the individual worker is excluded. Exploitation is a universal social *law*. The temptation to become emotionally absorbed in a particular individual is avoided. The emotional response is gigantic, but it is socialised.

The action covers one year. Its groundswell is that of everyday capitalism: slump—boom—slump. Thus monopoly capitalism's basic lack of a dynamic history, its vicious-circle life-story can be told in the space of a single year. It ends where it begins—or not quite, for the second slump is slightly deeper than the first. The apparently static picture has in fact a strategic social rhythm— inexorable decline.

The classic hero is modified, but he remains, with his rich inner life and nearness to the author's own standpoint. There can be no question of the individuality of the individual hero being 'drained' out into the hero-collective. The portrayal of Frank Owen shows that Tressell's great innovations should not blind us to the debt he owes to the classical realist heritage—or the debt which this heritage owes to Tressell. In one sense Owen is none other than that 'obscure', dedicated, puritan artisan who begins with Christian in *The Pilgrim's Progress* and is handed over to Tressell by Thomas Hardy in the person of Jude Fawley. He is Jude rescued, given, through the socialist vision and the objective exploits of his class, a new and practical perspective.

Much of the novelty and power of Tressell's impact lies in this synthesis of innovation and tradition, in our apprehension of the familiar as unfamiliar and new. Here again he is almost unique among our proletarian and socialist writers most of whom have tended to rely too readily on the aesthetic and politico-social interest of their material as such, and on secondrate or fashionable literary models. There have been exceptions of course, in the best works of Alan Sillitoe, in James Plunkett's *Strumpet City*, and in Lewis Grassic Gibbon's *A Scots Quair*. In the latter the line of tradition is rather to the older folk-culture, a source which plays little part in Tressell.

In view of the ambitiousness and novelty of his undertaking Tressell had to be extremely catholic in his cultural 'connections'. He took what he needed from wherever it offered itself. Thus his sources include elements from contemporary naturalism and from popular and 'low' forms of mass entertainment. He was an admirer of Bram Stoker's *Dracula*, and his body-snatching episode ('The Ghouls') stems from that quarter. In the 'Pandorama' scene he presses a piece of current 'sub-culture' into service—the magic lantern, a predecessor of the cinema. More important than these, the strong tradition of socialist political prose (pamphlets, speeches, lectures, debates, etc.) puts its unmistakable stamp on his narrative style with its marriage of precise, sober description and ferocious irony—and even on certain aspects of the structure, for instance Owen's dramatised lectures.

But his main relationship is to the heritage of classical realism. One of the hallmarks of this was its drive towards extensive totality. Dickens, the English bourgeois novel's last universal man, came closest to grasping 'the sorry scheme of things entire' as an integrated *system* of oppression. The English novel had to wait for the proletarian Tressell to complete this job. His portrait of the boss-class and its minions is essential to this. While bourgeois authors were plumbing the 'rich depths' of the inner life of this class's drop-outs and exceptions, Tressell goes to work on its everyday practitioners. Using techniques of caricature and grotesque derived directly from Swift and Fielding he isolates them as a Yahoo-species whose life-function consists in devouring and wasting the things produced by humanity (the workers), and in systematically negating the human essence itself, which is located in the latter.

This is epitomised in the destructive relationship of the bosses, etc. to the labour process. The extortion of surplus value at the point of production is the germ from which the whole ramified system of exploitation radiates. It is the point of naked confrontation between man and anti-man, and so, quite naturally, Tressell places it at the hub of his radial working-model of society. His is the most massive, contradictory and successful depiction of men at work in our literature. Alienated labour emerges as the chief source of man's woe, but work as such also as the chief potential source of his joy, his fulfilment.

Only once, at its very inception, had the bourgeois novel boldly put man's central activity, work, at the centre of aesthetic interest —in *Robinson Crusoe*. Increasingly since then the aesthetic burden which should chiefly be borne by work has fallen on something else, something apparently unaffected by alienation, something which although important to life and art, has played a part in the latter quite disproportionate to its part in social life— 'love'. It is interesting in this connection that Tressell jettisons the 'love interest' entirely. The neglected heritage of the first modern English novel is picked up and developed in our first great working-class novel. In the former the epic struggle is external to labour as such, being between worker-man and nature; in the latter, work itself becomes the arena of a life-and-death struggle between two classes of men and within individual men. This struggle inhibits and complicates the original and basic one with nature. We have already mentioned the workers' fight to retain a pride in work well done. True pride and fulfilment for Rushton and Hunter consists in *having work badly done*. It is in this that they put themselves beyond the human pale. The particular strength and emphasis of Tressell's approach here undoubtedly owes much to the ideas elaborated by William Morris, whom he greatly admired.

Across this chasm separating humanity and its negation, personal relationships can hardly exist. Nevertheless British revolutionary writers have tried again and again to express the facts of oppression through a plot based on just such personal-emotional involvements across the gulf. The only relationship which Tressell allows to be established across it is that of simple, impersonal cash payment—in art as in life. This is certainly a triumph of uncompromising realism, but how, then, does Tressell 'bind' his massive edifice and give it shape and unity?

He does so mainly through using two classical techniques inherited from Dickens. The first of these is a system of paradoxical contrasts. Those between bosses and workers, and between illusion and reality are self-evident. More unobtrusive are, for instance, those between the healthy reactions of children and the wrongheaded folly of their elders and parents, or between the spontaneous actions of basically sound workers like Joe Philpot and the petty calculatedness of opportunists like Slyme. The effect is as of a mosaic. This technique is eminently suited to revealing the true nature of the most paradoxical society in history.

The second 'technique' is inherent in the way he builds his images. These are so rich in concentrated typicality that they tend to take on an added dimension. As with Dickens, many of the complex single images become epitomes or metaphors for important aspects of society and of the statement of the book as a whole. Two examples: Misery, the manager, is always exhorting the men to 'slobber it over', to cover the dirt, cracks and structural weaknesses in the walls of the 'Cave' so that it looks all right just long enough for the firm to pocket money. This was, and is, the actual 'state of the nation' as a whole. Then there is Slyme, a working-man version of Uriah Heep. He insinuates himself into the Easton family with the aim of seducing Ruth, which he eventually manages. Later he leaves the seemingly sinking ship and the pregnant Ruth. Apart from its immediate social comment this 'symbolises' the role of evangelising religion and opportunism in subverting and betraying the working class.

Tressell's successors have been better placed to organise their plots round a picture of the developing organised class struggle, thus giving their picture a strategic forward movement and practical perspective absent in Tressell. But to rely almost entirely on this 'ready-made' organisational element, as so many have done, can lead to looseness and lack of *artistic* unity. Here, as elsewhere, there is much to be said for taking a leaf out of Tressell's book.

II

Patrick MacGill, the author of *Children of the Dead End*, was born of a poor peasant family in Donegal in 1890. In his youth 'he lived the life of the Irish migrant labourers and the itinerant navvies in Scotland. His autobiographical novel quickly became something of a classic among workers in Scotland. His success was used against him and his class. He was turned into a kind of 'official' working-class writer to put across the propaganda of the ruling class in the language and idiom of the workers themselves.

In 1914, however, he still had the stuff in him to take a different path. Broadly speaking *Children of the Dead End* expresses the same new quality of strategic working-class self-confidence which is to be found in Tressell. In the years between the Belfast strike of 1907 and the class war in Dublin in 1913 the organised Irish working class had come quickly from behind and now formed the vanguard of proletarian struggle. Although this coming of age is not directly reflected in the novel its impact is there in the self-confidence shown, in the broad (but not complete) rejection of bourgeois values and in the militant (if immature) class standpoint.

In one episode the two heroes, Dermod Flynn (the author) and the navvy Moleskin Joe, are discussing a poem which Dermod has written. Joe says he prefers the rough-and-ready ballad, *The Shootin' of the Crow*, by Two-Shift Mullholland, to Dermod's rather sentimental and derivative verses: 'It's a true song, so help me God! But yours!'[5] Joe was a real-life character whose sound advice on realism MacGill followed when writing *Children of the Dead End*. A new importance, a direct reference to life is demanded of art. Thus the autobiographical and documentary emphasis of *Children of the Dead End* (and of *The Ragged Trousered Philanthropists*) is important. But in both cases there is a new quality as against previous working-class autobiographies.

Now the everyday materials of the worker's own life are consciously and unashamedly transformed into art. A new type of
novel arises to which the term 'fiction' can no longer really be
applied, although they are no longer 'documentary' either.
Aesthetic principles which seemed eternal begin to reveal their
class restrictions.

The novel begins with Dermod Flynn's childhood in the fishing
and crofting village of Glenmornan in Ireland. The time is about
1900. In a series of very short chapters MacGill builds up a picture
of the Irish country people in the stranglehold of the landlord—
merchant—priest triumvirate. But things are stirring. Many young
people are beginning to question the right of the old clique to rule
over them—and even to have doubts about the God who was
supposed to have granted this right.

One of these budding rebels is young Dermod. Still a mere lad
Dermod has to go 'beyond the mountain' to make money for the
priest, the landlord and the growing family. With other agricultural wage-labourers he stands at the 'Slave Market' to be
inspected and bought by the more prosperous farmers. Being a
commodity encourages Dermod's process of mental liberation.

After varying fortunes at the hands of several masters he sets
sail with a group of Glenmornan acquaintances to work at the
seasonal potato-picking in Scotland (1905). One of the party is his
childhood sweetheart, Nora Ryan.

If conditions in Ireland are bad, those under which the pickers
have to live in Scotland are terrible. Dermod comes to reject a
God of personal concern, though not God as such. The naive and
ignorant Nora is seduced by a middle-class reformer, whereupon
Dermod squanders all his wages and has to remain behind when the
others sail for home. He sets out to 'seek his fortune' in Scotland
and meets up with Moleskin Joe, a rollicking, battling, self-
educated, class-conscious wit and itinerant navvy, who becomes
his friend and mentor.

After two years of drifting Dermod gets news that the 'fallen'
Nora is somewhere in Glasgow and goes to look for her there, but
without success. For a time he works as a platelayer along with
other Irish labourers on the railway. At this point he develops an
appetite for reading and tries his hand at writing verses. His
interest in politics is aroused by hearing socialists speak at the
street corner and he joins the 'socialist party'.[6] This is the last the
reader hears of the organised socialist movement.

Dermod studies Marx and Henry George. 'The former, the
more logical, appealed to me least.'[7] The misery and hazards of

work on the railway are fearful. He brings the men out on strike but the Irish labourers, ignorant, unorganised and intimidated, cave in after a few minutes.

In a 'model lodging house' Dermod defeats the celebrated bruiser, Carroty, and discovers a 'typical' Irish love of fighting in himself, of which the author thoroughly approves. Dermod, Moleskin and Carroty set out for a big navvying job at Kinlochleven in the Highlands. Scenes of digging and blasting, drinking, fighting and gambling at the camp—a Scottish version of Jack London's Klondike. The living conditions could almost do justice to a concentration camp. Dermod begins to write accounts of navvy life for the London papers.

Back in Glasgow looking for Nora, Dermod again takes work on the railway, lodging in slum doss-houses. He is isolated from his workmates 'who believed in clergycraft, psalm-singing and hymn-hooting.'[8] Eventually he runs into Nora who is, of course, a prostitute. The shock forces him to a new insight: 'The social system is not like a person; one man's anger cannot remedy it, one man's fist cannot strike at its iniquities.'[9] He soon loses sight of Nora again.

A London newspaper takes him on as a reporter on labour questions. When he is asked to go to Wales and report on the big miners' strike in such a way as to discredit the men he resigns. Back in Glasgow once more Dermod and Moleskin track Nora down to old Gourock Ellen's. She is in the last stages of TB and expires after the obligatory 'touching' reunion with her old love. Faced with this 'last great reality' Dermod and the redoubtable Joe get down on their knees and pray for the repose of her soul.[10]

In his Irish scenes he sees the world, as E. M. Forster would have wished the ideal artist to see it,[11] both steadily and as a whole. He knows exactly what he wants, so that his art is astonishingly economic, even laconic in a very modern sense. He paces from one strategic image to the next without the need of explanatory transitions, each image-scene being the crystallisation of a mass of potential material and capable of standing on its own as a miniature of the whole. The cumulative effect is a completely transparent, poetic 'working model' of Irish rural society.

The writing in these sections is of a kind one associates with folk-tales and ballads. It is rhythmic, but far less 'worked up' and closer to the actual speech rhythms of the peasantry than is Gibbon's narrative rhythm in *A Scots Quair*. MacGill had that gift of the revolutionary writer to make ordinary and worn words appear fresh and meaningful:

The wind was moaning over the chimney. By staying very quiet one could hear the wail in its voice, and it was like that of the stream on the far side of the glen. A pot of potatoes hung over the fire, and as the water bubbled and sang the potatoes could be seen bursting their jackets beneath the lid. . . . An oil lamp swung by a string from the roof-tree backwards and forwards like a willow branch when the wind of October is high. As it swung the shadows chased each other in the silence of the farther corners of the house. My mother said that if we were bad children the shadows would run away with us, but they never did, and indeed we were often full of all sorts of mischief. We felt afraid of the shadows, they even frightened mother. But father was afraid of nothing.[12]

For all the misery this Irish world is suffused with beauty. It is a valid world whose assurance of its own human dignity is the product of centuries of peasant struggle in which native culture played a powerful part, a community deeply imbued with the certainty that it will dance on the graves of its oppressors: 'The people when they saw this feared the new parish priest, but they never took any heed to the new God, and up to this day there are many good six-hand reelers in Glenmornan. And the priest is, dead.'[13] As in all truly popular and revolutionary art there arises a sense of the *tragic* contradiction between the quality of humanity achieved and the way it is thwarted and denied by existing social relations.

The further MacGill moves away from his Irish roots and the nearer he gets to the modern industrial city of Glasgow the less able he is to cope with his life-material artistically. He was equipped neither by sensibility nor by ideology to penetrate beneath the scum surface of degradation and alienation which lay over the much more fluid and complex urban proletarian community of modern Scotland. From being a supreme artist he now becomes, on the whole, a middling naturalist-type journalist in the fashionable vein of Jack London's *The People of the Abyss*.

In this City of Dreadful Night the nearest MacGill gets to the industrial workers are the Irish labourers on the railway. It is the lumpen outcasts such as the old semi-prostitute, Gourock Ellen, who stand representative of the 'common people' in the mass. It is true that MacGill shows—rather too insistently—that they have a heart of gold, that they are the true Christians, and so on, but it is the traditional humble humanity of the 'helping hand'. There is no real vitality here, no pride, no rebellion. In fact their humanity actually seems to depend on their being 'the dregs'. Thus the world of middle-class values, which MacGill rejects, is not, on the whole, contrasted morally with that of the working class as such, but with that of the social outcasts. Thus the moral contradiction between man and anti-man is moved outside of society proper and tends towards a contrast between the outcasts on the one hand and the *whole* of society on the other. There is an ominous tendency to *sentimentalise* existing degradation. Here MacGill runs counter to great contemporary proletarian writers like Maxim Gorky, Robert Tressell, and (a little later) Sean O'Casey.

This uncertainty in relation to the industrial city certainly reflects the author's position as an itinerant Irish labourer on the periphery of the organised mass struggle. But he was not alone in this artistic rout before the gates of Glasgow. Again and again this was to be the nut on which Scottish radical authors broke their teeth. It was the biggest unsolved aesthetic problem facing these writers throughout the period. Proletarian and allied artists in England seem to have had much less difficulty in coming to terms artistically with the industrial city.

In MacGill this was not only a failure to bridge the sensibility gap. At this stage the tough nut of Scottish industrial life and struggle could only be cracked with the tool of scientific socialism. MacGill rejected Marx in favour of 'human' or 'British' socialism. Militant though his class position is, it is also primitive and unstable. True to the Irish and popular traditions the anti-clerical strain runs strongly. But nothing coherent is put into the field against traditional Christianity as a social philosophy. The author's sentimental ILP brand of socialism could not fill the bill since it was itself but a variation on Christianity. So there is no real historical debate running systematically through the book. The glorification of the 'Fightin' Irishman' is a poor substitute for that fight for men's minds at the centre of Tressell's book, and it was the weak spot at which pressure was later applied to turn MacGill into an apologist of imperialist militarism. Equally ominous is the relapse into kneeling prayer at the end. The angels thrive in a vacuum. It is true that near the close Dermod does have a fleeting realisation of the inadequacy of 'one man's fist', but there is no lead on to participation in the organised class struggle and so the book entirely lacks a practical revolutionary perspective.

Why then did the workers take it to their hearts? Probably the main reason at the time was its dramatic exposure of the festering degradation in which millions were forced to exist behind the outward facade of the Edwardian 'Indian Summer'. But what has kept the book alive is undoubtedly the personality of *Moleskin Joe*, who stands outside all the criticisms I have made. In his life-style he is not one of the new Clydeside militants. An individualist and adventurer, a 'giant of the open road', his way of life has something old-fashioned and 'romantic' about it. He keeps himself clear of the normal industrial treadmill whenever he can. His qualities seem peculiar to him so that there is an ambivalent self-sufficiency about him. Yet strangely enough he succeeds in being a brilliant embodiment of the spiritual quintessence of the 'new proletarian' of his day. In fact it seems as if this 'untypical' outward life-style becomes a kind of metaphor ideally suited to express that new pride and self-sufficiency growingly characteristic of the rank and file since the late 1880s.

His literary ancestry lies partly with the heroes of the picaresque and ballad traditions. He is too cunning and irrepresssible for an environment which seeks to proscribe his humanity. His appetites, both physical and intellectual, are universal and Homeric in scale. In articulateness he outstrips Sillitoe's somewhat similar heroes, and in his sense of solidarity he leaves them far behind. The essential *self-confidence* of the man emerges in the following exchange. He asks a ploughman for a chew of tobacco:

'If you did your work well and take a job when you get one, you'd have tobacco of your own,' said the ploughman. 'Forbye you would have a hoose and a wife and a dinner ready for you when you went hame in the evenin'. As it is you're daunderin' aboot like a lost flea, too lazy to leeve and too afeard to dee.'

'By Christ! I wouldn't be in your shoes, anyway,' Joe broke in quietly and soberly, a sign that he was aware of having encountered an enemy worthy of his steel. 'A man might as well expect an old sow to go up a tree backwards and whistle like a thrush, as expect decency from a nipple-noddled ninny-hammer like you. If you were a man like me, you would not be tied to a woman's apron strings all your life. . . . Look at me! I'm not at the beck and call of any woman that takes a calf fancy for me.'

'Who would take a fancy to you?'

'You marry a wench and set up a beggarly house,' said Joe, without taking any heed of the interruption. 'You work fourteen or fifteen hours a day for every day of the year. . . . Your wife will get old, her teeth will fall out, and her hair will get thin, until she becomes as bald as the sole of your foot. She'll get uglier until you loathe the sight of her, and find one day that you cannot kiss her for the love of God. But all the time you'll have to stay with her, growl at her, and nothin' before both of you but the grave or the workhouse. If you are as clever a cadger as me why do you suffer all this?'

'Because I'm a decent man,' said the plougher.

Joe straightened up as if seriously insulted. 'Well, I'm damned!' he muttered and continued on his journey. 'It's the first time I ever got the

worst of an argument, Flynn,' he said after we had gone out of sight of the ploughman, and he kept repeating this phrase for the rest of the day. For myself, I thought that Joe got the best of the argument, and I pointed out the merits of his sarcastic remarks. . . .
    'But that about the decent man was one up for him,' Joe interrupted.[14]

Besides being a militant working-class art critic (see above) Moleskin possesses a spirit of universal enquiry that reaches beyond the stars:

'You cannot think of a place where there is nothing, and as far as I can see there is no end to anything. You can't think of the last day as they talk about, for that would mean the end of time. It's funny to think of a man sayin' that there'll be no time after such and such a time. How can time stop?'[15]

Joe in his anger states directly that tragic contradiction implied throughout the novel:

'It was always, "Slide! we don't need you any more," and then a man like me, as helped to build a thousand houses big as castles, was hellish glad to get the shelter of a ten-acre field and a shut gate between me and the winds of night.'[16]

It is as if some character out of Shakespeare had turned proletarian and shouldered his way back into English literature. Integrated, all-sided, full blooded and flamboyant, he is the militant affirmation of human personality and individuality at a time when these things were fading from bourgeois art.

III

John Macdougall Hay, the author of *Gillespie*, was born in 1881 at Tarbert in the Scottish Highlands. Son of a steamship agent he studied philosophy, literature and, later, divinity, at Glasgow University, financing the latter studies with freelance journalism. Always sympathetic to the downtrodden, he cultivated close ties to the poor members of his parish after becoming a minister of the Church of Scotland. According to Robert Kemp he once commented that if he had been a politician 'he would have been Labour'.[17] Hay died of tuberculosis in 1919. Kemp suggests that he was becoming increasingly alienated from the Church towards the end of his life.
    He probably started writing *Gillespie* in 1907, six years after the

publication of George Douglas Brown's *The House with the Green Shutters*. The two books have a common theme up to a point— the exposure of the self-made-man-cum-monopolist. Brown's book is accepted as a minor classic; *Gillespie* has remained in obscurity. Whereas the former traces the fall of the capitalist, *Gillespie* analyses the mechanics of his rise—a more dangerous subject.

By the 1900s the monopoly capitalist class had thrown off the mask of respectability worn by its Victorian parents. Murder and rapine abroad and at home, corruption rampant, luxury flaunted in the faces of the poor—to this queer end had the great and optimistic nineteenth century led, the century of the Self-Made Man. It was clearly time to take a closer and harder look at that popular hero. *The House with the Green Shutters* and *Gillespie* do just that. Two Scots novels—surely no accident. Coming into the running rather late, Scottish capitalists outdid even their English counterparts in unprincipled 'legal' brigandage and proverbial meanness. In the Scottish context it was easy to identify the villanies of the 'primitive' period with the grander but essentially similar practices of monopoly-capitalism in one and the same person. The Reverend Hay went to work on the myth of the self-made man with a *Calvinist* lack of compromise and Jehovian vengeance which finds no equal in English literature. Hay was an admirer to Dostoevsky, Balzac and Zola and his novel belongs more to this continental tradition of realism.

The story is related in highly wrought prose, great creative play being made with the Scots speech of the fishermen. In the following passage the local doctor and policeman are being ferried across a gale-swept stretch of sea:

'It was smooth watter oot tae the "Ghost"; but oh! boys-a-boys, it was blowin' good O! frae the suthard—fair glens o' seas runnin' oot on the Loch. We'd four reefs in, an', being close-hauled, I got into the fo'c'sle beside the bobby for the jib. Just wi' that we opened Rudh'a'Mhail an' she got the weight o' the sea, bow under. Ye ken in the deid o' winter we werena oot at the fushin'; an' beds an' nets were lyin' aboot' an' the hale laggery fetched away tae leeward, an' the bobby wi' them. If ye ever saw a greetin' bubbly-jock it was Cammel the bobby. His face was lik' a foozy moon in the fog. Weel, I cried tae Big Finla' tae ease her a bit till I got the jib on her—Lang Jamie was by him at the sheet; an' there was the bobby standin' at the break o' the fo'c'sle—the very worst place he could stand in. I told him tae come awa' doon aft beside the doctor, but he thought I was takin' a fiver oot o' him. So I just left him jaloosin'.'[18]

In the light of this the rhythmic talk of the folk-narrator in Gibbon's *A Scots Quair* is not so totally new and unique as has sometimes been thought.

The story of Gillespie Strang is set in the fictitious West-Highland fishing and farming township of Brieston in the late 1850s and 1860s. Due to a family blood-crime in the past a doom hangs over the house of Richard Strang, fisherman. It is predicted that the birth of a son will complete the pattern which will end in unnatural murder. A son is born—Gillespie.

At the age of twenty Gillespie dominates the house—the epitome of the 'hard-headed', cheese-paring, callous business-man of the Scottish school. By means of murder (usually done by proxy, for Gillespie has a well-developed sense of self-preservation), fraud, blackmail, intimidation and a vulture's eye for every unconsidered bawbee, he comes step by step to control the economic life of the whole district. His exterior is 'jolly' and 'soft-looking' and like Fielding's Jonathan Wild 'Gillespie explored warily the human heart, and laid his strategies on the instability and gullibleness of men.'[19] Before the people wake up to it he has established monopoly control over the fishing fleet, the crews, the victualling and supplies, the buying and selling of the catch, its storage and transportation by sea. 'A dim conception of the bigness of this man and of his audacity began to impregnate their minds. This man in one morning suddenly became gigantic, and the sparrows of Dothan saw that their day of hopping on the Quay was done.'[20]

Through a relentless account of that 'vulgar' detail which the English bourgeois author had spared his gentle readers, Hay reveals the true nature of that euphemism 'a fair day's business'. In this way a Black Book of incontrovertible evidence is compiled, documenting the 'innocent' process by which that legendary benefactor, the self-made man, made himself and unmade others. The untrammelled pursuit of self-interest is incompatible with the common weal. Also uncovered is the organic link between the self-made man and the monopolist.

He cheats his parents of their nest-egg, drives his mother to an early death, debauches his wife and finally drives her demented. He is responsible for drowning his elder son, Iain, through sending him out in an ill-founded boat, and earns the hatred of Eoghan, his younger son, in whom he has placed all his hopes. Those who would humanise the capitalist have always suggested that he keeps a conscience with the family silver. Not so Gillespie. There is no contradiction between the public and the private. He is all of a piece.

Gillespie is the object of hatred of both God and the common people whom he ruins. There are supernatural overtones strongly reminiscent of *The Rime of the Ancient Mariner* in the drought which strikes Brieston, bringing with it a derelict ship full of dead men. Plague breaks out. God is not mocked—or is He? Gillespie in fact exploits the suffering of the people to tighten his stranglehold and expand his capital.

But revolt is brewing. (Much of the dramatic tension of the book's realism derives from the refusal of so many people within Gillespie's radius to accept the passive role of mere victim.[21]) Farmer Lonend, Gillespie's double-crossed ex-co-conspirator, and Mrs Galbraith, whom Gillespie has cheated out of house and hold, plot in traditional Highland manner to wreak vengeance upon him. (He has peopled Mrs Galbraith's former steading with sheep; the terrible bitterness created by the Highland Clearances is reflected in this woman's reaction to her tormentor.)

This conspiratorial kind of personal vendetta is morally compromised from the start, because it uses means hardly differing from those of Gillespie himself. But there are other, more social forces at work: 'Gillespie however was unaware that times occur in the history of nations and of communities when Law is whirled away in the tempest of the people's revolt. Such a time was coming in Brieston.'[22] Encouraged by Lonend the desperate fishermen fire the fleet which was once their own dearest possession. 'A cool philosophy will recognise the necessity and worth of such an upheaval as overtook Brieston, for there can be no redemption without blood.'[23] The conflagration assumes supernatural proportions. God is in league with the people, it seems, and takes over where men can go no farther. 'The menacing dictum that Jehovah is a just paymaster was fulfilled upon his head.'[24] Or was it? The fire actually turns out to be another 'godsend' for Gillespie's plans of empire.

The tale ends in a welter of blood and horror. Lonend and Galbraith seem to be closing in, but the monster has a trick or two against them up its sleeve yet. The end comes when Morag, his demented wife, saws through her son Eoghan's throat with a razor while he is trying to comfort her. Her head is banged against the fender and she dies. The 'doom' is fulfilled. Gillespie contracts lockjaw through stepping on a broken whisky bottle lying beside Morag's corpse. He expires in horrible agony.

The realistic unity of the story is threatened at various points by the intrusion of supernatural agencies. Some play is made with current naturalist theories of heredity (though it should be noted that Gillespie's parents and his own sons are *not* like him; he appears as an alien intrusion in the chain of humanity). Calvinist theology leaves its mark in the idea of predestination (doom) and apocalyptic judgement. It is but a short step from this to Greek tragedy, and in fact the Reverend Hay, with his solid grounding in classical literature, imbues his subject with this atmosphere—an atmosphere, on the other hand, congenial to the introduction of national folk-elements from traditional Highland legend.

Nevertheless, if one removes all these 'props' the story still succeeds in making a totally realistic impact, with causes and effects of a very earthly origin: Iain has been drowned; Gillespie is talking to Eoghan—'"Ay! ay! blame me for Goad Almighty's storms." Eoghan answers—"No—I blame you for a rotten, ill-founded, undermanned boat." '[25]

That Hay believed in revolutionary solutions should be obvious from the quotations given. His closeness to the labouring people and his respect for their daily heroism emerges in the episode of ferrying the ridiculous representative of law and order across the water. These were the People. Seldom has such a powerful image been created of Humanity spat upon and derided as in Hay's picture of these titans of the sea at the mercy of the jackals of the fish trade:

On a june morning of perfect calm, when ducks were swimming about in the Harbour, a skiff was seen coming in at the Perch, deep to the gunwales. The men on the beams were sitting on herring as they rowed. She was followed by a second, a third, a fourth, and a fifth, under clouds of gulls. The smacksmen had refused to buy. The half-dozen buyers on the Quay were in a flutter, running about like hens, sharing their empty stock. They bought some seventy boxes between them. There yet remained four and a half boats of herring. The fishermen were now offering these at any price—instead of being offered; at five shillings a box, four shillings, three, two, one. Standing on the Quay and looking down upon these fishermen in their loaded boats, one caught a look of pathos upon their rugged faces, tawny with sweat threshed out of them in a fifteen-mile pull in the teeth of the tide. Their tired eyes were grey like the sea, their blue shirts with short oilskin sleeves were laced with herring scales; and herring scales smeared the big fishing boots which come up over the knee; their hands were slippery with herring spawn; even their beards and pipes were whitened. Everywhere a flood of light poured down. It stiffened and blackened the blood of the bruised fish, and the heat brought up that tang of fish and that savour of brine which have almost an edge of pain, so sharp, haunting, and fascinating are they in the nostrils of men who have been bred as fishers and have lived upon the salt water. The spectacle was compelling in its beauty, in its suggestion of prodigal seas and of the tireless industry and cunning craft of man; and at the same time sad with the irony of circumstance—niggard dealers haggling, shuffling, sniffing in the background. The dotard buyers shook their heads, though their mouths watered. They could not cope with one hundredth part of the fish. It was too early in the season for curing. . . .

A deep silence fell down the length of the Quay. One by one the fishermen, with dumb faces, sat down on the gunwales, the oars, or the beams, eyeing the load of fish. An old man seated on the stern beam of the second boat lifted a massive head slowly and took off his round bonnet. He seemed to be invoking Heaven. As they had come home-wards in the break of day to the sweep of the oars, he was given the tiller, being too old for that long pull. As he leaned upon the tiller he had dreamed in the somnolent morning of the spending of money. The sun glanced and shone on his round bald head. The streaks of grey hair were smeared with herring scales. . . . The old man bent and lifted a herring. He held it a moment aloft in the glittering sunlight; then he tossed it into the sea. It fell with a plout which seemed to crash in through the tremendous silence. Every eye followed it, wriggling down to the bottom. The old man nodded to the crews.

'Gull's meat, boys! gull's meat;' and he collapsed in the stern beam, huddled up, a piteous, forlorn wisp, stupidly nursing the old rusty round bonnet in his hands. An air of profound sorrow hung over the boat. She seemed chained in white, gleaming manacles. It was not precious food that was aboard any longer but ballast.[26]

The feast of nature is too rich for the puny digestions of those that buy and sell. The mighty rhythms of its seas and those that work them overwhelm the feverish jerkings of the marketeers, and yet are simultaneously frustrated and restricted by them. They are a monstrous insult to all that towering beauty, natural and human, turning it into a shining prisonhouse and dashing its generous gift out of men's hands. At one level the fishermen and the fish are synonymous (note the fish scales everywhere). In being forced to throw the 'silver darlings' into the water, these dignified sea-gods are being forced to throw their very selves away. The scene as a whole, it seems to me, is one of the few worthy descendants in our literature of Keats' blazing outburst in *Isabella* containing the lines '. . . with hollow eyes/Many all day in dazzling river stood,/ To take the rich-ored driftings of the flood.' Out of such poetic images of alienation the revolt of the people arises with the persuasive force of a natural law.

The revolt of the fishermen of Brieston is an imaginative development of the actual discontent and resistance of the poor Highland fishermen against their destruction at the hands of the big syndicates who were gaining a stranglehold on the industry in the last two decades of the nineteenth century. Gillespie's career epitomises this takeover. Also involved is that last peasants' revolt on British soil, the Crofters' War of the 1880s, with its land seizures and radical-revolutionary programme. It is the spirit behind the burning of the fishing fleet in *Gillespie*.

Hay is not able to advance to the point where he can see the working people as capable of overthrowing the Gillespies of the world. There is just a touch of Christian paternalism evident in the passage quoted, unconsciously embodied in the image of the narrator *looking down* upon their suffering from the height of the quay. Apart from this, Hay was half-fascinated—as was almost every petty-bourgeois artist of the time—by what he saw as the immense dynamism and single-mindedness of the monster he abhorred. It seemed, as Yeats wrote, that 'The best lack all conviction, while the worst/ Are full of passionate intensity.'[27] Lacking the key of the organised proletariat it seemed that such a man as Gillespie could not be overthrown by existing mortal agencies. Hence the Calvinist Jehovah who raises man-initiated conflagrations to the necessary apocalyptic proportions.

Gillespie's bloody end is, however, not engineered by any extra-natural force. It is the logical outcome of his whole career. Within the limitations of Hay's context it is a powerful poetic image hinting at the destruction of capitalism in a coming-to-a-head of the contradictions it has piled up for itself. Indeed, given the fact that Hay was unable to embody the larger ramifications of capitalism's effects and the revolt against them entirely in terms of themselves, the recurring hyperbolic images add an extra dimension which carries the implications of the action beyond the bounds of the purely local.

NOTES

1 Cf. Ralph Fox, *The Novel and the People* (London, 1937), p. 53.
2 Frederick Engels, Preface to the American Edition of *The Condition of the Working-Class in England*, in *Marx and Engels on Britain* (Moscow, 1953), p. 8.
3 Karl Marx, *Economic and Philosophic Manuscripts of 1844* (Moscow, 1961), p. 117.
4 *Ibid.*, p. 79.
5 Patrick MacGill, *Children of the Dead End, The Autobiography of an Irish Navvy* (New York, 1914), p. 170.
6 *Ibid.*, p. 140.

7 *Ibid.*
8 *Ibid.*, p. 255.
9 *Ibid.*, p. 269.
10 *Ibid.*, p. 305.
11 Cf. E. M. Forster, 'Forrest Reid', in *Abinger Harvest* (London, 1974), p. 95.
12 *Children of the Dead End*, p. 2.
13 *Ibid.*, p. 11.
14 *Ibid.*, pp. 161–2.
15 *Ibid.*, pp. 223–4.
16 *Ibid.*, p. 244.
17 Robert Kemp in his Preface to *Gillespie* (London, 1963), xi.
18 J. Macdougall Hay, *Gillespie* (London, 1963), pp. 60–1.
19 *Ibid.*, p. 178.
20 *Ibid.*, p. 147.
21 Cf. similar remarks by Bob Tait and Isobel Murray in their Introduction to *Gillespie* (Edinburgh and Vancouver, 1979).
22 *Gillespie* (London, 1963), p. 235.
23 *Ibid.*, p. 245.
24 *Ibid.*, p. 255.
25 *Ibid.*, p. 383.
26 *Ibid.*, pp. 173–39.
27 W. B. Yeats, *The Second Coming.*

Chapter 5

SILHOUETTES OF REVOLUTION: SOME NEGLECTED NOVELS OF THE EARLY 1920s

H. Gustav Klaus

Writing in May 1926, Ellen Wilkinson, the Labour MP and spokeswoman for the Left, contrasted a collection of newly translated Russian tales with the average English short story of the day. The crucial difference, she found, was apparent in the attitude to the everyday life of the common people. Whereas the Western stories were governed by one single obsession—sex—the Russians had succeeded in creating 'a literature of the job', they saw the human interest in a trade-union meeting and managed to dramatise the re-opening of a wrecked mine. 'Where is the literature of the British workers to answer this new note struck by Russia?'[1] she asked, and while admitting to some modest beginnings in poetry and drama she noted a lacuna in the field of fiction.

It was a complaint often voiced by the Left in the 1920s, and if one is to judge by the critical silence surrounding this period of working-class literature the assumptions underlying it are even today taken for granted. The 1920s are referred to as the pivot of the modernist movement, which is, moreover, seen to have celebrated its greatest triumph precisely in the field of the novel. These artistic triumphs have overshadowed a whole body of writing whose mere existence, given the difficult and discouraging conditions of production, is an achievement in kind. It is not a question of making extravagant claims for these writings, or of maintaining that the modernist works are unworthy of our attention. But it is essential for radical scholars with an interest in the 1920s to acknowledge the existence of this alternative tradition, and acknowledge it in the only adequate way, through the work of recovery and study, rather than to test for the *n*-th time, on the terrain of modernism, the latest critical weapon forged in some theoreticist smithy.

There has then never been any systematic enquiry into the working-class and socialist literary endeavours of the decade.[2] Such interest as there is for this kind of writing is usually reserved for the 1930s. Now this is clearly an untenable position. For one thing, the flowering of socialist fiction in the 1930s did not come out of the blue. As our survey will demonstrate, several writers who became better known in the 1930s—Ralph Fox and Harald Heslop, for instance—did, in fact, publish their first novels in the 1920s. Second, and more importantly, a real concern for socialist literature, if it is to be taken seriously, cannot limit itself to the study of one period which is currently enjoying a fashionable interest.

It would be misleading then to view the 1920s only in relation to—and as a precursor of—the richer harvest of the following decade. There is a distinctive group of novels in the early years which points back, if anywhere, to older, pre-war working-class literature, but which ought really to be taken as a body of work in its own right. It is these works I propose to consider; but first of all I would like to locate them in the movement of socialist fiction throughout the decade. The following are the divisions yielded by a first mapping of the field.

1 A group of about half-a-dozen works published in the years 1920–4, mainly by authors who, as writers, trade-unionists or politicians, had already played a role in the first two decades of the century; whose points of reference include the Russian Revolution (Barbor, Hamilton, Wells), the postwar social upheaval in Britain (Hamilton, Welsh) and, consistently, William Morris (Barbor, Carnie, Wells, Welsh).

2 A second batch of works produced by a younger generation of writers and workers published in the years 1928–30, with a different set of references: the experience of the General Strike (Heslop, Wilkinson), the spectre of unemployment (Hyde, Heslop), the construction of Socialism in the Soviet Union (Ashleigh, Fox, Le Gros Clark).

3 In between, covering the years 1925–7, or in terms of literary production 1924–6, a conspicuous lull with only one major work published (Ethel Carnie's *This Slavery*) which, however, as we shall see, really dates from an earlier period; another significant indication of this lull being the way in which one worker (Heslop) was forced to turn to Russia to make his literary debut.

These groupings reveal incidentally how arbitrary literary periodisation according to neat chronological units can be. Writers, when they compose or die, do not as a rule give much consideration to latter-day chroniclers. Nevertheless, a line has to be drawn somewhere, and since the principal aim of this chapter is to take stock of unavailable buried material it does not matter too much at this stage where it is drawn. In performing this task I have chosen to introduce as many writers as possible, limiting myself, however, to the discussion of one work each. This approach can best disclose the breadth and variety of fictional devices and socialist viewpoints.

I

James C. Welsh (1880–1954) was forty when *The Underworld* (1920), his first novel, was published. From the age of twelve he had worked in the mines of Lanarkshire interrupted only by a brief and soon regretted spell of emigration to New Zealand in 1906. Well before that date he had already become an active trade unionist and taken an interest in socialist politics. A member of the ILP, he stood for parliament in the first elections after the war but was defeated. Instead he became a full-time official in his union.[3]

From his mother, of whom there is a warm fictionalised portrait in *The Underworld*, Welsh had inherited a musical sensibility which is discernible in his first literary effort, the volume *Songs of a Miner* (1917),[4] and which adds an occasional lyrical note to some chapters of his novels. Of these *The Underworld* was an instant success selling fifty thousand copies in a few months and remaining almost continually in print for the rest of the decade. In a manner reminiscent of Wheeler's *Sunshine and Shadow*, but without the latter's stereotyped character-portrayal, the book follows the lives of two rivals, of middle-class and working-class origin respectively, from their schoolboy days to the age of maturity. Like its Chartist predecessor it focuses on the working-class figure and his evolution as a spirited fighter for the Cause, and mirrors his individual coming-of-age with the progress of the Labour movement in Scotland. But the life-story of the working-class hero, Robert Sinclair, is never allowed to absorb the reader's interest. Through a series of interspersed vignettes Welsh builds up a whole mosaic of life in a mining community: the working conditions on the coal-face and the permanent threat of accidents; the atmosphere in the homes and the role of the working-class woman; the sense of neighbourhood and locality; the relationship between the respectable and the less respectable members of the community, between strikers and blacklegs, socialists and working-class Tories; the liveliness and humour even under grimy and degrading conditions. A period of some twenty-five years is thus covered, from the 1880s to the Great Unrest, in which the local incidents, strikes, blacklistings, campaigns are connected, not always successfully, with the great national events involving the working class and the miners in particular. Welsh does not hesitate to introduce such historical figures as Robert Smillie and Keir Hardie and to give vivid descriptions of the magnetic effect of their speeches on working-class audiences, though, unlike Tressell, he refrains from reproducing these, or any other socialist lectures and discussions, probably because he presumed they would form an alien element in a novel.

A didactic intent is, however, not missing from the book. It comes through rather subtly, for instance in the magnificent chapter entitled 'The Conference' which demonstrates how the trade-union leaders, to Robert's disgust, are bamboozled by the clever manoeuvrings of the government representatives. In some very fine dialogues, which incidentally testify to the richness of what is only inadequately described as a restricted code, Welsh here drives his lessons home. Robert who is a newcomer to the council of his union asks a fellow delegate why everybody seems to be overawed in the presence of ministers:

'Ach, man; it's a right askin' that question; but efter thae chaps get round aboot you, wi' their greasy tongues, an' their flattering' ways, you jist begin to think that it's nae use to bother ony mair aboot resistin'. Look at that auld fermer-collier lookin' chiel, wi' his white heid an' his snipe-nose an' a smile on his face that wad mak' you believe he was gaun to dae you some big service. That's the smile that has made him Prime Minister. You'd think frae his face that he was just a solid easy-gaun kindly auld fermer, who took a constant joy in givin' jeelie-pieces to hungry weans. But when he speaks, and gets a grip o' you, he's yin o' the soopliest lawyers that ever danced roun' the rim o' hell withoot fallin' in. He'd do his faither, that yin. He wad that.'

'Then there's that ither chiel—I think he's on the Local Government Board or something. He's a corker, wi' a face like yin o' they pented cupids that the lasses send to the young men on picture post cards. Look at his nice wee baby's mooth, an' the smile on it too. It wad dazzle a hungry crocodile lookin' for its denner.'[5]

The Conference chapter not only affords a clear warning against 'national interest' phrase-mongery but also, through Robert's courageous example, in uninvitedly bursting out in a fiery speech, points to an aggressive strategy for the realisation of working-class interests.

Another lesson is embedded in a sub-plot which is built around Mysie Maitland's attempt to raise herself above her class. Despite being wooed by Robert this working girl elopes with Peter Rundell, the son of the colliery owner in whose household she has worked as a servant. Peter is not a deceitful seducer but actually prepared to marry her, but as the wife of a future employer the girl is expected to acquire the polish and refinement of her superiors so as not to bring disgrace upon their class. Welsh is at pains to demonstrate the unnaturalness and fallacy of this endeavoured assimilation. Once arrived in Edinburgh, where she is to learn how to move in the upper reaches of society, Mysie falls ill, she is estranged, unhappy and tormented by homesickness. Unable to resist her yearning any longer she steals away, returning home only to drop dead in the arms of her parents. The deathbed scene in which she unites the hands of the two rivals is crudely sentimental. But despite such false overtones Welsh's message is unequivocal: abide by your class, stand by your community, or as Mysie keeps repeating: 'It was a' a mistake.'[6]

Robert provides the positive example of this loyalty. This is underlined by the closing scene in which, at the news of a mining disaster, he throws himself into the rescue work in the course of which he perishes. On one level Robert has, of course, also moved beyond the traditional boundaries of his community: he has educated himself and he has travelled widely as a union delegate. But in doing this he is serving his community and combating 'the enemies of his class'.[7] Robert embodies the 'deep humanity'[8] that Welsh at one stage ascribes to Keir Hardie. In this he is not alone —his mother and a whole number of minor figures all contribute facets to this image so that there emerges what has been described as an 'artistic depiction of them as Humanity by definition, as ultimately undefeatable'.[9]

On the other hand, despite his firm roots in his class, Robert is also, partly as a result of his education and activities, partly because of his unfulfilled love for Mysie, a lonely figure. In this respect he resembles Owen, Larry Meath and Ewan Tavendale, to cite only names from some better known socialist novels. Isolation seems to be the price the working-class intellectual has to pay in this period. The question is why on top of this Welsh has chosen to let his hero die. Of the aforementioned characters only Greenwood's socialist suffers the same fate, whereas Tressell saves Owen from suicide and Gibbon sends Ewan to Communist Party headquarters. It seems to me that Welsh in this solution falls prey to his occasionally uncontrolled sense of drama. No doubt he deemed it fit to close with a last view of the underworld, i.e. the mine, and the toll it takes from the people who work it, so as to

remind us how (coal) production is bound up with the whole lives
of the people. No doubt he succeeded in presenting another
example of the splendid sense of solidarity the colliers have
developed, under the most adverse circumstances. But the 'killing'
of Robert seems to have no meaning beyond an individual
sacrifice.

The Underworld is Welsh's most sustained socialist creation. In
The Morlocks (1924) the author who had meanwhile won his
parliamentary seat is already wavering in his convictions. Though
his material in this second novel is more directly revolutionary
than in the first work—the postwar industrial confrontation with
the miners is once again in the forefront—Welsh is now more
preoccupied with the possible damage 'yin last desperate attempt
tae cause Revolution'[10] can do. *Norman Dale, M.P.* (1928), his
third and last novel, completes the shift to the Right.

II

The only other novel published in the first half of the 1920s which
is coloured by a comparable fighting spirit is *This Slavery* by Ethel
Carnie (1886–196?).[11] This book came out in 1925 but it clearly
bears the mark of an earlier, in fact, pre-war composition.

The very title seems to stem from an older rhetoric; Carnie's
fellow Lancashire writer Bart Kennedy, for instance, had published his novel *Slavery: Pictures from the Depths* in 1905. Then
there are the allusions to the Boer War and the SDF, and on one
occasion an impressive gallery of ancestors of the Cause is
presented which includes the names of 'Morris and Marx,
Carpenter and Liebnetch [!], Wat Tyler and John Ball, Ernest
Jones and Robert Owen, Shelley and Heine, and William Blake'[12]
but makes no reference to contemporary working-class leaders.

Finally we notice the intrinsic evidence, a distinct prewar
working-class sensibility or structure of feeling, manifest in a
strong emphasis on suffering and brutalisation which borders on
naturalism. This is an element we find in Tressell, where despair
looms never far in the background, and in Charles Allen Clarke,
another Lancashire writer, whose works contain some extremely
bitter episodes. It is a characteristic of the works published or
written in the first decade of the century because it corresponds to
the objective situation and subjective experience of the working
class, which is one of juridical attacks against its organisation and
of eroding real wages. By contrast, the literature of the 1920s
displays far greater confidence, even if the action is set before
World War I, as in Welsh, precisely because of the new organised

strength of the working class gained in the years 1911–14 and again after 1918. (It is as well to remember that Tressell, though his work was published in 1914, died in 1911 when the offensive of the working class was only just gathering momentum.)

This Slavery stands somewhere between these two groups of works. The description of agonising poverty and its pressure on working men and women links it with the earlier period, but its revolutionary ardour foreshadows the postwar works and indicates how much it owes to the 1911–14 unrest when industrial conflicts were spreading, and the deployment of troops against strikers, as related in the novel, was no unusual feature.

The novel is divided into two parts, of which the first part portrays a fatherless working-class family struggling below subsistence level as the two bread-earners, both of them girls, lose their jobs owing to a fire in the textile mill where they have been employed. To this ordeal the sisters, already differentiated in their tastes and temperaments, react differently. Rachel, a 'pugnacious agitator' who wrestles with *Das Kapital* by candle-light, becomes even more militant, picturing herself in some desperate moments with a shotgun in her hand. Hester, more beautiful and artistically minded, though not without socialist sympathies either, is at the end of her tether:

'I am tired of being a slave . . . I don't want to live, dreaming of an awakening in the people which never comes—like my father did. I don't want to go to prison, atoning for the apathy of people content to be slaves. The fact that they'll let their agitators go there and rot for striking their blows, is itself a condemnation of the working-classes. I suppose there is a cause for it all, but it won't be undone in my life-time, and I want life—Now.'[13]

Hester's path, like Mysie's in *The Underworld*, turns out to be another abortive attempt of a working girl to raise herself above her class, though here the marriage into the factory-owning middle class comes off. That it occupies greater space in the construction of the plot and is more convincingly motivated clearly results from the feminine sensibility of the author who has endowed her character with greater strength and independence. Welsh's working girl fulfils the female role in a conventional love triangle, that is to say she remains a basically passive figure. Carnie's heroines—her principal characters are always women—take the initiative, they deploy a quality of courage and loyalty which is in no way inferior to the male embodiment of such virtues and ideals in the works of male authors.

With the second part of the novel, in which the author picks up
the threads after a lapse of six years—did she leave the work in a
drawer for a similar period of time?—we move to the bosses' side
and to a major confrontation between Capital and Labour.
Hester, though gratified at first by the wealth of her husband and
the bliss of a family life—both of which remain denied to Rachel
who meanwhile has been wrongly sentenced to prison—feels
gradually estranged in her new surroundings. Yet the real test is
still to come, and it eventually comes with the outbreak of a strike
in the cotton industry which quickly deteriorates into a kind of
class war of attrition with each side hoping to exhaust the other.
Hester's sympathies are all with her roots now, she regrets the
'defection' from her class but still accepts the validity of the
marriage bond. Only after the death of her son, caused by an
epidemic but precipitated by her husband's negligence, who is too
much concerned with building up his business, does the rupture
become irreversible, though she holds out for a while mainly in
order to communicate to the strikers the strategy of the bosses that
she overhears being discussed in her house. The individual
motivation is thus still, if somewhat feebly, upheld; but Carnie, I
think, here sacrifices probability for a lesson in class loyalty which
she sees as reemerging, if only deeply enough engrained, in times
of emotional and social crisis. This is even more obvious in the
ending in which Hester, who has in the meantime been detected as
a 'spy' and turned out by her husband, is fatally hit by a bullet as
she entreats the soldiers not to shoot on their class brethren. As
Mary Ashraf has commented:

the abrupt and enigmatic ending of the book fails in the artistic sense, and
where earlier episodes have movement and substance, the last chapters
have an air of unreality. For just when the reader should be brought
closer to the rising tension of the masses coming into action, the
concentration is on the turmoil in Hester's mind.[14]

A contemporary reviewer argued on similar, if more derogatory
lines when he accused the author in *The Sunday Worker* of selling
out to bourgeois fictional conventions by having 'the usual love
situation as the pivot of the machinery of the whole tale.'[15]

Carnie's vehement rejoinder proves that despite her absorption
in an earlier period her socialist commitment was unflagging. She
emphatically defended the love-interest on the grounds that just
like the bread-struggle it was an elemental part of human life and

pronounced herself 'against shimmy-shake, "intellectual" criticism.'[16]

Carnie deserves special attention for being one of the very few female working-class novelists of any period. As articles elsewhere in this book illustrate, there were a good many women writers with a socialist perspective in the late nineteenth century, and they were around too, to a lesser degree, in the 1920s and 1930s; but almost without exception these came from the middle class. Again we have documentary evidence of working women, by way of interviews or autobiographies written late in life, but the case of a female proletarian novelist is surely unique. One can speculate as to whether it was the double burden of mill drudgery and housework which deprived working women of the little leisure time there was or whether other factors were involved.

Ethel Carnie had worked in a Lancashire cotton mill from the age of nine. She became a vigorous trade-union campaigner and at one time edited *The Woman Worker*.[17] Like Welsh she ventured first into poetry (*Songs of a Factory Girl*, 1910) before tackling the more demanding novel form (*Miss Nobody*, 1913). In the 1920s, having a husband and two children to look after, she established herself as a professional writer but seems at first to have withdrawn from active politics, though contacts with the radical left remained, as her sketches and tales published in *The Sunday Worker* show. Late in 1926 she figured on the committee of the newly created Workers' Theatre Movement. By that time, however, her creative powers had passed their zenith. Her last work came out in 1931 though she appears to have lived well into the post-1945 period.

III

Very little is known about H. R. Barbor. The catalogue of the British Library lists three works: *Jezebel: a Tragedy in Three Acts* (1924), *The Theatre: an Art and an Industry* from the same year, and the novel *Against the Red Sky: Silhouettes of Revolution*, published in 1922 and reprinted in 1926. Of these the pamphlet on the theatre, which starts with an indictment of the commercialisation of the West End stage and closes with a passionate plea for the unionisation of actors, still makes impressive reading today, if only for its pioneering demand for an equal share for actors in the running of a playhouse. The author had first expounded his views in a series of articles in *The New Age*, the liberal monthly whose long-standing editor A. R. Orage had a tradition of Fabianism and Guild Socialism behind him.

Barbor's name also crops up on the contributors' page of an even more progressive, albeit shortlived, journal with the name of *Germinal*. Like *The New Age* this 'illustrated Monthly'—of which only two numbers seem to have appeared, in 1923—showed a keen interest in the new Russian literature, printing contributions from Gorky, Blok and Akhmatova. The social leaning and cosmopolitan outlook of this venture comes through not only in the naming of the journal but also in an editorial statement couched in the characteristically archaic diction which is a mark of the whole journal: 'Others have sung of the States, but I sing of the peoples. I sing the peoples united; I sing the peoples creative; the peoples alert without master, of themselves they are master.'[18]

The New Age and *Germinal* ambit delineates some contours of the intellectual milieu in which Barbor moved. In *Against the Red Sky* we witness, through the eyes of a young writer, a socialist revolution taking place *and* succeeding in Britain. Richard Constable one morning blunders into some street-fighting in the heart of London in which, more spontaneously than deliberately, he joins the armed workers against the forces of order. Yet once he has fought side by side with them he accepts full responsibility for his choice and eventually rises to the position of President of the Revolutionary Tribunal. The account of the fighting with its unmotivated emphasis on the bloodier side of the skirmishes, the absurd suggestion that an insurrectionary force would accept a complete stranger in their ranks, a middle-class intellectual at that, and quickly promote him to a leading position are among the least convincing parts of the book. But granted the flimsy elements of the plot, granted furthermore the unsatisfactory treatment of the working-class revolutionaries, there comes a point where seriousness and sincerity take over. It is as if the author had undergone a conversion in the act of writing, as if what began as a pure flight of imagination had suddenly taken a real grip on him. The change is readily apparent in the mind of the protagonist. Constable's first encounter with the workers reads like a Day Lewis poem from the early 1930s:

They were a mixed crowd . . . showing in hand and features the signs of toil, and their dress the economy that is the lot of the manual worker. Yet there was something in the presence of these men that impressed the young intellectual, something potent, dynamic, indefinable, some irritation of purposeful personality. . . .[19]

The protagonist's inner journey from reservation and haughtiness to identification with the proletarian cause is mirrored and, in fact, accelerated by his move to the East End. The consideration of what the bourgeois side has to offer—'Security: perhaps for the few, but at a price few could pay. Security—ending with gout and double chins—and wars and oppressions at each end of it. Culture: the less said the better'[20]—this consideration does not occupy him for very long. His journey 'Eastward Ho' (Chapter VII) ends with a definite crossing of borders, the acquisition of a new identity, outwardly recognisable in the adoption of a new, more popular name (John Smith), emotionally enacted in a new love relationship with an Irish comrade, which supplants the old *liaison dangereuse* with a married countess.

Part of the novel's relevance then lies in the illumination of the frame of mind of a young literary intellectual who, disillusioned about the state of bourgeois culture and the gloomy prospects it holds for his kind, throws in his lot with the working class. In this respect *Against the Red Sky* is a remarkable fictional anticipation of the real leftward move of the English intelligentsia a decade later. However, where the fictitious Constable/Smith differs from his latter-day real-life epigones is in the consistency and loyalty of his stand. He has made his choice, which is to work for the revolution, and subsequently does not lament the abandonment of his literary career. His is not a split personality, hovering between poetry and politics, with the resultant danger of becoming ineffective and perhaps paralysed in both realms. Only on the very last pages of his book, with an easing of the immediate pressure after the triumph of the revolution and with the return of his first love, does the hero show signs of a lessening of his political fervour.[21]

Perhaps the audacity of *Against the Red Sky* can best be measured when compared to another novel which envisages a socialist revolution in England, J. D. Beresford's *Revolution*, published the previous year. In this work the middle-class protagonist, shell-shocked ex-World-War officer Paul Leaming, though clearly fascinated and attracted by the personal sincerity of a trade-union leader and his cogently argued manifesto, never joins the Left. Instead he chooses to act as a mediator between the forces of reaction and of revolution and sees himself as the voice of reason and humanity in the midst of turmoil, his mission being to save a small Midlands parish from the throes of terror. Beresford's novel is a curiously detached intellectual experiment —the depiction of the revolutionary course stops at the village border—which ends, significantly, with the counter-revolution in the saddle and Paul becoming an apostle of a visionary humanism which 'could never be reached by a change of Government'.[22]

To note that Constable/Smith in *Against the Red Sky* has substituted the gun for the pen does not imply that he is not concerned with the 'poetic life' (Upward) any more. On the contrary, at every spare moment his thoughts wander to the future for which the present struggle is waged. The workers

were so obviously concerned about the material bases of life; for them revolt meant boots, housing, cheese, rolling stock. For him it meant the inbreathing of free air, the counterplay of ideas, self-expression, fidelity unbiassed by commerce. . . . When they thought factory, he thought theatre. Beyond the newly-organised industrial community which they saw outstepping from capitalist bondage, he conceived the dim immensity of a faithfully democratic future.[23]

This is from the early stages of the revolutionary process and still betrays the sense of separation from, and somewhat patronising attitude towards, the workers which, with regard to cultural matters, he never quite manages to overcome. Yet the passage also reveals his intense preoccupation with the construction of a socialist society, as does his later project for the establishment of municipal repertory theatres for every town of over a thousand inhabitants.

Barbor's narrative resources are as unbalanced as his ideological position. When dealing with the sequence of revolutionary events which occupy much of the book he all too often succumbs to an historiographical style, untainted by any resolved attempt at representation. Luckily this weakness is offset by the insertion of two self-contained, extraordinarily colourful episodes, in which the focus shifts from hero and metropolis to the common people in the country. In one of them a station-master, who has hitherto led a quiet uneventful life, runs a locomotive into a train loaded with White troops and armoured cars killing himself in the act but succeeding in holding up the reactionary force and causing considerable damage. Such solitary acts of heroism are to be found in every war and revolution, and Barbor here pays homage to their unknown originators. These stories combined with the cautious approach to a revolutionary stance, held the promise of greater achievements, but their author, for whatever reason, fell into silence.

IV

If *Against the Red Sky* betrays certain utopian features, it is nevertheless set in the near future. By contrast, the tomorrow of H. G. Wells's *Men Like Gods* (1922) is so far removed from the present that it needs one of the author's time-travelling procedures to span the distance from the contemporary world. The visitor to the new world, the liberal journalist Mr Barnstaple, here does not remain on his own but is eventually joined by a whole band of people, not necessarily a cross-section of English society but certainly a fair sample of some of the author's best-hated men: a war minister, a peer, a capitalist, a priest, a cinema king and, alas, two chauffeurs who have to pose as representatives of the working class. The presentation of these two feeble creatures has led to irritation in some socialist quarters. Now it is true that here as everywhere in Wells's work it would be futile to look for a positive historical role attributed to the working class. As Caudwell wrote:

> he is unable even to imagine what workers are like. As he acknowledges, he does not know them, has not talked to them, cannot understand them. All he has of them is childhood memories of the proletarian abyss below the *petit bourgeois* . . . the proletariat does not exist for Wells. The change therefore can only come from within the bourgeois class.[24]

But does such knowledge justify an outright rejection of *Men Like Gods*? Another criticism frequently levelled against Wells's utopias is that they present a 'cellophane world'[25] (Morton), scientific and ordered, hygienic and sterile. Again we have to recognise the validity of this stricture, and we can even subsume the god-like inhabitants of Utopia under it, so bloodless do they appear. And certainly if this were indeed all that could be said about the novel we would be better to move on at once to the next work.

Yet a genuine utopia does not exhaust itself in the projection of an ideal society, it is as much defined by its critique of existing society. I would suggest that while the book does not succeed on the level of its vision of the future it has real merits in its savage exposure of imperialism.

To give but two illustrations. As it happens, the Earthlings import germs into the purified world of Utopia where disease-carrying insects have long been exterminated and contagious diseases are virtually unknown. This causes an epidemic among the utopians who quite naturally react by putting the infectors in quarantine. Quite naturally, that is, in the view of Mr Barnstaple and the by now sympathetic reader, but not for the entrepreneur Mr Burleigh who fails to see the logic in this measure:

'Here are we—absolutely the only perfectly immune people here—and we—*we* are to be isolated.'
   'They say they catch things from us,' said Lady Stella.
   'Very well,' said Mr. Burleigh, making his point with his long white hand. 'Very well, then let *them* be isolated! This is—Chinese; this is topsy-turvy. I'm disappointed in them.'[26]

To the colonialist who likes to parade as the emissary of civilisation, to the churchman whose main concern is the spreading of the Gospel among the natives, to the imperialist for whom his metropolitan homeland is the hub of the universe, the idea of making sense of 'savage thinking'—i.e. the measures taken by the utopians against the infectors—can only appear abstruse. This trio forms the hard core of the earthly expedition. It is they who hatch out a vicious plan by which to take control of the entire planet. How carefully Wells strives to render the machinations of the imperialists can be seen in a row which arises between the English and the only Frenchman in the party over the partition of the prospective colony.
   Mr Catskill, a thinly disguised Winston Churchill,

stood at the end of the table explaining that he had used the word Empire loosely, apologising for using it, explaining that when he said Empire he had all Western Civilisation in mind. 'When I said it,' he said, turning to Mr. Hunker, 'I meant a common brotherhood of understanding.' He faced towards M. Dupont. 'I meant our tried and imperishable Entente.'
   'There are at least no Russians here,' said M. Dupont. 'And no Germans.'
   'True,' said Lord Barralonga. 'We start ahead of the Hun here, and we can keep ahead.'
   'And I take it,' said Mr. Hunker, 'that Japanese are barred.'
   'No reason why we shouldn't start clean with a complete colour bar,' reflected Lord Barralonga. 'This seems to me a White Man's World.'[27]

Wells not only tears the mask of civility from these brigands, he also gives his readers the pleasure of witnessing, how, for once, they burn their fingers.
   The reason why this castigation of imperialism is so much more effective than the proffered counter-image of utopia is quite simply that this critique is rendered in a fictionalised satirical

manner whereas the 'advantages' of Well's educational and scientific State are brought home in tiresome lectures and conversations. Behind this qualitative difference lies, of course, the fact that Wells had a much clearer notion of the enemies than of the potential allies on the road to progress, of the deficiencies of the prevailing system than of its ideal successor, no matter how much he racked his brain for ever-new models.

There is another aspect of *Men Like Gods* which, in view of the author's vacillating stance on this issue, deserves special mention. Wells does not hesitate here to embrace the concept of Socialism and to call utopia a 'practical communism', a term directly borrowed from Morris. 'I had never thought before that socialism could exalt and ennoble the individual and individualism degrade him, but now I see plainly that here the thing is proved.'[28] Again, it is true that when it comes to a fleshing out of these concepts he often fills them with his own highly idiosyncratic brand of meaning, and it is equally true that the 'Great Revolution' to which Mr Barnstaple resolves to devote himself 'soul and body'[29] on his return to Earth is not Marxist-inspired. But with the horrors of World War I and the allied interventions in revolutionary Russia at the back of his mind, Wells harbours no illusions about the duration of the struggle to install the new order or the amount of suffering inevitably accompanying it—two issues on which some of his early communist critics displayed a more blissful optimism than Wells in his supposed state of innocent confidence.

V

In Mary Agnes Hamilton's *Follow My Leader* (1922) the best passage occurs towards the end when the heroine, a sensitive upper-class girl who stands between a dominating father and a no less commanding lover, after a long mental struggle, musters up the strength to recognise that impartiality is a sham. As she accepts the need to take sides, Jane Heriot meditates on the implications of her conclusions:

To be a Socialist . . . was no isolated decision; it coloured every part of a man's thinking, acting, feeling; made the life of the individual continuous with that of the community and the life of the community itself a conscious whole. Only when individuals felt and thought so, could it be realized. It was not a thing a man thought about now and then, at elections and in political arguments; it determined how and why he lived in all relations. There was no issue, however great or however small, to which it was not applicable.[30]

It has been a long way to travel for the daughter of employer, newspaper magnate and Conservative Cabinet Minister Designate John Heriot. And she would not have reached the destination without the companionship and attraction of the trade unionist Sandy Colquhoun.

Yet this crowning moment of achievement and assurance, however anxiously the author is trying to render it as a triumph of surmounted class barriers, cannot entirely dispel the ambiguous impression that the depiction of Jane's first encounter with the working class in action has left behind. This episode, conveyed like the rest of the novel through the eyes of the heroine, is no doubt meant to lay bare Jane's initial class perspective. But there are moments when the distance between protagonist and narrator breaks down, when Jane's point of view intermingles with the authorial ideology, when class prejudice and class condescension, instead of being made transparent, are actually mystified.

The scene is a strike meeting to which friends of Colquhoun have taken her. To Jane the whole atmosphere in the hall appears 'thick' and 'fetid with the smoke of cheap tobacco'. She is at once repelled and frightened 'by this undifferentiated mass, cruel and ugly beyond anything she had ever seen'. To her horror she hears 'crude incitements', 'false reasonings' coming from the mouth of a 'windy and preposterous' agitator who every now and then 'spat the word "Capitalist" out of his mouth'. Inevitably there is the 'pervading smell' of these people but then Jane suddenly is overcome by a feeling of sympathy, as she notices the 'helplessness of the massed ranks of the auditors'.[31]

Notice how the mood shifts at the end from repulsion to pity, how the working class thus becomes an object of upper-class philanthropy. What is disturbing is that this picture of the working class, and of radical oratory, is never modified or relativised in the remainder of the book. How little Jane has changed in basic class attitudes is revealed right at the end when, despite her new faith, she still cannot hide her fears about the 'dark moving swaying masses' and 'their terrible possibilities'.[32] It needs to be recalled that this novel comes from the pen of a writer (1882–1966) who stood for parliament as an ILP candidate (on this occasion unsuccessfully) in the year following the publication of the novel; from a politician who was a close collaborator of Ramsey MacDonald and, later, Arthur Henderson; from a journalist who was on the board of the *New Leader*.[33]

As in the case of Wells, an (unsatisfactory) treatment of the working class cannot be the sole criterion for an assessment of a work, but in *Follow My Leader* there is little else to make up for this weakness. Indeed the author's eagerness to dissociate herself from everything that savours of class struggle and revolution makes her uncritically adopt the vocabulary of the fiercest anti-Communists ('Bolshie', 'Red Peril', etc.) as well as denounce the ongoing socialist experiment in Russia. Instead she preaches moderation and amelioration to the point—as the solution of the novel suggests—of class reconciliation.

After his by-election victory over Colquhoun Mr Heriot can afford to make a graceful conciliatory gesture to his future son-in-law because he has convinced himself of one thing:

'Is this fellow Colquhuoun a Bolshevik?'
'Lord, no. He's a parliamentary Revisionist of the MacDonald type. . . . Oh, no, Colquhoun's not Red at all. Industrially he's a bit wild, but politically quite straight. I don't agree with his ideas, but he has ideas. I believe he'd be quite useful in the House. . . .'[34]

Since the dialogue from which this is taken contains not a trace of irony, the author has evidently provided here a piece of unintended parody. The reader is left to guess to whom the domesticated working-class leader would be useful.

It is not only the dubious nature of her socialism that raises doubts about Mrs Hamilton's position. From a feminist viewpoint the treatment of Jane is hardly more satisfactory. As David Smith has observed, the novel gives an effective picture not so much of the heroine 'torn between two creeds, as of her being torn between two dominating men.'[35] In this conflict Jane's identity can never develop to the full. It is not exaggerated to say that she leads an existence only as daughter and lover, in relation to men, that is, and that ultimately she is converted to socialism because she marries a socialist.

This is all the more striking as the author seems theoretically familiar with the problem of female subordination:

'In a novel', she said, looking up at him with a little smile, 'no woman could be in my position. They've never let a woman bother, really, about what she thought.'
'Oh, novels,' said Sandy, with contempt.
'Women in novels,' Jane went on, 'never have any minds; not what I would call operative minds, not minds that matter.'[36]

Yet the construction of the plot and the presentation of the central character do not bear out such momentary insights. Jane

Heriot has nothing of the sturdy independence and sheer stamina of Ethel Carnie's unsophisticated working-class heroines. And she is almost a negative counterpart of Joan Craig, the central figure in Ellen Wilkinson's *Clash* (1929) who is likewise confronted with a choice between two men yet makes her deepest convictions the basis for her decision.

VI

Several of the novels discussed here came from the presses of the Labour Publishing Co. which in these years was the only publishing house of the Labour movement to pay more than lip service to creative socialist literature.[37] For the overwhelming impression one gets from leafing through the Reviews and Books Received sections of the labour periodicals of the early 1920s is that the meaning of literature has been narrowed down to tracts, pamphlets, textbooks. Yet even the Labour Publishing Co., despite its indubitable merits for the propagation of a different notion of literature, was not exactly discriminating when it came to the ideological texture of a novel, volume of poetry or collection of short stories. Its sponsoring of the works of Theodora Wilson Wilson[38] and Stacey W. Hyde is a case in point.

Perhaps the keenest observers and mentors of socialist and working-class literature throughout the decade sat not in London but in Moscow. The Russians translated Welsh and Heslop, they dedicated articles to Hyde and Heslop, had visits by Wells, Fox and, later, O'Flaherty and Lionel Britton. They read and attacked MacGill and Carnie. They arranged for Robert Ellis and Heslop to attend the international conferences on proletarian and revolutionary literature (1927, 1930).

The internationalisation of socialist literature—of which these Soviet activities are but one sign—would, at a later stage, assume concrete shape in the translation of Soviet and German revolutionary novels into English, in the formation of writers' associations, in the convening of writers' conferences. One could argue that in the early 1920s the British contribution to this process of internationalisation lay precisely in the imaginary enactment of revolution. For the war which had toppled thrones and unleashed revolutions on the Continent had left the basic structures of power in Britain intact. It had led to social upheavals but not to a revolutionary situation. Hence the silhouettes of revolution discernible in the novels under review are really those of Eastern and Central Europe transposed into an industrially shaken but politically stable Britain.

What was executed in imaginary terms and aspired to by one group of writers, gave nightmares to another. The 1920s witness a host of anti-revolutionary novels ranging ideologically from the Christian-inspired *Revolt* (1928) by George Lissenden[39] to the downright fascist *The Blueshirts* (1926) by the anonymous J.J.J. It is a mark of the bankrupt 'sensibility' of these works that they continued to pour out when the silhouettes of revolution had long disappeared from the political stage in Europe and from their imaginative enactment in British novels alike.

For when, after a lapse of three years, the socialist novel emerges once again, in the works of Fox (*Storming Heaven*), Wilkinson (*Clash*), Heslop (*The Gate of a Strange Field*), Le Gros Clark (*Apparition*), Ashleigh (*Rambling Kid*), it is rather different in character. These works are by and large carried by a more strongly grounded belief in socialism. What they may lack in immediacy they make up in patient exploration. Except for two cases (*Storming Heaven, Rambling Kid*) which are clearly conceived as *Bildungsromane*, novels of growth and development, the journey of a protagonist towards the embracement of Socialism is given rather less prominence. Another difference is that whereas in the early 1920s socialist attitudes were most deeply rooted in the worker-writers (Welsh, Carnie) they have now their strongest hold in the intellectuals (Ashleigh, Fox, Wilkinson, Le Gros Clark). The novels of two worker-writers, creative in these years, are either devoid of a socialist perspective (Hyde) or uneasy in the adoption of any definite line (Heslop) but, in any case, manifest reservations against the representatives of the organisations of the working class.

NOTES

1 *Plebs* XIX, 5 (May 1926), p. 178.
2 Individual aspects have been treated, if somewhat cursorily, by Leonard A. Jones, 'The British Workers' Theatre 1917–1935', unpubl. PhD thesis (Leipzig University, 1965); David Smith, *Socialist Propaganda in the Twentieth-Century British Novel* (London, 1978), pp. 39–47; Stuart McIntyre, *A Proletarian Science. British Marxism 1917–1933* (London, 1980).
3 See the entry in the *Dictionary of Labour Biography*, vol. 2 (1974), pp. 399–401 contributed by the two editors Joyce Bellamy and John Saville.
4 'Introduction' to James C. Welsh, *Songs of a Miner* (London, 1917),

p. 8; Bellamy and Saville, *Dictionary of Labour Biography*, p. 400.
5 James C. Welsh, *The Underworld* (London, 1920), pp. 203–4.
6 *Ibid.*, p. 238.
7 *Ibid.*, p. 207.
8 *Ibid.*, p. 163.
9 Jack Mitchell, 'The Struggle for the Working-Class Novel in Scotland 1900–1939', *Zeitschrift für Anglitik und Amerikanistik* XXI (1973), p. 391.
10 James C. Welsh, *The Morlocks* (London, 1924), p. 284.
11 Though the greater part of her works were published under her later name, Ethel Carnie Holdsworth, I continue to use Ethel Carnie because this is how she is best known.
12 Ethel Carnie Holdsworth, *This Slavery* (London, 1925), p. 97. The only one alive on the list was Edward Carpenter while the Liebknecht mentioned is almost certain to be Wilhelm, the elder one. To a later list the author adds, interestingly, the names of Lenin, Maclean and Rosa Luxemburg, see *The Sunday Worker* of 26 July 1925.
13 Carnie, *This Slavery*, p. 121.
14 P. M. Ashraf, *Introduction to Working-Class Literature in Great Britain, Part II: Prose* (Berlin, 1979), p. 190.
15 'Peachum' on *This Slavery*, *The Sunday Worker*, 5 July 1925.
16 *The Sunday Worker*, 26 July 1925.
17 Cf. Ashraf, *Introduction*, pp. 176–7.
18 *Germinal* I, 2 (1923). Note the Whitmanesque ring in this quotation.
19 H. R. Barbor, *Against the Red Sky* (London, 1922), p. 76.
20 *Ibid.*, p. 66.
21 Though to make of this a case of cynicism (Smith, *op. cit.*, p. 47) is to misread the novel.
22 J. D. Beresford, *Revolution* (London, 1921), p. 212.
23 Barbor, *op. cit.*, p. 84.
24 Christopher Caudwell, *Studies in a Dying Culture* (London, 1938), pp. 82, 85.
25 A. L. Morton, *The English Utopia* (London, 1969), p. 240.
26 H. G. Wells, *Men Like Gods* (London, 1976), p. 129.
27 *Ibid.*, p. 143.
28 *Ibid.*, p. 203.
29 *Ibid.*, p. 221.
30 Mary Agnes Hamilton, *Follow My Leader* (London, 1922), p. 237.
31 *Ibid.*, pp. 57–9.
32 *Ibid.*, p. 273.
33 See the entry by Margaret Cole in *The Dictionary of Labour Biography*, vol. 5 (1979), pp. 97–9.
34 Hamilton, *op. cit.*, pp. 269–70.
35 Smith, *op. cit.*, p. 41.
36 Hamilton, *op. cit.*, p. 145.
37 Martin Lawrence, the Communist publisher, only started translating Russian novels, by Gladkov, Fadeev, Panfero and others, from 1929.

38 I am indebted to Sabine Hilker for information on this writer's *Jack o' Peterloo* (1924) which appears to be a 'historical' novel more in the sense of belonging to the past than treating it from a twentieth-century perspective.

39 This work ought not be confused with the anti-fascist novel *Revolt* (London, 1933) by A. P. Roley.

Chapter 6

WORKING-CLASS, PROLETARIAN, SOCIALIST: PROBLEMS IN SOME WELSH NOVELS

Raymond Williams

I

First they had to be recovered, those novels by working-class writers, and those and others about working-class life, which had been read out of the literary tradition and even the literary record. The recovery is by no means yet complete, but real progress has been made: as part of the research of a new generation, from the 1950s, in cultural studies and social history; also in the research of scholars from outside Britain, who at times moved more confidently past the native cultural blocks that had been set in place.

But recovery only as research, a new department of academia, is at best the beginning of the story. Significant recovery begins when at least some of the novels are put into active circulation again, for the readers and the children and successors of the readers among whom and sometimes for whom they were written.

There is then one difficulty. A certain recirculation, of selected examples, had already occurred. Where, you might ask, from the 1950s onwards, were the working-class novels of the 1930s? Why, there on the shelves, in paperback editions: Walter Greenwood's *Love on the Dole*; Richard Llewellyn's *How Green was my Valley*. These stood for the others, were the most representative, the most successful, the best.

Few knowing the wider body of work would consent to any of those or similar adjectives, except 'successful'. The success was a success is a success. But as this began to be said, the work of recovery became, and not only from educated habit, internally evaluative, discriminatory, critical. Read *Chwalfa* and *Black Parade* so that you can learn to 'place' *How Green was my Valley*. Read *All Things Betray Thee* to find a mode beyond any of these. And so back to literature, and to criticism.

But not entirely. For the work of recovery is also, indeed sometimes exclusively, a political impulse. Already *The Ragged Trousered Philanthropists*, now also *Cwmardy* and *We Live*, have direct political interest. New questions then: the political line; its difficulties; its contrasts with the non-political, the non-aligned, the romanticised, the reactionary. Simple questions, or at least simple answers, since we know in hindsight what the correct line might, could, should have been.

Yet in the end questions as difficult as those other, persuasively simple, critical questions: how well written; how vigorous; how convincing. Intellectually difficult questions, and the answers depending, in large part, on the position from which they are asked. A familiar position: what did those working-class writers, that generation, do for us? The only question that is easily admitted into bourgeois discourse on this topic: did they do enough for us? Did they serve us well?

'Piss off', would they say, if they were here to speak for themselves? That is not the language of an intervention in a discourse. 'Go blow your own trumpet, fight your own battles, write your own novels.' That is getting more like it. It is the beginning of the discipline of working-class culture. But only the beginning. Active solidarity, rather than informed retrospective sympathy. No room then for reckoning mistakes? For learning the lessons of history? 'Well yes, admitted. In our own time we blew up the old buggers who stood in our way. And honoured a few of them, come to that.' So that *we* could do better. Try to do better. We didn't manage too much of it. How about you?

II

The simplest descriptive novel about working-class life is already, by being written, a significant and positive cultural intervention. For it is not, even yet, what a novel is supposed to be, even as one kind among others. And changing this takes time. As late as the 1830s the English middle class had still to persuade themselves that their own lives were interesting enough for a novel. The aristocracy, its romances and its scandals, that was where the blood flowed. Flows. Commerce, family, the individual picking his way: how to make these fictionally moving? It was done; had in part been done already while many writers and readers still wondered if it was possible, or concluded it was impossible. But in the end done so thoroughly that impressed readers will have no other: serious fiction, refuse all substitutes.

Or now the other way round: the bourgeois novel; the classic realist text. Change commerce to industrial labour and it is not nearly enough; the family is still there, and the individual picking his way. They have not done enough for us: where is the class? A question asked, but more practically, in these actual novels. A place, a community, a type of work, families, collective actions, failures to act, solidarities, divisions, factions, struggles, local victories, defeats, changes of mind, emigrations. Who wants a class like that?

Because we are here we shall write about ourselves. To try to get it clear and to let others know about it. If they don't like it that's up to them.

III

That they have not, in general, liked it, and for an ever-lengthening list of reasons, we shall have to live with, die with. We. We die, we live. History moves on; our history and that bigger history made for, imposed on us. Can we not then ask, with respect, about the practical problems and about the changes? Ask, whether they like it or not, so that, still being here, we may know a little better what we have done and failed to do, and what we could still do and try to do.

Because we are here. Because the Depression, suddenly, is not a historical period, for the recovery of documents and memoirs. Because it has come back, is again being imposed on us, and we thought that could never happen. Not a literary or historical experience. Unemployment, closures; political defeats and divisions; advice to emigrate; anger.

It is being lived as well as written. It was always being lived as well as written.

IV

The terms are often in everyday practice interchangeable: working-class, popular, industrial, proletarian, radical, socialist, regional, Welsh. They are confused as terms because they are confused as experience and practice. Thus we endure their confusion, necessarily endure. But then to change we must think about them, begin to make some distinctions for ourselves.

Popular: yes and no. We had to write the life of a people. Popular in that sense, yes. Popular in the other sense: not really. We were read by some, but most even of those we wrote about were at the cinema and then the television, or reading penny dreadfuls and twopenny loves.

Regional: yes, we were admitted as that. New exotics for the English to read about. Funny people the Welsh. Talking and singing like mad. And yes suffering of course. 'Something must be done.'

Welsh: yes and no. It was a special problem for us. We had a literature, *in* Welsh, that was perhaps the oldest continuous body of writing in Europe. Except that by the twentieth century it was no longer our majority language, and as part of the same history Wales had changed, had a majority of urban and industrial workers, was to that extent separate from the life within which the received forms were generated: tribal, feudal, pastoral, religious; a many-sided tradition which did not, however, include realist prose narrative. By the twentieth century that may have been old to the English; it was new to us.

Industrial; well, certainly. But there is the problem. There were novels about English industrial life from the 1840s: *Mary Barton*, *North and South*, *Hard Times*, *Shirley* and so on. A Welshman grouped them as English industrial novels. He was right and wrong. As a group they had been read out of the tradition; it was right to insist on the group. But then 'industrial'; that is so many things. It was textiles, that group: the first wave of the Industrial Revolution. Except that there were already iron and coal as their base: iron and coal that were already, by the 1840s, changing the face of Wales. If you look at the range of work that was represented in nineteenth-century novels, you will find, on the one hand, the full middle-class spectrum of businesses and professions; on the other hand a very limited working-class range, with the textile mills predominant. Agricultural labour made some headway; rural and urban craftsmen were there; in the city, and especially London, a wide variety of occupations, including the humblest, and among them the sweatshops. But of industry, in its developing sense, comparatively little was visible. Nobody was writing novels which more than glanced, if that, at the ironworks, the rapidly developing coalmines, the docks, the shipyards, the chemical works, the engineering shops. Of if they were, we have still to recover them.

This is the groundwork for analysing the remaining terms: radical and socialist; working-class and proletarian. For on the one hand there was already, by the 1830s, a self-organising and self-conscious working class, predominantly radical in politics, only beginning to be touched by socialism but—as at Merthyr and elsewhere—already moving at times into local insurrection. By the 1890s this was a much more general movement, with established unions and the beginning of a move into parliamentary representation. These phases of organisation and conflict can be found in English novels from the 1840s. In novels written by middle- or upper-class observers, some of them initially sympathetic but predominantly to working men or women as individuals within a total condition, rather than to a class marked by its own forms of independent organisation. Almost invariably there is hostility to the active factors of class, even alongside sympathy with the conditions of the class. And because this is so, class relations are elements of the organisation of such novels, but relations as seen from outside the working class. This tendency actually strengthened during the century. There can be a shared radicalism—the old working-class/middle-class alliance—in Mrs Gaskell, in Mark Rutherford; even, in mediated ways, in Kingsley and George Eliot. But, as the active working-class developed, the specific hostility of Dickens—still enclosed within a generalised radicalism—became the active hostility and contempt of Gissing. The subtitle of his *Demos* was *A Story of English Socialism*. The conscious class issue, in its modern form, had been joined.

On the other hand, all through the nineteenth century, there were working-class writers. Only they were rarely writing novels. Verse of several kinds, and some vigorous work-songs. In prose, pamphlets, memoirs, autobiographies. That is either writing in the direct service of the cause, or writing as a record of it. Or, as in the increasingly popular form of the autobiography, of which hundreds of examples are still being recovered, the story of an exceptional man who had served the cause, or had become important through the cause, or who had 'risen' from the class to some other eminence. A mixed history, but the accessible form individual, even when middle-class fiction was already, in its own terms, social.

V

Novels by writers born or still living in the modern working class are then predominantly a twentieth-century phenomenon, occurring up to a century after the economic and political formations of the class. And still, in the earliest phase, over a narrow spectrum of working-class life. *The Ragged-Trousered Philanthropists* includes building workers in a seaside town; at the outside edge of modern industrial organisation. The socialist who mocks and instructs them, and who so memorably shows up their exploiters, is an immigrant. So, significantly, was the writer.

Then the first example of one of the two main kinds of working-class writer: (i) the writer born in a working-class family, moving out of it typically through education and his profession as writer; (ii) the working-class adult who writes a novel. Noonan (Tressell) becomes an example of (ii). The central English example of (i) is

D. H. Lawrence. And with Lawrence comes a central sector of working-class life: coalmining.

Eighty years on, with the spectrum remarkably broadened, we have not yet mapped these emergences. We shall have to do this, if we are to answer all the questions about working class and proletarian, socialist and anti-socialist or 'neutral'. I know only one map in reasonable detail: that of the Welsh. It raises all the questions. The answers come less readily.

VI

The first novelist I know of who had worked in a coalmine was Joseph Keating (born Mountain Ash, 1871). He left the mine at sixteen, became a clerk and a journalist, published novels·from the 1890s. He shows us some of the difficulties. He describes colliery work with remarkable power. But he centres his fiction in a different class, of coal-owning families and managers, or the old landed families. He had a shrewd sense of what novels then were.

Yet beyond these difficulties (which I have discussed in more detail in *The Welsh Industrial Novel*) Keating marks a specifically Welsh situation. For reasons internal to its social history, the writers and intellectuals of twentieth-century Wales are much more often working class in origin than their twentieth-century English counterparts. Thus the novels of Welsh working-class life are, in great majority, written in one way or another from inside the class.

In one way or another: that is where the problems start. But first a necessary word about class. As people organising and organised by work, and by the specific fact of selling their labour, the working class is very widely extended, with relative strength or weakness in particular trades but still with a national form. There are then variable degrees of relation between this economic class and different types of community. In the coalfields, in the docks, in the shipyard areas there are special kinds of community formed by the relative singularity and uniformity of employment. The majority are workers but also neighbours, interrelated families, inhabitants of a particular locality: in social relations which in no way contradict, which on the contrary strengthen, their economic ties. Is it then only a coincidence that it is in just such places, where different kinds of social relations strengthen the economic ties of class, that socialist consciousness has been and is to this day strongest? At the other extreme, as now in south-east England, there are millions of workers, the majority organised in unions, who live in more heterogeneous communities and who work in a variety of jobs which have physical contiguity but no other visible integration. In such areas, socialist consciousness has been and still is weakest. And then there are not only the extremes; there is a very complex range of intermediate cases.

For the novel, several consequences. In fact most of the working-class novels have come from the coalfields, the shipyard areas, the docksides, together with the continuing examples from the textile mills. But they come not only with these advantages, of the inspiring consciousness of a working-class community, but with the associated disadvantages—or are they disadvantages?; that is now where the argument turns.

First, that the very intensity of the community can be self-enclosing. It is the only and sufficient thing to write. But then the working-class novel can become a 'regional' novel: 'regional' not in the prejudicial sense of metropolitan criticism, where anything that is not London or Home Counties is 'regional' = 'provincial'; 'regional' in that more serious sense that the novel is written as if the region were autonomous. For Welsh mining families, in a novel, that can be in effect so; they are miners, Welsh, neighbours, families, members of chapels or parties, in one broad defining dimension. And one part of this dimension is working-class consciousness, in these terms. But then a working class, at its most general, and in any socialist perspective, is really a formation within a much wider system: not only the much wider national and international economy; but also the relations between classes, including that other alien class, those other alien or indeterminate or irrelevant classes. The stronger the sense of class singularity, in that defining place, the more difficult, in fictional terms, the true sense or presence of a differently defining system.

So a number of possibilities. The descriptive novel, not now by the sympathetic outside observer, but from within the class community. Thus not 'objective realist fiction', in the bourgeois mode, but subjectively descriptive, with the class community as subject. For example Gwyn Jones's *Times Like These*. Or is it? For the most accessible fictional centre, grounded in the reality of this kind of class community—the community of workers always within the community of families—is of course the working-class family, all the levels meeting or seeming to meet there. But can a family then represent a class? In these local terms, yes. In wider terms, including especially the more systematic elements, no. But then to follow the system, in any normal fictional terms, would be to go beyond the community which is the immediate subject and inspiration. Hence the predominant feelings: suffering; strain;

pressures on the family to break up, emigrate, losing the community and the family and becoming, where you can, economic man; indeed the family and community feeling at its strongest and most moving when it is being broken and dispersed by economic depression. Compare the structure of feeling of Rowland Hughes' *Chwalfa*, in another intense locality, the quarrying villages of North Wales: the full dimension and its breaking, dispersal.

Second possibility. The wider system is not realised in the novel, because that would involve going beyond the boundaries of the community which forms it. Only local representatives and subordinates of the alien class are at all visible. But there is then internal struggle, not only with these, but between different versions of the nature of the system, as they affect and run through this intense local life. The struggle within the class, as between militant socialism, reformism, subordinate adjustments, collaboration. A struggle highlighted in certain major events, notably strikes, and crucially in South Wales the general strike of 1926 followed by the months of the miners' lockout. For examples, Lewis Jones's *Cwmardy* and *We Live*. Socialist novels, as distinct from working-class novels? That change of emphasis is right but especially in *We Live* carries the marks of its specific formation. The identification of the system is not only locally generated and fought out; it is also attached to imported, unrealised, versions of what is happening elsewhere. And then what really happens elsewhere can kick back to blur the internal version. A lived and substantiated movement can become a party line. But only at that level. In the main the novels have moved much closer to the class as subject, though for economy still centrally the class as family, as distinct from the other possibility, the family as class.

Third possibility: historical formation. The advantages of locality retained and even strengthened; new perspectives made possible by moving through periods and generations, a working class being made, and changing, rather than simply, descriptively and substantially, present. For example, Jack Jones's *Black Parade*. The same Jack Jones who in *Rhondda Roundabout* had sketched the internal variety rather than the class uniformity or the mainly political diversity of the people of the valley. In neither kind socialist, for there are other destinations of that turbulent and diverse history. But in *Black Parade* powerful; a novel of the making, the struggles, the defeats of a class. An ironic question, aside. Can the initial form of the socialist novel—its committed perspective added to the descriptive local identity—include defeats (of which there were many) except as springboards for new

struggles or as lessons for final victory? The commitment, as in
Lewis Jones, is inspiring. The victory, or even the avoidance of
further defeats, is still due. The problem reaches to the known
boundary of the novel as a form.

Fourth possibility: the process of composition itself. The composition of a history, and the composition of a writing of that
history. For example, Gwyn Thomas's *All Things Betray Thee*.
Most of the localising marks taken out. The particulars of struggle
given a general form. At the centre of the novel the problem of
finding a voice to articulate them. The hesitations, the actual
limits, of art; the final commited articulation almost inarticulate,
but moving because it has included the struggle in its most general
form. A struggle which includes finding the voice of the history,
beyond either the flattened representations or the applied ideological phrases.

VII

Each of these possibilities was worth attempting and achieving.
And each is still a possibility, given the vast area of unrecovered,
unwritten, popular and labouring and working-class experience.

But in the period since the 1950s, some new problems, within
some new opportunities. Among 'working-class writers' there has
been a heavy shift of proportion between the two kinds: those
born in the working-class but moving out, in some sense, through
education and writing; working-class adults beginning to write.
The drift of the culture, and of the organisation of publishing, have
worked to multiply the former, through now two or three
generations; to diminish the latter, though in some vigorous local
developments of community publishing it is clear that many of
them are still there, waiting for openings. Some political differences also. The Left in the 1930s, and especially the Communist
Party, consciously sought adult working-class writers, and made
openings for them: with some disadvantages, in the consequent
political direction, but still releasing new cultural forces. The
postwar Left has not done this, in any central way. The Labour
Party and the unions have failed, throughout, even to see that the
cultural struggle is a major element of all political and economic
struggles. It is only on the fringe, in radical community publishing,
that this has been recognised; but then indeed as yet on the fringe;
marginally.

And meanwhile a quite different major force has been unleashed. In the general advancement of the working class, and in a
rapidly expanding cultural market—led by radio and television but

with important effects in print, there is now major commercial production in the area of working-class life and for working-class publics. Once this has happened, the problem of distinctions within the general category, 'working-class writing', becomes acute. Especially the problem of the meaning of 'socialist' or 'proletarian' writing within this now general category.

We can try to distinguish some kinds.

(a) The novel of working-class childhood, and of the move away from it.

(b) The novel of a past period of working-class life, typically just at the edge of living memory; unconnected to the present.

(c) The novel of contemporary working-class life, naturalised, depoliticised, reproductive.

(d) The novel of working class–middle class encounters, within newly mobile and mixed communities.

We cannot yet make any full inventory, but it seems clear that (a) has been predominant in the literature of the period. It corresponds to a typical social movement of the majority of writers who enter this area at all. From *Sons and Lovers* on, it is a significant English form. The working-class childhood is strongly written; the move away from it is given equal force. It is less common in Welsh writers. Thus Gwyn Jones, sharing the same apparent trajectory of educational mobility, centred not on the individual move away, but on the broader and persistent family experience. For much the same reasons, I wrote *Border Country* and *Second Generation* against this pattern, including the child-hood and the mobility but making them interact with a persistent adult working-class life.

There has been important work in (b), which again fits the trajectory of the socially mobile writers. Through education and research, combined with local and family memories, they can recover a period. Compare *When the Boat Comes In* and *Days of Hope*, finding an outlet first now in television, and then moving to print. It is often moving, valuable work. But it connects to the present in mood and idea rather than in social experience. Hence the numerous weak commercial forms of the same apparent kind: what it was like yesterday; not like today. Poverty as nostalgia reaches through the cultural spectrum, even into advertising. Of course a simple, decent, wholesome poverty. A distinction then within this kind: the distinction between period and historical fiction. Period fiction is enclosed in its time, is an object—often colourful—of spectacle. Historical fiction, even where it makes no deliberate connections, or is not fully consequent, has movement and challenge.

Work in (c) is the predominant commercial form. It has many local reproductive fidelities. It extends to relatively vigorous 'low life' fiction. The treatment of politics is often the key. Naturalistically it can indeed be seen as marginal; much of that has happened, in the wider history, though it was never for long as central and general as some work in type (b) suggests, or as in the work which came out of exceptional crisis—the Welsh novels of the 1930s. Marginality is one thing; the eccentricity, comicality, of politics—the 'local red'—is another. A great deal of this.

Commercial work also in (d), at simple levels of contrast of life-styles, often overlapping with (a). In any serious way still comparatively rare. The pulls of (a), (b) and (c) are much stronger.

VIII

Some criteria then perhaps. There is a still workable descriptive classification of working-class fiction. Very simple. The majority of characters and events belong to working-class life. For some time yet, given the persistent dominance of other classes in fiction, a distinction worth making.

But only to lead on to further distinctions, as above. And for some of us as an impulse to distinguish socialist writing within the expanded general form.

Easily done? The author, or a decisive character, offers a socialist interpretation of what is happening, what happened, what might have happened, what could yet happen. Heavily warned off by the dominant culture. No preaching in novels. No ideas in novels! To hell. Do it.

But interlocked with this necessary defiance, some harder decisions. An interpretation of what? Look at the kinds again. In (a) the necessary socialist shift; what ought to have been a more general human shift. The working class is not a childhood family, although of course it includes that experience. The socialist writer has to interpret not only the childhood but the mobility and the immobility and the consequent problems of relationship, at every level from the most directly personal to the social and economic and political.

In (b) the simplest mode of interpretation, but with dangers. Not just the heroic period, as inspiration. The working class is not a past tense. At this stage, for a socialist writer, the necessary inclusion of interpretation of defeats and failures, and the relations between these and subsequent adaptations. Possible only in the historical novel, whether like *Black Parade* or the quite different *All Things Betray Thee*. Overridden by the period novel. A reflection for socialist writers. We have many period novels. We have a few historical novels. We have only the beginnings of a historical materialist novel, yet it ought to be one of our three major forms.

Nothing in (c), as it stands, but an obvious need for work which can recognise, without either stabilising, promoting or recommending, the altered political and social conditions of the now exceptionally diverse contemporary working class. The inclusion of continuing struggles within what is frankly recognised, also, as in majority a predominantly reproductive mode. The interactions between these, especially those starting now, as the new slump presses on the new acceptances.

Much for socialists in (d). The purity of 'working-class fiction' refused, sometimes, for the exploration of class relations and class developments, and for that difficult contact, beyond local interactions, with what is truly systematic, the working class visibly *within* a system. Recognitions indeed of the working class still making itself, though now in diverse ways. Recognitions also of it being made, remade, deprived of its identity for a bargain. The risk, here, of proletarian pieties. Stick to the fact not the idea of a proletariat, and seek forms in which the changes can be shown and interpreted, rather than the received shapes imposed. Changes within the class, but then also the contradictory class locations: not only intellectuals but technicians, some managers and administrators; these not only in their subjective traverse from working-class childhood to adult relocation or contradiction; also in their objective trajectory, towards contesting places in a contested and precarious and at once determined and determinable system. Socialist writing of classes and between classes, and of people moving and changing in and between classes and class gaps and class contradictions. Beyond piety to realism.

IX

A reach exceeding our grasp? Not exceeding *our* grasp. From historical objects—working-class writers of the 1930s—to historical subjects: our fathers, our comrades, who worked and would expect us to work. Learning from them to change and go on.

Chapter 7

THE LANGUAGE OF THE WORKING-CLASS NOVEL OF THE 1930s

Ramón López Ortega

The more important moments in working-class and socialist literature have usually coincided with periods of profound social and economic crisis. The Hungry Forties, the Great Depression of 1874, the years of the Great Unrest, and even the time that followed World War II, provide many examples of this. The 1930s are no exception. A considerable number of novelists turned their attention, often with great success, to the industrial scene and working-class life. Yet in English literary history there has been a reluctance to admit the importance of their contribution.[1] In the following pages I will make some comments on their use of language and try to establish the place they occupy in English literature.

The Depression was at once the fuse that fired and the cement that bound these writers together. The spectre of unemployment and industrial conflict haunts the pages of their work; it lurks behind all the recurrent images—poverty, the fruitless search for work, life on the dole, the Means Test, the hunger marches, the strikes. These events conditioned the writers' perspective and, ultimately, their literary consciousness. Thus, whatever may have been their specific political convictions, they all attempted to enlist the sympathy of their readers, striving for solidarity with the working class. A strong faith in socialism as the only possible way to a new social order animates their novels, because, as one of these young writers declared, 'the creed of socialism is a great deal more than a political programme'.[2] Of course, this does not mean that the sensibility of all the 1930s writers was rooted in and sustained by this new vision, this new 'humanism' as Jack Mitchell calls it;[3] many simply limited themselves to 'novelising' party lines and political programmes, but we must be wary of any generalisation that might include all these revolutionary authors. To put it in Jack Lindsay's words, we cannot continue 'at the mercy of tendentious accounts belittling or ridiculing the developments which then powerfully occurred'.[4]

A threadbare cliché that has been applied to these writers is an alleged contempt for the formal and stylistic dimensions of literature and a neglect of the mainstream; this again is a half truth that has often led us astray.

Admittedly, it is true that some of the English supporters of *proletkult* theories repudiated literary tradition by asserting that culturally, and even linguistically, they were starting out from scratch. For the novelist Alec Brown, literary English since the arrival of the printing press in England was but a jargon invented by the dominant classes; it was he who fathered the preposterous slogan: 'WRITTEN ENGLISH BEGINS WITH US'.[5]

Nevertheless it is equally true that in the same decade voices of other revolutionary writers were raised recognising the value of technique and the richness of literary heritage. Lewis Grassic Gibbon, the author of the most successful working-class novel of the 1930s, was one of them. 'It is not a decayed and decrepit dinosaur who is the opponent of the real revolutionary writer,' he said, 'but a very healthy and vigorous dragon indeed.'[6] And furthermore, Ralph Fox and Amabel Williams-Ellis, two of the leading authorities of the day, openly advised imitations modelled on the classics of the Great Tradition or on the aesthetic doctrines prevailing at the close of the nineteenth century.[7] Incidentally, they were often responsible for the exaggerated naturalism that charac- terised some of the 1930s novels, and for their stylistic stagnation.

One thing remains clear: even among those who offered the most naïve 'literary' solutions, it is still possible to perceive an awareness of the difficult relationship between language—and form in general—and content. Of course, this awareness is perfectly evident in the most gifted writers—not only in Grassic Gibbon, but also in Edward Upward, James Barke, Lewis Jones, and even in Walter Brierley—who strove to forge a new literary form, a vehicle adequate to express a distinct point of view and a new flow of imagination. For them, the declaration of the Writers' International Association—'Journalism, literature, the theatre, are developing in technique while narrowing in content'—was more a lament over a lack of concern for 'the events and issues that matter' than a deliberate discouragement of new uses of language.[8]

In 1929, the year of the Wall Street Crash, a novel appeared that made its author an honorary member of a literary movement to which he never belonged.[9] The author was Henry Green: his novel was *Living*.[10] It is neither the best working-class novel of the

Depression as Walter Allen imagines—let alone the only one as W. Y. Tindall thinks[11]—nor does its tone relate to the time in the way later novels did. Nevertheless, some circumstances came together in the making of *Living* that could well have provided a valuable lesson for the revolutionary writers of the 1930s.

To begin with, Green felt compelled to share as widely as he could the personal experience he had working in his father's factory in Birmingham. Ironically his account of it is closer to the world of the working class than those of some socialist or worker-writers themselves. His was only a vacation job, but somehow it begot in him a 'living' enthusiasm—the title of the book is not fortuitous. For the first time he seemed to realise in the act of work itself that he was a man, the act of work becoming indeed a total absorption in the factory and the world centred on it. It was an awakening or, in his own words, 'an introduction to indisputable facts at last, to a life bare of almost everything except essentials'.[12] Perhaps it was this full immersion into work that made possible Green's sensitive documentation of it in its innate dignity; this is nowhere more vivid than in the portrait of Craigan, a lifetime worker whose very being is rooted in the factory, and a man who has to come to terms with retirement from it.

Then, because of this need to commit his overwhelming experience to paper, Green felt equally compelled to find the language which would express that firsthand insight into working-class living. He soon realised he was dealing with new material, really a different way of life, for the rendering of which most available literary conventions seemed inadequate. At the same time, and unlike Alec Brown and his kind, he understood that it was not possible to shed a literary inheritance. While successfully mining the resources of working-class and current idiom, he was equally aware of the strengths of earlier English literary forms.

The result is a terse, energetic and eliptical prose which, as Edward Stokes observes, is 'essentially the industrial workers' style'.[13] The linguistic economy of *Living* certainly catches the factory atmosphere and the ethos of the working community. But this statement requires clarification: it does not mean that Green's almost telegraphic prose literally mirrors the sparseness characteristic of a proletarian environment. His artifice in my opinion is far more subtle: a consistent use of parataxis and asyndeton allows the fundamental facts of working-class life to stand out more clearly. As I see it, his solid style well translates the main features of the restricted code usually employed in working-class communication. This is a legitimate interpretation, I believe, of

Green's often quoted statement: 'I wanted to make that book as taut and spare as possible to fit the proletarian life I was then leading.' His astringent and economical paragraphs emphasise what is important and are meant to heighten the reader's awareness since, as the author continues, 'the more you leave out, the more you highlight what you leave in'.[14] Giorgio Melchiori compares this technique to that of the Impressionists and notes that Green intensifies 'the emotional quality of the picture by concentrating on the really significant features'.[15]

In order to achieve this effect the author went not only to ordinary speech, but also to literary tradition. His elision of articles, or their replacement by demonstratives, has been attributed to Anglo-Saxon influence; and perhaps this also explains his frequent omission of the non-adverbial 'there'. In dialogue, on the other hand, he normally retains the article—and this makes one wonder whether the alternative explanation usually given (a possible influence of the Warwickshire dialect in which apocopation makes the definite article barely heard) is valid.

The foundation of his narrative is the simple sentence and the careful reproduction of vernacular dialogue; yet his syntax is full of bold deviations from the norm (abrupt inversions and distortions of word-order) which jog our minds. The picture of the foundry epitomises the controlled and even cadenced severity and compactness of this verbal world:

In the foundry was now sharp smell of burnt sand. Steam rose from the boxes round about. On these, in the running gates and risers, metal shone out red where it set. On Mr. Craigan's huge box in which was his casting Mr. Craigan and Jim Dale stood. They raised and lowered long rods into metal in the risers to as to keep the metal molten. Steam rose up round them so their legs were wet and heat from the molten metal under them made balls of sweat roll down them. Arc lamps above threw their shadows out sprawling along over the floor and as they worked rhythmically their rods up and down so their shadows worked. (p. 34)

However harsh the style of *Living* may be, it is never arid. From time to time touches of lyricism gentle the realistic description and glimpses of poetry help to make solemn moments memorable. The best-known example is perhaps the passage in which the singing of the Welsh worker Arthur Jones interrupts the running of the factory and keeps his workmates in ecstatic suspense. Green closes it by telling us in one sentence, in which the laconic phrase echoes Biblical words, the reason for Jones' joy: 'That night son had been born to him' (p. 90).

Henry Green, perhaps like D. H. Lawrence, may have failed to grasp the whole potential of the working class; a better appreciation of the possibilities behind the squalor and misery would have contributed to a fuller picture of this collective hero in their novels. Yet, in spite of this shortcoming, their artistic rendering of proletarian experience remains a model worth imitating.

Unfortunately not every writer of the 1930s recognised it as such. Pieces like *David and Joanna* (1936) or *They Won't Let You Live* (1939) by George Blake and Simon Blumenfeld, respectively, rank among the saddest examples of literature overrun by political doctrine. But perhaps none of them in this respect is as bad as Alec Brown's *The Daughters of Albion* (1935). This book reveals the sterility of its author's theorising.[16] Brown imagined that proletarian simplicity could be conjured out of some orthographic vagaries and a random scattering of colloquial conventions (for example, 'N-no, dont, d-d-dont, d-d-d . . .', 'Ye-e-es', 'havent', 'isnt', etc.). As a result of this, his social and political views, however acceptable in themselves, do not live in his images and characters; he has to 'explain' his episodes. David Smith sums up all this by saying: 'His innovations seem to consist, in fact, of an indiscriminate omission of capital letters, apostrophes, and hyphens, such contractions as "alright", and such onomatopoeic eccentricities as "she turned to the lamp on the low table beside her narrow bed and puff! puff! puff! blew it out"'.[17] George Blake and Simon Blumenfeld also weigh down the action of their works by insistent authorial intrusion. Because of their obsessive intellectualising, all that happens in the story is dredged through a sieve of ideology, and so the necessary balance between commentary and dialogue is lost. Persistent insinuation destroys the seed of literary life, and consequently language becomes more and more abstract. In George Blake's work, for example, we find that Joanna is suddenly and inexplicably enlightened; and the author, unable to allow this character to mature naturally, is also forced to 'explain' the nature of her illumination:

Vaguely but with certainty she knew that the struggle was not as he described it: not a local affair of radical antagonisms and injustices. It was the struggle of simple, imprisoned people, of David's and Joanna's everywhere, to escape into freedom and peace, wherein love might blossom sweetly and life be full in simplicity. And she knew, while Durward ranted, that for all that had happened to her, the will towards that life was not dead within herself nor the future necessarily empty. In a private flush of gladness, but cooly, she made herself a tally of the elements in her own case. On the one side were poverty and oppressive custom, and these she did not undervalue; but on the other were youth, strength, a precedent, and her own renascent will. (p. 383)

Likewise, Simon Blumenfeld is himself the dominant character in *They Won't Let You Live*. After having failed to make his characters come to life, the concluding words of the novel sound like a pamphlet:

His father's world was dying, although in its convulsions it might set continents aflame. It seemed too late now to avoid a clash, but probably it was for the best; if it had been better last year than now, it was better now than in three month's time, or in six, which held about the full limit of a Nazi promise. He had to look ahead, after the conflict, to see that this never happened again. The survivors, young people, would build a newer, saner world, where middle-aged men were not lopped off like dead twigs because they did not fit in, where violence in private and public affairs had no place, where prejudice and lies could no longer dim the vision of decent folk. They would establish a society where the whole of life could flower harmoniously, whose fabric would never more be endangered by one shrieking lunatic straddling Europe. Enough of retreating, of whining and pleading; let the dead past bury the dead. No more crying to the sea, and having pity sigh back with the wind. Clear-eyed, with a million others, he would stand out boldly in the tempest and shake a fist at thunder. (p. 251)

However, it would be inadmissible to say that this is the pattern of every novel of the Depression. George Blake himself had written another work, *The Shipbuilders* (1935),[18] in which many of the flaws of *David and Joanna* are absent. The small critical attention it has received seems to concentrate on its failures. Shortly after its publication it was classed as 'topical journalism'.[19] In part the charge is true, but when considered in its entirety, the novel possibly deserves better treatment. George Blake success-fully depicts the pride of a skilled worker in his craft when it is threatened by the machine. Danny Schield's decision to 'stick to [his] own trade' (p. 254) and refuse any other kind of work when the economic crisis finally drowns a dying industry, may not be the best response in such a situation, but pride in the skill of his hands is the only thing the Slump has left him. Somehow this old type of hero, in spite of the prevailing pessimism of the story, provides a breath of hope.

Walter Greenwood's *Love on the Dole* (1933)[20] and also Walter Brierley's *Means Test Man* (1935), despite the negative evaluations they are usually given, offer in my opinion a lively and convincing picture of Britain during the 1930s.

In *Love on the Dole* Greenwood presents a wide range of characters and, however contrived his prose at times may seem, allows us to listen to a working community in the throes of the Depression. Sometimes we hear it in probing self-reflection, verging on inner monologue, as in Mr Hardcastle's about his daughter's desertion of the family and its moral assumptions (pp. 249–50); sometimes in the familiar complaint of an apprentice, made in tough colloquialisms, remembering that as soon as he and his workmates are entitled to a full salary, 'They give us the bloody sack an' don't care a damn wot becomes of us' (p. 180). More often perhaps, we hear the community speaking in the words of Larry Meath, a convinced socialist who is so fully identified with it. Greenwood's creation of a collective hero and the appropriate environment has given the novel the status of a trustworthy documentary of the decade. Historians like A. J. P. Taylor and Arthur Marwick in fact used it as such.[21] Characters such as Mr Hardcastle or Harry experience the sufferings of the majority in their own lives—perhaps the need to pour out these feelings is responsible for the melodrama that occasionally tinges the story—while Larry Meath is the interpreter of their anger and aspirations.

Larry, a character having much in common with Robert Tressell's Owen, is a familiar figure in proletarian literature: the typical autodidact who puts his education at the service of his class. In contrast to most of the other characters, he speaks in Standard English, but this does not separate him from the rest; for them he is a 'credit t' t' neighbourhood' (p. 96). The best worker-novelists —including W. E. Tirebuck and Robert Tressell—always present this type of worker hero either gradually abandoning his native dialect as he matures politically, or expressing himself in educated English from the beginning. One cannot object to *Love on the Dole* on this account, because whatever our opinion about this attitude to language may be, the novel only reflects what has been the case with the most politically conscious working-class leaders in real life. The general flow of Greenwood's novel is not marred by occasional inconsistencies,[22] and from time to time it achieves a beauty comparable to the passage quoted from *Living*:

The foundry! What a place.
Steel platforms from which you saw great muscular men dwarfed to insignificance by the vastness of everything, men the size of Ned Narkey who had charge of the gigantic crane. Fascinated he saw the cumbrous

thing, driven by Ned, unseen, move slowly along its metals; leisurely, its great arm deposited an enormous ladle by the furnace. A pause; a hoarse shout; a startling glimpse of fire then a rushing, spitting river of flames that was molten metal running out of the furnace's channel into the ladle until it brimmed. The river of fire was damned, ceased as by magic. The crane's limp cable tautened; slowly the ladle swung, revolved, white-hot, a vivid, staring glare that stabbed the eyes; slowly it swung, twenty tons of molten metal to the moulds. (pp. 48–9)

In Walter Brierley's work the Means Test man is presented as a threat to family unity and even personal equilibrium. Yet it would be unfair to accuse this realist writer of overloaded pessimism or melodrama when living memory and the chronicles of the 1930s corroborate that this was the prevalent feeling. 'The most cruel and evil effect of the Means Test,' wrote Orwell in *The Road to Wigan Pier* (1937), 'is the way in which it breaks up families' (p. 70);[23] and Arthur Marwick quotes an unemployed worker as saying: 'The Means Test and the capitalists . . . prevent me from having a decent life, but at least I will have a decent death.'[24] Brierley gives these events literary form by juxtaposing passages reminiscent of the stream-of-consciousness technique with the crudest naturalism. The resulting picture is profoundly sad, monotonous; but this is the effect he sought. The clock acts as a constant reminder of the gradual spiritual death of Jack Cook. The lack of movement adds to this process of depersonalisation and psychological destruction. Brierley never indulges in facile solutions. Cook is not even supported by the solidarity of his family and his neighbours. A miner goes as far as to taunt him to his face:'Ere ar've bin thumpin' mi ribs ert a' dee far no moor than that begger's gerrin' on t' dole' (p. 99).

Like many out-of-work men during those days, Cook is haunted by the idea of suicide. But this appears more as an act of angry frustration than of total despair, because he is fully aware of the roots of the social malaise; 'His hate', the book tells us, 'was against the fact that such a system could be' (p. 87). Undeniably the novel has weaknesses, but they are not the alleged fantasies of psychological fiction or an indulgence in sterile naturalism. Quite the contrary, the use the author makes of psychology and naturalism is attuned to the atmosphere the novel requires, and this helps to make the book an adequate metaphor of the decade.

Belonging really to this same group in date and outlook, there is a handful of novels separated from it slightly not only by quality but also by the introduction of some financially more privileged characters who now find themselves equally victims of the Slump. This somewhat bigger canvas of the Depression is well represented in James Barke's *Major Operation* (1936) and in James Lansdale Hodson's *Harvest in the North* (1934).[25]

Major Operation is basically built on an intellectual debate between Anderson, a well-to-do member of the middle class, and MacKelvie, a militant shipyard worker. Yet it would be too simplistic to dismiss the novel as a mere debate. Anderson's life, seriously affected by the Depression, undergoes fundamental changes that finally lead him to death, a victim of police violence in a hunger march. In brief summary these events may smack of fantasy, but in the story they are entirely plausible within a well-devised plot. Ill, financially ruined, and out of work, Anderson encounters socialism in the person of MacKelvie while convalescing in hospital after a serious operation. When his wife decides to run away with his rich former friend and partner, MacKelvie—by then unemployed himself—becomes Anderson's only material and spiritual support, taking him home with him. There MacKelvie, in a more relaxed atmosphere, tries to enlighten him. At the end of the novel, after much hesitation and not without considerable misgivings—Anderson is on the verge of suicide—a series of events lead him to join the workers' demonstration.

The transformation wrought on Anderson's mind, a major operation indeed, is immense, but the author manages to make it credible. In order to effect these rapid shifts in fortune, convictions, and even social setting, Barke tries different styles with considerable success. Within the framework of a symmetric structure he jumps from the depressed scenery of the slums to the luxurious surroundings of the wealthy. An almost episodic pattern imitating film techniques makes the rendering of this contrast possible. For instance, in the first part of the book, significantly subtitled 'The Two Worlds', in fast sequence Barke gives us pictures of Rowat's world, one of banal discussions, and then scenes from MacKelvie's, in which there is only time for the pressing issues of the day (pp. 63ff). But a few pages later, in the section labelled 'The Smells of Slumdom', this agile style is suddenly replaced by a controlled naturalistic prose that conveys the real misery of the times.

Jack Mitchell, in what seems to be the best critical commentary on this novel, refers to this stylistic variety observing that Barke borrowed from Dos Passos 'the impressionistic newspaper-headline or telegrammic style', and that he also made 'attempts, not always unsuccessful, to apply a modified surrealistic stream-of-consciousness technique'. Later, he describes MacKelvie as 'a heroic placard devoid of any real conflict' and as 'a damp squib'.²⁶ This may be going slightly too far because, while there is some truth in the criticism, one should not forget that MacKelvie is not the main character of the novel—not even a central one, although at a first reading it may appear otherwise. He is rather, in my opinion, a peripheral figure whose role is to serve as a counterpoint, almost a reference point, to make Anderson possible. MacKelvie is one of those figures who have to be judged more in terms of their function within the fabric of the novel than as characters in their own right.

In *Harvest in the North* a full economic cycle is completed in the life experience of the Renshaw family. Within a short space of time this working family knows the prosperity of an economic boom and total ruin. Harriet, the wife of the now jobless head of the house, personifies the pride of her class. The words of contempt she throws at her husband's former boss bear evidence of it: 'He was very useful to you, wasn't he, when you were floatin' companies?' (p. 247).

A clear understanding of economic and historical law permeates and to a certain extent governs the whole story without endangering the earthiness of its image and scene. The liberation of the working class, for instance, is seen in the same historical perspective as the liberation of the bourgeoisie, not in an abstract way but through a telling anecdote. Edward Houghton, the owner of a moribund textile industry, shows understanding of the rightness of the workers: 'I've a good deal of sympathy with the pitman who asked the duke how he came to own all the coal. The duke said: "My forefathers fought for it." "Good," said the pitman, slipping off his jacket, "I'll fight *thee* for it"' (p. 111). Characteristically, Houghton is not referring to one of his own mill-hands, but to a miner. The miner was always in the vanguard of the labour movement and in the forefront of most of its struggles. In many of the novels of the time he is an almost indispensable character.

The cluster of novels with the most clearly defined personality within the 1930s movement all deal with mining life and were often written by miners themselves. Perhaps the best examples are Harold Heslop's *Last Cage Down* (1935) and, especially, Lewis Jones' *Cwmardy* (1937).²⁷ *Times Like These* (1936),²⁸ by Gwyn Jones, although its author's background is different, also deserves mention. These writers had a local culture at hand which had nourished a whole literary tradition—not only the works of D. H.

Lawrence, but also some more consciously working-class pieces such as *Miss Grace of All Souls* (1895) or *The Underworld* (1920), by W. E. Tirebuck and James Welsh, respectively. Lewis Jones' and Gwyn Jones' heroes share with Tirebuck's and Welsh's a full sense of solidarity and unusual clarity of consciousness; and what is more important from a literary viewpoint, their dialogues have the raciness and directness of vernacular idiom and ordinary speech. Curiously, in some of these novels we find bilingual situations recalling *Sons and Lovers*, although the motivations are not always the same. Their aim is not only to confront 'educated' speech with the miners' idiom (and when this is the case the author's stand is far less hesitant than Lawrence's).

The setting of *Last Cage Down* is a coalfield and the antagonism between men and owners its *leitmotiv*. Heslop's strong and honest miner, James Cameron, has the qualities most admired by his workmates, and a knowledge of the mines such as is possessed only by one born of mining stock. His genuine love for the job does not make him oblivious to the sub-human conditions and the absence of safety precautions under which the work is done. In a scene which could be considered paradigmatic, Cameron, as the embodiment of all the miners, speaks with the mine manager, Tate, about the dangers to which they are exposed. No solution is reached. It is when the dialogue breaks down that Cameron, in response to Tate's hostility and obstinacy, utters his threat: 'Listen . . ., the first man you kill in that seam . . . do you hear? . . . The first man you kill. . . . I'll kill you, that's all' (p. 38). Shortly afterwards the danger Cameron foresaw becomes a reality with the death of his brother Jack. Throughout eleven chapters Cameron has been a prey to the obsession that the mine would claim another victim. Now, when his fears prove well-grounded, almost spontaneously we are on his side, ready to understand, and perhaps justify, any act of vengeance that might take place. The known frequency of mine disasters at the time does not strain the credibility of the story when another one occurs making Tate himself the new victim. James Cameron then gives an unforgettable lesson in humanity and generosity, placing himself at the forefront of the rescue brigade. His duty as a miner is unhesitating; he must save a workmate, even though he may be an enemy.

Cameron followed them, carrying his burden—John Tate. He was smiling grimly to himself. Tate was at his mercy—but Tate had to be saved. And he was going to save him! But all the time he was feeling that he was being a fool. (p. 351)

Any 'industrial' novel of the early Victorian period could have ended here, having imparted the inevitable moral lesson. But, although Cameron's behaviour deserves all praise, the miners' problems are not resolved by it. The mine is closed, the conflict begins, one which is neither haphazard nor blind, but organised and directed against a well-defined enemy:

'It's the only way,' Joe burst out.
'What's the only way?' she demanded, entering the room.
'Fighting the boss,' replied Joe. (p. 351)

The miners' struggle also inspired Lewis Jones' *Cwmardy*. It is based on actual events during the early years of the twentieth century. They are narrated with great imagination and one is aware of the author's purpose in linking them with the 1930s, when the novel was published. This device provides the author with the perspective required to handle the subject. As in *Last Cage Down*, in Lewis Jones' novel the action necessarily leads to conflict and violence. The earth also swallows up the lives of the best miners. The scene of the funeral of fifty-nine of these men after a gas explosion takes on an unusual pathos. Dai Cannon, the spiritual leader, solemnises the ceremony with an oration in which the voice of indignation and protest is accompanied, but by no means silenced, by the echoes of Job's patience and endurance (p. 102).

The men are profoundly conscious of the precarious conditions under which they work. 'Cattle are not treated like us. A farmer takes care of his cow when it is bad, but we be no use to anybody' (p. 130), says Len, the self-taught collier, in a weaker form of the local speech. (Len, following the usual pattern, gradually shifts to Standard English as his political awareness grows.) His father, Big Jim, makes the same complaint in his accustomed dialect: 'What do us men count? We be cheaper than chickens' (p. 89).

In a farcical enquiry that the company makes after the accident, a dialogue takes place in which Big Jim's vivid vernacular clashes with the clichés and evasive jargon of bureaucratic English. The questioner asks for his opinion—'can you, as a practical and an experienced miner, advance another theory as to the probable cause?'—but Jim is unable to understand the alien code: ''Scuse me, 'o'nt you? . . . I be not much of an English-speaking man and some of your words do come strange to my ears' (p. 99). The scene and the antagonism it generates, give us in a nutshell the very essence of the story.

The Federation listens to the growing radical voices of the

miners, who are tired of being forced to subsist under such conditions. One more Dai Cannon openly proposes strife as the only way out of poverty. 'The octopus', he declares, 'is closing his tentacles about the living bodies of our women and children. . . . If we are to starve, let it be in the sun with God's pure air around us. If we are to die let it be fighting like the slaves of old Rome. I stand, like Moses, for my people' (pp. 148–9). The miners fully identify with Dai, however distant the form of his language may be from theirs. The situation is serious. The author, however, refuses to translate it into melodramatic terms: Jim innocently adds a touch of humour that deflates the solemnity of Dai's rhetoric. 'By Christ, old Dai is a good speaker, mun,' he says to Len, 'but what did he mean by octopus testicles?' (p. 149).

After one of the strikes some of their claims are met. Len assures a group of his pit-mates that solidarity, a new ingredient in their social life, has wrought the miracle. 'We won the strike because we were united and organized, but we can easily lose all we have won if we go back to the old way of every man for himself' (p. 220). *Cwmardy*, the plot of which spans a whole lifetime, reveals a new class consciousness manifest in the cohesion of a mining town, which transforms the very nature of the struggle. In a brief early review, W. H. Williams pointed out that the evolution of class-consciousness—something 'lacking in D. H. Lawrence'— added a new note to the novel.[29] What Williams detected in *Cwmardy* was obviously the power of a new sensibility reaching forward into the future. The novel shows the inadequacy of mine-management, and opens up the possibility of control by the miners themselves. It must be stressed at once, however, that *Cwmardy* is permeated (but never buttressed) by this underlying idea.

The strength of its characters springs from dialogue; authorial exposition is reduced to the minimum. Big Jim, one of the most memorable of them, resembles and often equals Lawrence's miner Mr Morel. At first glance one may think that Jim's function is simply comic, like that of most dialect users in folklore, or that his language is a mere assembly of the conventional features used traditionally for the literary rendering of Anglo-Welsh and non-standard English in general. True, the conversation of Jim and the other miners does indeed manifest the phonological, morpho-logical and syntactical characteristics of his dialect: loss of initial semi-vowel *w* before back-rounded vowels—''o'nt', ''oodn't'; frequent apocopation of polysyllabic words from Latin origin— ''spect', ''member', 's'pose', ''sactly'; analogical levelling of verbal inflections, including those of *to be* and *to have*—'I be', 'the grass have been red'; unusual past tenses that result from the addition of dental suffixes to verbs which in Received English change their stem—'gived', 'knowed'; interrogative constructions by simple subject-verb inversion with verbs that normally would require the operator *do*—'Think you I be 'fraid of any man'; use of cumulative or so-called double negation—'don't cry no more'; and so forth. But Lewis Jones is not content with a timid reproduction of a few stereotyped dialectal traits, a trick Shakespeare himself used to give us Fluellen in *Henry V*. His is a balanced synthesis which allows the portrayal of well-rounded characters. Jim has a linguistic personality—an idiolect—that makes him unmistakable; and still more important, in *Cwmardy* a collective hero finds a voice.

Finally, it is worth considering Gwyn Jones' *Times like These* (1936). The battle waged by a whole community against an oppressive company forms the centre of this novel. The true hero is a mining village; its men, in fact. Not even Edgar Evans, Ike Jones or Oliver and Luke Biesty, the most outstanding characters, eclipse the other miners. In fact, it is within their community that their lives take on meaning: the situation demands the toil and effort of all. Like other novelists of this decade, Gwyn Jones depicted the working-class struggles of the immediate past. In *Times like These* he sets the action back ten years to link it with the days of the General Strike. The choice of this event as the background of the story is not fortuitous. The atmosphere of unemployment and poverty brought about by the Depression made the 1930s resemble the years of the previous decade. The author then appears to invite us to remember the lesons of 1926, just as, in a similar context, Oliver Biesty urges his fellow workers to recall Black Friday of 1921 (p. 15).

In 1926 the British working class, after nine days of total struggle, felt defeated, and particularly the miners who had to face the desertion of the rest. These factors were decisive in reaffirming the workers in the nature of their struggles. Once again the words of Edgar Evans, the leader of the miners' Federation, express the feelings of the majority:

Strike or lockout—call it what they will—it don't signify. I prefer to call it a fight—a fight between you and the men who want to see you slaves, beaten down, miserable, spiritless; a fight between you and the men who are willing to take the bread out of your mouths and the clothes off your backs that they can live in luxury; a fight between you and the men who

will grind down your families, your wives and your children, into the
deepest pit of poverty. We start that fight tomorrow. (p. 98)

The consciousness of class, an awareness of belonging to an
important group, pervades the entire novel. In it, the rejection of
individualism in the interest of the macrocosm, the class, is
complete. A total harmony between feeling and language con-
tributes to convey this. The most urgent issues find expression in
vernacular dialogue. Mary's gradual separation from her community in favour of middle-class values and refined tastes runs
parallel to a conscious abandonment of dialect. She does not speak
like the others; nor do the mine owners or managers and their
families. Louise, the English wife of one of the officials, provides
perhaps the most ludicrous example. Edgar Evans' language, on
the contrary, even when he uses an older model of radical rhetoric
traditionally realised in Standard English, is not wholly alien to the
miners' ears. In his long speeches (pp. 95, 172) we find the images
dearest to the working men and some of the main traits of local
talk and colloquial language: short and simple sentences, full of
expressive similies and sayings, irony and humour; unusual im-
perative constructions—'don't let's be afraid'; a preference for
older pronominal forms—'um' (< ME *huem, hem* < OE *heom,
him*) instead of 'them'; unusual regularisation of the past tense of
some verbs—'hurted', etc.; adverbial use of adjectives, a vestige
perhaps from an Old and Middle English dative form which
functioned adverbially—'you work dangerous'; and so on. Evans'
is not the empty language of a demagogue but a genuine piece of
trade-union oratory. At first glance his words may seem reminiscent of those of the harangues Dickens inserts in *Hard Times*.[30]
But a careful scrutiny reveals profound differences. Slackbridge's
sentences are totally alien to the culture of the working class. They
are mere rhetorical formulae, bereft of meaning, with a style
characterised by facile resort to a language echoing the apocalyptic
homily. The sources of this oratory can be found neither in the
working-class movement, nor in the legacy of the radical democratic culture; rather it is a mixture of the rhetoric of the baroque
pulpit and the thunderings of contemporary dissident preaching.[31]

Conversely, Evans' voice is that of his community. He embodies
the workers' hopes and his conviction that their cause will prevail,
springs from a fuller consciousness: 'We are the workers and we
must win' (p. 98).

When the strike fails, Evans addresses the people in words filled
with resentment against the rest of the population. In the past, as

he points out, hunger and bosses had undermined most strikers, but now the youth of the middle class—'*clurks* with motor cars, boys and girls from the Colleges who have never done a day's work in their lives' (p. 173)—have joined them. The novel is far from being doctrinaire and triumphalist, and neither does it portray reality in the manner of a dry social tract. There is a human dimension about it which puts it on a different level. It is the discovery and development of the potentialities of that community which are at stake. The angry cry of Ike Jones—'It's the system. . . . We aren't human beings. We are just like pick handles or old mandrils' (p. 294)—is the same as Oliver Biesty's and many others. The miners know victory and defeat, work and unemployment. These contradictory experiences alternate in the flow of Gwyn Jones' narrative, producing a characteristic rhythm. Luke Biesty strikes the final note: at the end, down-and-out and almost desperate, he is overcome by the feelings so familiar to the unemployed—impotence and destroying frustration, apathy and uselessness.

Harold Heslop, Lewis Jones and, to a certain extent, Gwyn Jones, were the product of, and legitimate spokesmen for, a local culture. In this they linked hands with the author who was supreme among all those who were part of this movement. A unique merit calls for special attention.

To speak of Lewis Grassic Gibbon is to speak of someone whose writing was not simply different in quality: it was different in kind. His assured craftsmanship came to full tide in *A Scots Quair* (1946),[32] the trilogy of his novels separately published as *Sunset Song* (1932), *Cloud Howe* (1933), and *Grey Granite* (1934).

A Scots Quair is centred in the recent history of the Scottish Lowlands and the consequent upheavals caused by industry in its rural communities. It was Gibbon's historical sense which shaped a story of enduring social conflict. His technique is especially well-geared to so rich a subject, a changing social situation in which human pawns strive to grasp the meaning of their economic and spiritual destiny. A radical evolutionary process threatening their survival requires collective decisions to forge a future. Because of this and the dynamic quality of his experience and understanding, Gibbon had to use a prose both mixed and multivalent.

Much has been written about the epic and cyclic nature of the plot, its progression from the tilling of the land to heavy industry, but the technique employed has received scant attention, and the debatable character of the conclusions reached leaves much room for further discussion.

The language of *A Scots Quair* successfully echoes the country speech of the North Eastern Lowlands, usually known as Lallans, Synthetic or Braid Scots, a direct descendant from the Old English dialect, Northumbrian. Views may differ on Gibbon's use of it, but sentence-structure, word-order, and internal rhythm rather than less significant features which might exclude a larger public, convey the essence of the vernacular. In Gibbon's modified syntax literary English intermingles with the flow and cadence of conversational Scots, 'the twists of the Scottish idiom'[33] to use his own words, showing the characteristics that, as Norman Page[34] has noted, mark spoken language, namely, intimate signals—'losh', 'och', 'feuch', etc.—incomplete sentences, colloquial repetition, hesitations, verbal omissions, anacoluthon, and other grammatical 'inconsistencies'. It is an oral style with uncommon poetic power. This poetic cast owes much to the predominance of the Doric in it. It is the language of the most memorable characters in the first two volumes, and of the everyday communal gossip throughout the trilogy. Even Ewan, 'who so seldom spoke it' as the author tells us, reverts to Scots in moments of emotion (*GG*, p. 464). English is employed almost always in opposition to Scots, and this opposition reflects sharp class distinctions. Inner conflict, too, usually manifests itself as a linguistic one—for instance in the case of Chris (*SS*, p. 37). As the language of the gentry, English is both despised and admired by the common folk. Ellen Johns, the English girl who believes that her name is a misspelling of Helen (*GG*, p. 382), fails to integrate into the community partly because of her language. In *Grey Granite*, the *Tory Pictman*—a conservative paper—is said to be 'full of dog Latin and constipated English, but of course not Scotch' (p. 485). In sociolinguistic terms, two different communication systems—the literary rendering of an elaborated code and a restricted one—are placed in permanent conflict. The metaphoric and aesthetic potential which, according to Basil Bernstein, a restricted code may have,[35] is revealed in many passages exemplified in the wedding 'invocation' of McIvor the Highlander (*SS*, pp. 123–4).

This language, far from being contrived, is spontaneously elicited by the nature of the story. Recurring alliteration and rhythmic anapaestic prose show the traces of a past that still survives, and reproduce the pulse of living and working. Careful use of polysyndetic coordination heightens the tempo when the plot demands it, yet at times this effect is complemented with the vigour of frequent asyndetic paragraphs which, in *Grey Granite*, also recall the style of Henry Green's *Living*. Other stylistic devices such as similes taken from nature and frequent anadiplosis endowing the elders' speech with an arcane, proverbial quality, enrich the poetic vein. This is in no way diminished in *Grey Granite* (pp. 363–4).

A sustained internal rhyme and the familiar Scots vocabulary add the rural colour so often mentioned by critics—'We can hear the earth itself speaking,' as Neil Gunn said.[36] Yet the tone is harsh, increasingly so in pace with the narrative; this is no gentle poetry, but a strong and insistent harmony, a recurring note in the final book of *A Scots Quair*. Occasionally, as if to remind us that literary language is an artifice even when based on popular speech, Gibbon uses more bookish and archaic forms ('meikle', 'childe', etc.).

With this semi-colloquial structure, often built on an evocative indirect style and a peculiar distribution of the generic and self-referring 'you'—both in modified direct and indirect speech[37]—the novel is an antiphony whose voices tell of deep social rifts. This plural style without the novelist's intrusion is a technical advance over his fellow writers and even his working-class literary predecessors. In this subordination of the author's voice to those of his characters, Gibbon ranks with major twentieth-century writers: he only organises the material. The diverse voices embody opposing forces in work and action.

At times echoes of an age-old culture blend with the new sounds of unrelenting class war, endowing inherited forms with a new revolutionary meaning, proverbs and sayings mingling with slogans and pamphlets, Biblical allusions with the aggressiveness of the political or trade-union harangue (*CH*, pp. 214–15, 240); political speeches—Jock Cronin's is of a piece with those found in other working-class novels of the 1930s (*CH*, p. 268)—alternate with the voice of the land, the rural gossip that carries the stigma of prejudice and custom; but it is in Robert Colquohoun's revolutionary homilies that the boldest synthesis of old and new is to be found (*CH*, p. 349). The semantic markers of a lingering piety, such as the ejaculatory prayers towards the end of *Cloud Howe* ('LORD, REMEMBER ME WHEN THOU COMEST INTO THY KINGDOM'), give way to revolutionary mottoes in *Grey Granite* ('DOWN WITH THE MEANS TEST AND HUNGER AND WAR'), and the occasional verses from hymns and traditional songs in the first two volumes, become in *Grey Granite* the militant verses of 'The Internationale' (p. 395).

At other times some voices spring out from the continuum of the prose, indicating the irreconcilable poles of the struggle; in the last

volume, in moments of crisis the voices raised in confrontation—
the Town Council, the Church, the Labour Party, the Press, the
Police—are no longer 'murmurings' embedded in the narrative,
but rather recorded as a series of clippings from different sources
(pp. 441, 485–6, 491–2); the effect of this multiple perspective on
a single event is almost Brechtian.

The novel's unity and vitality raising it to the rank of a genuine
national epic, result from this intricate weaving together of
contrasts, and the rhythm generated by such a tension is one of the
work's achievements. In the anonymous narrator of *Sunset Song*
one can already detect an ironic overtone which betrays a conflicting, dialectical view of the history of the powerful families which
he recounts. From Ewan Tavendale comes the political speech,
the radical language of the 1930s (*GG*, p. 457). These are perhaps
the first and last echoes of the 'communal' voice, as it has been
rightly described, of the poliphony which is at the core of the
'quair'. All this somehow reminds one of *The Waste Land*—T. S.
Eliot, incidentally, had a high opinion of Gibbon.

The supposed linguistic and compositional flaws found by
almost all the critics of *Grey Granite*, even by one as sympathetic
as MacDiarmid, seem to me non-existent. Changed circumstances
exact a change in style: language is once more moulded to fit the
new scene, the great industrial city, adapting itself to a new
rhythm, that of the machine, more monotonous, mechanical,
repetitive. Because *A Scots Quair* tells of the dissolution of the
Scottish peasantry and the emergence of the industrial proletariat,
the last rites of a pastoral will be witnessed in the ineluctable
demise of its image, and in a change in the nature of its poetry.
The new hero is bound to be less individual, more anonymous and
impersonal—perhaps less memorable. But this is not a stylistic
flaw of the author; rather, it is a merit. At the end of the book, as if
reminding us of the deliberate change, there is a return to an
Arcadian style, when Chris decides to go back to the country (*GG*,
p. 496).

Bearing all these facts in mind it is easy to trace the literary
tradition from which, as most critics agree, Gibbon comes: the
ballads, the poems of Burns, Walter Scott's historical novels, the
works of George Douglas Brown and William Morris, the styles of
William Alexander and J. Macdougall Hay, *The Ragged Trousered
Philanthropists*, Dos Passos' innovatory narrative, and the poetry of
Gibbon's great friend and compatriot, Hugh MacDiarmid. To
complete this brief survey of Gibbon's literary forbears—however
indirect their influence may have been—reference should be made

to the Chartist writers and those nineteenth-century Scottish poets whose verse has as its main subject industrial exploitation and poverty. The Chartist Ernest Jones and the Scottish poetess Ellen Johnston are the names that readily spring to mind.

Even without the evidence provided by *A Scots Quair*, a quick reading of all the other novels which have been discussed would be enough to invalidate the assessment made by Leavis, mechanically repeated by critics after him, that 'in matters of literature it was a barren decade'.[38] The movement has been judged more by the noisy and untenable theories of a few, than by the quiet and creative work of its true representatives. Grassic Gibbon, James Barke, Lewis Jones, Walter Brierley, and even Edward Upward never pretended to be making a *completely* different kind of literature by integrating their working-class experience and perspective into the novel form; nor did they share the belief that their fiction demanded a *totally* new language. Yet in their works both language and form are markedly affected by the requirements of a new subject matter and by a corresponding shift of focus, to an extent that is both considerable and differentiating. Unlike those who announced that literary English began with them, the real novelists of that generation knew how to tap the wealth of everyday speech and, at the same time, how to make use of the literary tradition. Through a balanced fusion of the world view peculiar to a developed working-class consciousness and the components of a radical legacy still alive in popular culture, these novelists wrote coherent works bearing no relationship to that pamphleteer literature in which all possibility of life is smothered by the heavy intrusion of the author, and in which problems are not really felt but simply analysed and observed. The strength of Grassic Gibbon's work and that of Lewis Jones, for instance, certainly lies in an adequate use of the working class' own means of expression, that is, the political speech, the trade-union debate, and even the pamphlet, but it also lies in the incorporation of popular and vernacular language, and of the rich literary tradition of oral radicalism. It is no accident that these writers should have drawn freely on the inexhaustible cultural resources of Scotland and Wales. What is revolutionary about their technique is a mastery of the spoken word and the endowment of old literary forms with the most modern devices of radical expression already referred to. The images of these novels emerge from immediate experience, and conflict (the class struggle) is never treated as an abstract or allegorical battle between two opposed forces in a moral fable; rather, this here-and-now quality prevents their characters from falling into mere abstractions. In this sense not only is this group of novels an excellent documentary of the pre-war years, but above all an eloquent and epic vision—almost a collective biography—of the working class during the Depression. The alleged imbalance in some of these works because there may be more of the boarding house, hospital, and union hall, or even of the street, than of the workshop or the factory in them, is refuted by the reality of the years themselves. They were years of mass unemployment; the very silence of the factory and its unfamiliar remoteness is itself the dramatic element. The scenes of unemployment, unusual trade-union activity, strikes, demonstrations and hunger marches were a necessity in order to portray the impossibility of finding a job and leading a full life. This literature is not just a detailed catalogue of squalor and poverty, nor does it simply rely on the insistence on that ugliness which characterised the turn-of-the-century naturalists. Even the most negative aspects of proletarian existence are always viewed in a more hopeful light; because, unlike previous working-class writers, these novelists knew that in literature the perspective of a new collective consciousness is not revealed simply by recording a certain set of living conditions; instead, it must be translated into the expression of that class engaged in an ongoing struggle for survival and for the fulfilment of its own identity. On the actual plane of textual composition all this implies, as we have seen, a use of different registers and levels of speech that transcends the mere function of providing 'local colour' as in previous literature.

Not only do the best of these novels convey the 'pastoral feeling about the dignity of that form of labour' referred to by William Empson in his contemporary essay on proletarian literature,[39] but, moreover, they reveal the dignity of a form of struggle. A better understanding of this movement must surely contribute to a fuller appreciation of the more recent English novel.

NOTES

1 Some noteworthy exceptions are these studies: Jack Mitchell, 'The Struggle for the Working-Class Novel in Scotland: 1900–1939', *Zeitschrift für Anglistik und Amerikanistik*, 21 (1973); David B. Smith, 'B. L. Coombes', *The Anglo-Welsh Review*, 24, no. 53 (Winter 1974); Roy Johnson, 'The Proletarian Novel', *Literature and History*, 2 (1975); and H. Gustav Klaus, 'Socialist Fiction in the 1930s', *Renaissance and Modern Studies*, 20 (1976). I have also considered the main working-class novelists of the 1930s from this perspective in

La crisis económica de 1929 y la novelística de tema obrero en Gran Bretaña en los años treinta (Salamanca, 1974), and in *Movimiento obrero y novela inglesa* (Salamanca, 1976).

2 The words are Randall Swingler's. See *Left Review*, 1 (December 1934), p. 78.

3 See Jack Mitchell, *Robert Tressell and 'The Ragged Trousered Philanthropists'* (London, 1969), pp. 23–48.

4 *After the Thirties* (London, 1956), p. 29.

5 *Left Review*, 1 (December 1934), p. 77.

6 *Left Review*, 1 (February 1935), p. 179.

7 See Klaus, *op. cit.*, p. 22.

8 *Left Review*, 1 (October 1934), p. 38.

9 Walter Allen, *Tradition and Dream* (London, 1968), p. 214.

10 Edition quoted: The Hogarth Press (London, 1970). Subsequent references will appear in the text.

11 See Allen, *op. cit.*, pp. 234–5; and William York Tindall, *Forces in Modern British Literature: 1885–1956* (New York, 1956), p. 49.

12 *Pack My Bag* (London, 1940), p. 236.

13 *The Novels of Henry Green* (London, 1959), p. 199.

14 Quoted by Terry Southern, 'The Art of Fiction XXII', *Paris Review*, 5 (Summer 1958), p. 75.

15 *The Tightrope Walkers* (London, 1956), p. 193.

16 In a note at the end of the novel Brown makes statements such as these: 'The printed word was from the start associated with all artificial language, and the history of "literary English" is the history first of the adaptation of English words to latinising minds, and then of the making of that artificial latinistic lingo more and more flexible, as if to disguise it as natural English. . . . Caxton and company were obliged in their printed language to crystallise the separateness of the class which used the printed books. . . . Literary English, being from the outset, in its printed form, the privilege of a ruling minority, was obliged to be differentiated from the English of the people. . . . Indeed, so long as there are two classes in the country, there must be this artificial language of the ruling class; and any class or group of a class which merely takes the place of an older ruling class is not only bound to fail to create a literary English which is real English, but is bound to go farther still from real English' (pp. 669–70).

17 *Socialist Propaganda in the Twentieth-Century British Novel* (London, 1978), p. 81.

18 Edition quoted: Collins (London, 1970).

19 *The Times Literary Supplement*, 14 March 1935, p. 158.

20 Edition quoted: Penguin Books (Harmondsworth, 1969).

21 See A. J. P. Taylor, *English History: 1914–1945* (Harmondsworth, 1970), p. 436; and Arthur Marwick, *Britain in the Century of Total War* (Harmondsworth, 1970), p. 238.

22 For a dissenting view, see the excellent commentary by Johnson, *op. cit.*; cf. also Carole Snee, 'Working Class Literature or Proletarian

Writing?', in Jon Clark *et al* (eds), *Culture and Crisis in Britain in the 30s* (London, 1979).
23 Edition quoted: Penguin Books (Harmondsworth, 1970).
24 *Op. cit.*, p. 238.
25 Edition quoted: Cedric Chivers Ltd (Portway Bath, 1969).
26 Jack Mitchell, 'The Struggle for the Working-Class Novel in Scotland', pp. 409–10.
27 Edition quoted: Lawrence & Wishart (London, 1979). This edition contains a very useful introduction by David B. Smith.
28 Edition quoted: Lawrence & Wishart (London, 1979).
29 'A Working Class Epic', *Left Review*, 7 (August 1937), p. 428.
30 Compare the opening words of both speeches: 'Oh my friends and fellow-men!' (Slackbridge) and 'Men . . . fellow workers' (Edgar Evans).
31 Elsewhere I have dealt with this in more detail: see 'La lengua de Slackbridge y la ideología de Dickens en *Hard Times*', *Atlantis*, 1 (1979), pp. 7–24.
32 Edition quoted: Hutchinson (London, 1971).
33 From a letter to Cuthbert Graham in 1933; quoted by Geoffrey Wagner, 'Lewis Grassic Gibbon and the Use of Lallans for Prose', *Aberdeen University Review* (Autumn 1952), p. 333.
34 See his *Speech in the English Novel* (London, 1973), Ch. I.
35 See his 'A Sociolinguistic Approach to Socialization', in J. J. Gumperz and D. Hymes (eds), *Directions in Sociolinguistics* (New York, 1971), p. 420.
36 Quoted by Ivor Brown, 'Foreword' to *A Scots Quair*.
37 On this see, Graham Trengrove, 'Who is you? Grammar and Grassic Gibbon', *Scottish Literary Journal* (1974).
38 F. R. Leavis, 'Retrospect of a Decade', *Scrutiny*, 9 (June 1940), p. 71.
39 'Proletarian Literature', in his *Some Versions of Pastoral* (London, 1935), p. 8.

Chapter 8

MILITANCY, ANGER AND RESIGNATION: ALTERNATIVE MOODS IN THE WORKING-CLASS NOVEL OF THE 1950s AND EARLY 1960s

Ingrid von Rosenberg

I The New Wave: Dimensions and Character

The 1950s and early 1960s, or to be more exact the years of Conservative government between 1953 and 1964, appear to have been, from the point of view of the history of the working-class novel, years of an amazing paradox. Although a period of economic boom, at the time proudly, today rather nostalgically called the years of 'affluence', and in fact the one period in the history of industrial Britain when at least the great majority of the working class were freed from the spectres of unemployment and want, those years brought a flood of working-class literature, mainly novels. This seems to belie the rule Keating had formulated in his book *The Working Classes in Victorian Fiction*: 'It is only during moments of social crisis that any significant number of English novelists have attempted to write fiction centred upon working-class life.'[1] The picture offered by the 1950s and early 1960s proves that obviously working-class literature can bloom just as well in times of relative prosperity.

The number of publications, beginning with an average of one or two new titles a year between 1953 and 1956, rose constantly till 1960, when it reached a peak of ten, to sink slowly again to an average of four or five new novels in the years following till 1964. All in all at least fifty novels about various aspects of working-class life were published between 1953 and 1964. By comparison, in the following ten years, hardly more than two or three new books came out every year, sometimes only one or even none, so that the whole amount does not even reach half that number published during the previous decade.[2]

Although there were a few professional writers among the authors like for instance Clancy Sigal or Nell Dunn, a few left-wing

intellectuals like Margot Heinemann and a few who were both like
Jack Lindsay, the great majority were themselves workers, when
they started to write, or were at least sons of workers. This is not
exactly a new phenomenon. Already in the 1930s much of the
working-class literature had been written from firsthand experience. Yet there is hardly any evidence that the writers of our period
had any knowledge of their predecessors: the tradition was cut for
various reasons. That workers in this century were at all able to
write about their own affairs contrary to the situation of the nineteenth century was, of course, partly due to the improved
educational chances of the class though, needless to say, many
inequalities continued to exist. After the war shorter working hours
and full employment, which made it a bearable risk to give up one's
job for a while, acted as additional favourable circumstances.
Among the critics of working-class, especially socialist, literature it
has become the habit to argue that the authors' own class background is of only negligible importance. My impression is a different one: I think it is a highly significant phenomenon if the bulk of
working-class literature in a certain period is written by people from
that class. Since they can be regarded as in some way the voice of
self-representation of the class, these works form an interesting
subject for literary-sociological research.

   To the astounding flood of publications in our period corresponds
a likewise astoundingly broad reception. Quite a few of the new
novels, like for instance Alan Sillitoe's *Saturday Night and Sunday
Morning* (1958), Stan Barstow's *A Kind of Loving* (1960) or John
Braine's *Room at the Top* (1957), after having won considerable
immediate recognition on their first coming out in hardcover
editions, were made into extremely successful films and subsequently published by one of the big paperback publishers like
Penguin, Corgi or Panther. To give only one example: *Saturday
Night and Sunday Morning* made its appearance in hardcover in
1958, was made into a film by Karel Reisz with Albert Finney.
starring, which won the British Film Academy Prize in 1960, and
was published as a paperback in the same year. Until 1975 the novel
had sold 2.679.000 copies, hardcovers and paperbacks, in Britain
and America.[3]

   One group of novels has to be excepted, though, which did not
meet with nearly half such a friendly and widespread reception.
They were the novels that can be called socialist in the stricter
sense, novels written by Communist authors, and with the exception of Jack Lindsay's books, were all published by Lawrence &
Wishart, the Communist publishing house. Only a very modest

number of copies could be sold of each novel, in some cases under one thousand, and in 1964 Lawrence & Wishart stopped publishing fiction altogether.[4]

But leaving them apart for the moment, it seems a fair guess to say that such a great audience as the bulk of fiction on the subject attracted could hardly have been an entirely working-class audience. Indeed, the hints are strong that people from all strata of society read the books and saw the films, thus proving an almost universal interest in the affairs of the working-class totally new in the history of working-class literature.

The explanation for this widespread interest has to be looked for in the general social situation of the class. The war had considerably increased its prestige in the eyes of the middle and upper classes. The impoverished, shabby masses of the prewar period had proved indispensable for winning the war through their performance in the forces as well as in the war-industry. The union leadership's clever policy that procured influence and even a share in the government for the unions unheard of before did further this process, even though left-wing critics have blamed their steps as co-operation with the ruling class. But one more factor may even have been more influential. Steady employment during and after the war had turned the working class into so many potent buyers, all the keener for their strong backlog demand, and the different branches of the consumer goods industry had started to cater eagerly for this new group of costumers. In a capitalist country this may well have been the decisive change to wring respect from the moneyed as well as powerful classes.

The way to a broad favourable reception was probably smoothed further by the almost complete absence of descriptions of want and misery, hitherto characteristic of all working-class literature and very likely an obstacle to the interest of that great part of the bourgeois reading public that sought entertainment in novels more than anything else.

Lastly, the writers' own attitude was of importance too. It seems that in the process of social change they had developed an attitude completely different from that of their predecessors in the 1930s. Where those had always shown an acute awareness of the class structure of British society and its injustices, the new generation of writers—always with the exception of the CP writers, of course— seemed almost indifferent to questions of class concerning their audience. They wrote their novels, addressed to no one in particular, and trusted them, and, as we have seen, justly, to be published by one of the big publishing houses, whose programmes were naturally mostly bourgeois in outlook. This shows a remarkable self-assurance, which again seems to find its explanation in the improved economic situation of the class as well as in its newly acquired social prestige. The writers no longer show that grim pride in the separateness of their class, born from its very underprivileged and deprived position, which had dictated all that militant pro-letarian literature of the past. They show a pride that is funda-mentally different, almost the opposite: it is pride in their in-tegration, in having become a respected part *within* the existing society at last.

The authors' very choice of their favourite literary form can be interpreted as a proof. For as has been well known ever since Hegel defined the novel as the 'bourgeois epic',[5] the novel is the genre produced by and characteristic of the middle classes' ascent to power. If worker-writers prefer this form so clearly, they sub-consciously prove a desire to compete with the middle class on its own cultural ground.

The same holds true of their motives as they were uttered in various articles, interviews and letters. They are anything but declarations of the intention to write social criticism. On the con-trary, the writers show some anxiety to cover up any such aims even where they are obvious and to claim merely aesthetic motives. Thus such a clear-sighted observer of social reality as Alan Sillitoe de-clared: 'I write as it comes, without subject or theme, with love and patience, and nothing else.' [6] Even the Communist writers con-formed to some extent when they unanimously insisted on the primacy of art over the political message. One finds all the well-worn arguments of the bourgeois tradition, which, on closer scru-tiny, boil down to the myth of the poetic genius and, particularly in the case of the less politically ambitious writers, to the theory of *l'art pour l'art*.

If working-class authors, deliberately or subconsciously, adopt originally middle-class attitudes to their own artistic activities, it seems justified to speak of a symptom of embourgeoisement. Al-though the truth of the theory of embourgeoisement could not generally be proved, it unexpectedly finds confirmation in the limited range of the cultural field. A strong proof that this is not mere extravagant conjecturing is the later career of most of these novelists: apart from the CP writers, who in the majority gave up writing fiction after two or three attempts, most of the others gradually turned away from their original subject-matter and became more or less successful professional writers, their work focusing like that of many of their middle-class colleagues on the theme of the problematic individual in an intellectual or arty setting.

When I speak of a tendency to embourgeoisement, I do not mean to say, though, that all this working-class literature of the 1950s and early 1960s was acquiescent and lacked a critical point of view. Bourgeois culture and literature itself, if not in its popular debased forms, has always been a critical reflection of social reality. The new working-class literature, following in its steps, did preserve this element too, even stressing it in the majority of cases.

Still, in spite of the strong influence of the prevailing bourgeois culture, the subject-matter of these novels was definitely working class. Thus they represent a complex phenomenon. On the one hand speaking of the ambition to win recognition from the same quarters as bourgeois literature, they on the other hand present a picture of a distinct working-class culture. At the historical moment when general economic and social changes diminished social inequalities with the consequence that differences of behaviour, habit, dress, etc. between the classes were being blurred—a process in which of course the mass media and their overall influence had a strong share, the worker-writers adopted an ambiguous attitude. While their subject-matter proves a desire to preserve the special character of working-class life as it had developed over the last hundred years,[7] they at the same time helped to further its dissolution as a separate culture by their own adjustment to the standards of bourgeois culture or, which is the same, the literary market.

II Political Novels: the Communist Contribution

The working-class novels of the 1950s and early 1960s fall easily into two groups: the smaller group of political or socialist novels on the one hand and the great majority of what I would like to call descriptive working-class novels on the other. A few novels cannot be ranged in either of these categories although they show similarities with one or both of them. I am here thinking of novels like Raymond Williams' *Border Country* (1960) and *Second Generation* (1964) or of Walter Allen's *All in a Lifetime* (1959). They clearly contain a political perspective or, in Williams' case rather a philosophical perspective, but not of the same colouring as the CP authors' novels. We shall have to leave them unconsidered here, for they deserve a closer examination than would be possible within the limited range of this chapter.[8] The largest contribution to the group of socialist novels was made by Jack Lindsay, who wrote a series of nine volumes collectively called 'novels of the British Way.' The first one came out in 1953, and the series finished in 1964, thus stretching precisely over the whole space of time under consideration.

The first four 'novels of the British Way' (*Betrayed Spring, Rising Tide, The Moment of Choice, A Local Habitation*), published between 1953 and 1957, form a tetralogy, covering the years 1946–51. Drawing on historical facts like the Peace Movement, the squatters and certain strikes, Lindsay weaves a picture of the British social situation just after the war, or rather of then prominent oppositional movements, presenting them as if seen through a magnifying glass, that is to say in a very optimistic light. Describing the actions and fates of a set of working-class and middle-class people in four industrial areas of Britain, he contrasts the higher morals, warmer humanity and idealistic political zeal of the working-class characters to the corruptness of most of the middle-class figures, although there are always some, like Lindsay himself, who become partisans to the working class. In spite of Lindsay's efforts to insert authentic working-class speech, the novels fail to come to life because the characters are made to move in rather a too stereotyped pattern and the political preaching gets too shrill at times. The remaining novels (*The Revolt of the Sons, All on the Never-Never, The Way the Ball Bounces, Masks and Faces, Choice of Times*) avoid these mistakes, though they are not free from others. The course of the historical development had forced Lindsay to give up some of his brash political optimism, and he no longer idealised the working class as a whole, although there are always a few admirable individuals protrayed. But he now tried to mirror the social situation more faithfully by including examples of working-class men or women confused or even corrupted by the new possibilities to make and spend money easily, as is especially the case in *All on the Never-Never* and *Choice of Times*.

Beside Lindsay there were at the time only two, or strictly speaking only one more intellectual novelist writing about aspects of working-class life from a socialist point of view: Margot Heinemann in *The Adventurers* (1960) tried to give an overall impression of the activities in the various branches of the working-class movement, her Communist protagonists playing a subsidiary, but important part. Dave Wallis, who in *A Tramstop by the Nile* (1958) had painted rather a heroic picture of Communist activity, but in a colonial setting, had by the time he wrote his two novels dealing with contemporary British life apparently lost much of his political enthusiasm. *Paved With Gold* (1959), which among other things gives an example of the struggle between the old and a new brand of capitalists in the London business world, shows two young people with a working-class background, a girl and a boy, taking advantage of the opportunities offered by the affluent society at the expense of their private happiness. And *Only Lovers Left Alive* (1964), dealing with the new phenomenon of the young emerging as a kind of new class, envisages an apocalyptic utopia, in which the teenagers have completely taken over, all the 'squares' committing suicide, and all culture being destroyed.

But, beside these professional writers, four worker-writers made their appearance: Len Doherty published *A Miner's Sons* (1955), *The Man Beneath* (1957) and *The Good Lion* (1958), which just like Lindsay's later novels marks a move away from the outright pro-paganda novel, David Lambert wrote *He Must So Live* (1956) and *No Time for Sleeping* (1958), both set in the 1930s, Herbert Smith *A Field of Folk* (1957) and *A Morning to Remember* (1962) and finally Robert Bonnar contributed *Stewartie* (1964).

All the socialist novels of the 1950s and 1960s have to be seen in close relation to the CP's cultural policy which they were deliber-ately written to support. To call well-known facts briefly to mind: the position of the party within the spectrum of left-wing groups had deteriorated a great deal since its heyday in the 1930s. Soviet Russia's ambiguous foreign politics during the earlier part of the war, later the Cold War, the Berlin Blockade, the news about the Stalinist terror of the 1930s spreading like wildfire in the Western world after the Twentieth Congress of the Russian Communist Party in 1956, and finally and probably above all the invasion of Hungary and the rigid line taken in Poland in the same year—these were factors that cost the CP, failing to condemn clearly any of the Russian party's moves, many of its supporters' sympathies. As a probable further negative influence something took effect which the party was not responsible for: the 'affluence' of the period had an appeasing effect. Thousands of members resigned from the party, above all the intellectuals: the party was on the defensive.

The new party programme *The British Road to Socialism*, first published in 1951, in an attempt to correct the course, insisted on a national character of the CP's future policy. Above all the pro-gramme renounces the theory of revolution and advocates taking part in parliamentary democracy, mostly by way of supporting the more powerful institutions of the Labour movement, the Labour Party and the trade unions.

Within the side-field of cultural politics the same careful course was adopted. While lip-service was still being paid to Soviet literature as the great model for any socialist writer and the theory of socialist realism accepted as a matter of course, questions of a specifically British form of socialist literature became more and more the centre of interest in cultural debates.[9]

The novels written within the framework of this policy are clearly designed to reflect the British social reality of the time in such a way as to convince a working-class audience of the necessity to continue the political struggle in spite of the 'affluence', even if not necessarily within the ranks of the party. All the characteristic features are tinged by the strong propagandist intention.

The setting in these works is usually a threefold one. We see the protagonists at their working place, at political meetings or at home. Surprisingly, descriptions of the conditions and of the process of work are not so frequent and not so extensive as one might expect from working-class novels, particularly if written by worker-writers. Where they do occur, it is not the aspect of alienation which is stressed, but rather the opposite. Apparently intended to inspire their audience with a feeling of pride in their social function, the descriptions tend to emphasise the satisfying or even, especially when the industry is mining, the heroic aspects of work. Thus: 'With powerful two-fisted swings of the short-handled six-pound hammer he drives the prop home as tight as he can.'[10] Herbert Smith in *A Field of Folk* voices the ideological reason for this amazingly rosy view of industrial work, when he lets the Communist Tom Barrett tell the young operative Kathy: '"Whether you like it or not, Kathy, what you're doing is vital; you're an important person, for it's the nation's wealth you're making here."'.[11] But some of the metaphors Smith uses for describing machine-work show that overstressing its positive aspects holds the danger to defeat his purpose. When Kathy is given the advice: '"Introduce yourself to it (the machine) politely; caress it a bit and then it'll do wonders!"'[13], and when in *A Morning to Remember* 'furnaces were coaxed and subdued'[13] and the factory is described as a 'huge existence' in whose life the people 'living near it' join[14], an admiration for machinery is expressed that comes dangerously close to acquiescence in the submission of man to machinery.

The political issues are, in contrast to some novels of the 1930s, of rather a small scale: usually they consist of strikes, mostly 'wildcat' strikes, caused by grievances arising from the immediate working conditions of the protagonists. The scenes of action are as a rule limited to the shop floor, meetings of the local union branch or, at the most, of the local CP cell. Issues of national or world-wide importance are included merely on the level of discussion. Only the works of the middle-class writers make an exception, as the brief survey of them may have shown. Margot Heinemann for instance, to exemplify this just a little more, lets her heroes take part in such events of national interest as the first post-war elections and a TUC conference, where topics such as the German rearmament and the atomic armament of the British forces are being discussed. The limitation in the worker-writers novels seems a genuine drawback because the conflicts thus appear isolated, and their connections with the general social and political situation are not made transparent.

The events that trigger off the action are as a rule attempts of the management to cut down wages, to sack employees, to introduce time-saving new methods or machinery or to save money by neglecting safety precautions. In some novels, though, like in Doherty's *The Man Beneath*, in Smith's *A Morning to Remember* and in a way in Bonnar's *Stewartie* too, the central event is not a strike, but an accident. In any case these starting-point situations are used as testing grounds for the protagonists' true mettle. And it is usually the Communists who come out best. Even though in agreement with the political creed, which the authors wish to propagate (some novels, that is Smith's and Lambert's, have a collective hero) there is always at least one outstanding figure who leads the battle, and in most cases he is a member of the CP like Bill Omond in Lambert's *He Must So Live*, Tom Barrett in Smith's *A Field of Folk* or Robert Mellers in Doherty's *A Miner's Sons*. But true to social reality as well as to the party programme, neither the single figures nor the party as a whole are represented as being able to lead the fight alone. Instead the Communists are always shown in close alliance with, if not in a serving position to, the more influential organisations of the Labour movement, sometimes a symbolical bond of close friendship existing between the Communist semi-hero and one of their representatives. Two examples of such friendships are the relationship between Jim Harris and Johnny in *The Man Beneath* or the one between Tom Barrett and the foreman Albert Ewings in *A Field of Folk*, but there are more. The Communists impress their fellow-workers not so much by lecturing them on political theory, but by the example of their admirable personalities. Warm-hearted, friendly, always ready to advise, help and sacrifice, responsible, fearless and good organisers, they combine all good qualities required for the supreme working-class virtue of solidarity.

What all these novels try to achieve in the end is to open up a utopian perspective as required by the theory of socialist realism.

The deepest significance of all the strike actions is, by representing a strong picture of working-class solidarity, to suggest the possibility of more and even bigger such upheavals in the future until finally a socialist society will be realised. The Communists kindle the flame, but then the strikes or demonstrations are carried by a mighty collective of workers from the various organisations of the movement and even from the unorganised rank-and-file.

Political theory is not quite neglected, but is looked at from a somewhat surprising angle. The economic aspects are hardly ever mentioned. Instead throughout the humanistic aims are stressed. Thus Tom Barrett in *A Field of Folk* holds the following image of the socialist future: 'an image . . ., promising a land with better homes, wider lives, and labour that was an honour instead of a wretched sixty-an-hour sweat.'[15] And in *A Miner's Sons* the question '"What would *your* world be like?"' is answered:

'Very different. Shaped to satisfy all men's needs. . . . It would have all that men wanted for all men to enjoy. . . . When men count more than just what profits they represent, when all men have equal right to develop as they want, they're given room to find themselves. They're allowed the leisure to discover their real abilities. . . .'[16]

Perhaps this was meant to be a clever policy in the age of 'affluence': setting too much store by the economic advantages of socialism may not have been considered suited to rouse the fairly saturated British working class of the 1950s, whereas with respect to personal freedom and self-realisation there was much still to be wished for. But then the shift of focus to the more personal implications of the theory also means a shift of interest from the collective of the proletariat to the single individual, a shift that, as we shall see, is paralleled in the descriptive working-class novels, where it is certainly much more prominent.

That it has actually taken place, if probably unnoticed by them, in the minds of the political novelists too, is further confirmed by a peculiar way in which they sometimes interpret the act of joining the party. When Herbert Mellers in *A Miner's Sons* has been recruited, Doherty comments: 'Now he had something to go by— now there was something to fall back on and regain strength for life from.'[17] In such a statement Communism has undergone a subtle, but nevertheless significant change from an objective political theory to the merely personal importance of a stabilising factor in a person's life. The grand revolutionary perspective has shrunk to the narrow dimensions of a quiet inner consolation, a help for the individual to endure the meaninglessness of present-day life. The very meaning of Communism is thus being reversed. Here, behind the authors' backs, so to speak, and in spite of their conscious intentions which definitely were to keep awake working-class militancy, the objective historical trend of the period breaks through: the relative stagnation of the movement finds expression in this basically resignative view of socialist theory and politics.

The description of the workers' private lives is used to reinforce the didactic effect. Everywhere we get images of intact families, not just of couples in love, on whom the bourgeois novel, above all concerned with the individual's claim to self-realisation, has focused over the last 150 years. There is warmth, comfort and solidarity in these working-class families, which provide the single members with the strength necessary to fight their battles in the outside world. If in some cases the harmony is not perfect right at the beginning, it is being achieved in the course of action as in Doherty's novels. Both the worker-writers and the intellectuals convey this picture with an emphasis, which is not always free from pathos.

Although I do not wish to deny that mutual help and solidarity may be stronger in some working-class families, this image is, nevertheless, too rosy if judged by the standards of realism. As one may learn not only from a flood of sociological literature, but from simple observation, the stress of modern life bears heavily on human relationships, and not least so in working-class families where the effects of the alienation of work and social insecurity are felt most strongly. If proof is wanted, one need only think of the thousands of battered women and children, of the figures of juvenile delinquency and of the statistics of divorce. Besides, in our particular period the combined influences of both the relative new wealth and television, which was beginning its triumphant advance, were at work in such a way as to threaten the traditional close companionship within the working-class family even further: the young saw pictures of and possessed the financial means to obtain pleasures outside the home. If the political novels omit these features, the only plausible reason can again be the authors' propagandist motivation. Wishing to represent the proletariat as the agent of great future historical changes in as favourable a light as possible, they obviously thought to do so best by showing them sticking to the traditional set of behaviour. But the trouble is that this conjuring up of the solutions of the past lacks the power to convince precisely because the contemporary conditions are faded out under which they would have to prove their strength.

With respect to their artistic means the writers, not unlike the bourgeois novelists of the time,[18] make use of existing models of earlier bourgeois literature, thus proving less inventive and daring than some of their forerunners like Tressell, MacGill or Grassic Gibbon had been. Worse yet, the worker-writers among them, whose knowledge of good bourgeois literature may well have been limited, even made indiscriminate use of writing techniques to be found in its popular debased form of appeasing popular fiction thereby in a way counteracting their own conscious political ambition.

The narrative point of view is throughout that of the omniscient author, who arranges his material with a sovereignty serious bourgeois novelists have found impossible to administer ever since the contradictions in the social set-up have become overconspicuous about the turn of the century. If Communist writers, on the other hand, return to this point of view, this is a feature that need not be explained by their adherence to popular fiction, where it has of course survived, but can be considered as a logical consequence of their political belief. To a Communist the world is not a mystery as to many a bourgeois mind, but moving according to the fixed laws of history on a predictable course to the final goal of a socialist society. But this narrative perspective has its disadvantages for a political novelist. If every single thought the protagonists harbour or deed they do is commented upon by the narrator, hardly any room is left for the reader's independent reactions. Instead of his critical capacities being stirred, they will more likely be lulled to sleep. The protagonists, thus strictly under control of their creators, are grouped into a certain pattern of types, or rather of 'flat characters', for they have hardly enough body to meet Lukács' definition of a type as a literary figure typical of his class at a certain moment of history. The technique is a simple black-and-white manner: all the bosses are baddies, and most of the workers are intrinsically good, even though some of them may err.

The outward appearance is used to indicate the inner qualities of a person in much the same way as in the popular novel, which serves as a rich stock of models. The descriptions of the factory owners and managers are visibly stamped by the physical contempt of the manual worker for the man in the white collar. Mostly bald and fat, with cold eyes and thin lips that never smile, thus denoting their sinister intentions, they resemble the villains in detective or adventure stories. The middle-class authors naturally draw a more differentiated picture of the representatives of their own class.

Particularly in Lindsay's second group of novels the characterisation is sometimes finely wrought in an attempt to do justice to the
influences of the contemporary social conditions on the individual
psyche. But even in his work the majority of his middle-class
figures is stereotyped as morally rotten.

The description of the workers, on the other hand, falls in with
the general tendency to idealisation. To their moral and political
integrity corresponds a strong and handsome physis which again
finds a direct parallel in the portraits of the heroes in popular
fiction. In the portraits of the working-class girls the problematic
aspect of this idolisation becomes most obvious. Wishing to make
them appear no less attractive than the heroines of the traditional
bourgeois novel, the authors allow no signs of stress and fatigue to
show in their immaculate features, thereby definitely falsifying
reality. Again the model of the popular novel is apparent:

The girl, she was no more than twenty, maybe less, had all the slender
grace of a young deer wary in its movements. Jet black hair cascaded
loosely to her shoulders in a foam of curls as she brushed the loose strands
off her cheeks with a nervous gesture as she walked. . . . Within the dark
halo of her hair her face seemed small and rather pale for youthful health.
Yet the great dark eyes were alive enough as she responded to the many
'Hello, Jean' calls greeting her along the way.[19]

Probably without realising it the writers equip their heroines with
attributes that in popular literature signal all the virtues required
by the traditional passive female role: cleanliness, diligence,
simplicity of mind and submission.[20] This seriously hampers the
authors' overt attempts at inspiring women readers with an
interest in politics by telling examples of girls or women engaged in
union politics or at least being understanding companions to their
politically active husbands.

Style and language, like all the other elements, are shaped to
serve the didactic aim. The simple and straightforward narrative is
hardly adorned by metaphors or descriptions of the settings, which
is certainly one of the reasons why almost nowhere a sense of a
particular atmosphere is being conveyed. Dialogue prevails, a
convenient vehicle for the political message. What seems remarkable is that, with the exception of Bonnar, none of the authors
makes use of a distinct dialect. In order to keep their books
universally understandable, they let pass this one more opportunity to provide their stories with a particular local flavour. A few
characteristics of working-class speech almost to be found every-

where in Britain like short sentences, a missing -s in the third person singular, etc. suffice them to indicate the social background of their protagonists. Bonnar alone wrote *Stewartie* in a strongly rhythmical language, interspersed with Scotticisms, reminiscent of Grassic Gibbon, whom he very much admired.

Summing up why the CP novels of the decade failed to achieve what they were designed for, it has become obvious that it was from too much of a good intention. Too eager in their wish to win over their readers, the authors tried to persuade them by simplifying the social situation, by idealising the working class and by calling up almost exclusively the readers' intellectual capacities, leaving their imaginary needs unsatisfied. But the readers, far too much guided in this way, are deprived of an opportunity to judge for themselves, which seems the indispensable first step to any political move. Moreover, in some features we even found the authors subconsciously advocating the *status quo* like in their purely positive view of industrial work or in their too careless reliance on the resources of appeasing literature. These novels may have been reassuring reading for the already converted, but they were not of the stuff to fascinate and win new allies to the movement as for example Robert Tressell's *The Ragged Trousered Philanthropists* (1914) had been.

III Descriptive Working-Class Novels

As these novels are so much better known, it seems justified to deal with them more briefly, even if they made the greater impact on the literary scene. To list them all here would be impossible. It may suffice to name a few writers to give an impression of the amazing dimensions of this type of novel: Alan Sillitoe, Sid Chaplin, David Storey, Stan Barstow, John Sommerfield, Hugh Munro, John Braine, Keith Waterhouse, Bill Naughton, Nell Dunn, Colin McInnes, Frederick Grice were among them. Literary history so far has grouped some of their work together with novels by the so-called 'Angry Young Men' like Kingsley Amis and John Wain, but this grouping led to a disregard of such books that told a different story from the recurring theme of the discontented scholarship-boy.

If the authors of the descriptive novels do not wish to propagate a certain political creed, this does not mean that they are without a sense of the political situation, or a critical attitude, for that matter. Perhaps just because they were unbiased by any particular theory they on the whole reacted to the national as well as international social and political reality more sensitively. But the class-war was no subject for them, not even in its reduced form as an industrial dispute in a certain plant. Instead they show themselves deeply impressed by the two phenomena of the time that probably made the greatest impact on people's lives, at first sight bearing rather conflicting implications: the fear of the atomic bomb and, on the national level, the new 'affluence'. The fear of the bomb, for which the United States and Russia appeared likewise responsible, is the great shadow looming in the background of their books. The texts rarely speak directly of it, shunning the topic like a taboo, but the few instances are telling enough, like the following example taken from Sommerfield's *North-West Five* (1960): 'They lived under the threat of the cold war, the hydrogen bomb, radioactive fall-out, all sorts of nightmarish disasters whose reality seemed remote from the narrow world of everyday life. . . .'[21] In the face of such apocalyptic threats the class-war may well have seemed of minor importance to many. Still the novelists do not revel in bleak despair, but react like the majority of men have reacted to the present day: by psychological repression and escape, turning their attention to the more immediate problems of everyday life. The new prosperity and the Welfare State had by no means produced only positive results, but had in an unforeseen way created a set of new difficulties for the working class, more or less of a psychological nature. For old people the predominant feeling may well have been relief. Like Arthur Seaton's father in Sillitoe's *Saturday Night and Sunday Morning* they were grateful for the greater sense of social security and happy to be finally able to enjoy some small luxuries like as many cigarettes and pints as they wished for and, of course, a TV set.[22]

But for the young things were different. The unprecedented flow of money into the pockets of their Teddy suits at a very early stage of their life meant the means for unwonted pleasures, but also a source of confusion. The pattern of behaviour, which generations before them had developed for necessity's sake and even their parents had still clung to—exactly the one which the Communist authors glorified—had lost its inevitability for them, and they started out to experiment with new forms. Now, that the basic needs of food, warmth and shelter were gratified, more subtler needs made themselves felt. Like so many bourgeois individuals before them, in real life as well as in literature, the young working-class individuals now launched on the search for self-realisation. But while the traditional set of behaviour had offered a certain psychological stability even if it meant repression of individual desires, the now open prospects did bring feelings of disorientation, insecurity and loneliness along with the promise of new pleasures. It is on this ambiguity that the descriptive novels focus, concentrating on a feature of contemporary life the CP authors had wilfully left unconsidered. They do so by following the fortunes of a single young man, in this, as in many other characteristics of their work, coming even closer to the model of the bourgeois novel than the CP authors had done. An image of working-class life ensues which is in many ways different from that of the Communist novels and which, due to the authors' greater susceptibility to impressions and their unbiased observation, seems truer to life.

The differences begin with the representation of work. Such scenes take up even less room than in the CP novels, but where they do occur the aspect of alienation is stressed most strongly. The descriptions in Alan Sillitoe's *Saturday Night and Sunday Morning* are the best known, but there are other examples like this one taken from Hugh Munro's *Tribal Town* (1964): 'Few of its [the factory's] employees knew what they were making. For whom. Or why. Except for their own wages, of course.'[23]

What seems remarkable is that the heroes no longer adhere to a particular trade, in which they could take a certain pride, like the working-class heroes of tradition, but, in accordance with the conditions of full employment, wander from 'job' to 'job' in the course of the action, none of which is described as holding any interest in itself, not even if it is the means to climb the social ladder like rugby playing in Storey's *This Sporting Life* (1958). The only aspect under which all these occupations mean anything to the protagonists (and to the authors) is the aspect of earning money, and as much money as possible. For money is considered as the key to the gratification of the deeper longings stirring obscurely in the breasts of the juvenile heroes.

A consequence of this new attitude to work is that the heroes take hardly any interest in either their fellow-workers or their bosses. In vain does one look for the traditional working-class solidarity or for its counterpart, the common hostility to the 'gaffers': the new heroes act as 'lone wolves'. Relations to fellow-workers are restricted to personal friendships or even a competitive relation as the one between Billy Liar and Stamp or the one between Machin and Arnie in *This Sporting Life*. Employers and managers on the other hand have lost much of their frightening stature and are represented as either dubious or ridiculous figures, the juvenile hero's contempt for their age playing a more important role than the traditional mistrust of the exploiter—Uncle George in Chaplin's *The Day of the Sardine* (1961) or Shadrack and Duxberry in *Billy Liar* (1959) are examples—or even as friendly helpers and furtherers like Van Huyten in Barstow's *A Kind of Loving* or Hoylake in Braine's *Room at the Top*. By far the greater part of the novels is reserved for the description of the hero's private life which, in view of the alienation of work, appears as the only possible sphere for self-fulfilment. Sillitoe's title *Saturday Night and Sunday Morning* can be looked upon as symbolical of the whole genre.

According to the workers' more practical cast of mind, bred by the long experience of want and misery, these working-class heroes seek their self-realisation not so much in a philosophical search for a 'meaning' in life, like so many bourgeois heroes, but in the much more concrete hunt for physical delights and private happiness. If Storey's Arthur Machin or Braine's Joe Lampton are socially ambitious, it is not so much for the more symbolical satisfaction of being admitted to the higher ranks, but for the solid advantages of being able to buy and enjoy things hitherto unobtainable for people of their class.

However, to the heroes' deep and painful surprise, happiness does not automatically follow. In particular the social upstarts pay dearly for their career. Machin as well as Joe Lampton lose the women they love through their own fault. This seems an interesting feature deserving closer notice. Machin and Lampton live out what Hoggart termed the new 'working-class hedonism' fostered by the new prosperity of the class.[24] Hoggart regretted this: he feared that the working class would become too materialistic in outlook and lose its best quality, that is, the capacity for solidarity. Storey and Braine, in giving a tragical ending to their stories, display the same anxiety which, on closer scrutiny, appears to be a symptom of a guilty conscience. All three authors seem to feel uneasy at the sight of members of their class enjoying material pleasures. Here remnants of the Puritan heritage seem to come to the surface, in whose name the ruling class has for centuries justified the suppression and exploitation of the labouring classes. If worker-writers give voice to these morals, it shows just how much the exploited class has internalised the denial of their own claims to the sweets of life.

The heroes who stay in their class are not much happier. It is interesting to note on what they spend their fairly good wages: on clothes to wear after work, on motorbikes, occasionally even a car, on girls, pub visits, drink, in short, on means of escape, escape not

only from a drab eight-hour job on the lathe, but from the narrow-
ness of home life as well. Where the heroes of earlier working-
class literature and the CP novels had sought relaxation and
comfort within the family and neighbourhood, the new heroes
seek, if any, the company of their own age group: the novels
illustrate the emergence of youth as a separate social and cultural
group in those years, wearing their particular clothes and developing their own code of behaviour. But as a rule they do not find
what they are craving for. The 'gangs', as for instance described by
Chaplin in *The Day of the Sardine* or by Colin McInnes in *Absolute
Beginners* (1959), cannot offer the same stable support and steady
warmth as the family of tradition had done, because they are made
up of members who all follow their own interest first and foremost,
and who are ready to leave the group any moment if they are
crossed or grow out of it.

But the relationship from which the young heroes expect the
most satisfaction is love. Here we have another characteristic the
books share with the traditional bourgeois novel, and, indeed, it
may well have been one of their main attractions for the bourgeois
reading public. One finds the young men entangled in at least one,
sometimes in a whole series of rather complicated, more or less
freely described love affairs, which on the whole, though, fail to
bring them permanent bliss, though keen enough temporary
pleasures. The social reasons are partly made visible: we see the
frustration at work, and we get to know their parents and
understand that their upbringing did not prepare the young to
have and cope with more refined feelings. So love itself turns out
to be one more experience to shake the hero's mental stability
rather than to fulfil his longing for happiness and self-realisation.

Of course, the novels do not all tell the same story. Some are
more pessimistic in outlook than others. Some leave their heroes
after a series of upsetting adventures, all turning out to be
frustrating in the end, leaving them high and dry in a state of utter
bewilderment or bitter cynicism. This is true of Storey's *This
Sporting Life*, Braine's *Room at the Top*, Chaplin's *The Day of the
Sardine*, Sillitoe's *The Loneliness of the Long-Distance Runner*
(1959) and Waterhouse's *Billy Liar*. In other novels, after much
the same strain of experiences, if not wilder ones, the authors
finally make an effort to give a happy ending to their heroes'
search. Interestingly enough, they, just like the Communist
authors, turn back to the solutions of the past, concentrating on
the private aspects, needless to say. Sillitoe in *Saturday Night and
Sunday Morning*, Sommerfield in *North-West Five*, Chaplin in *The

Watchers and the Watched (1962), just like the CP novelists, show their heroes finally and happily accepting the role of husband and member of a large family, prescribed for them by the rules of tradition. In the words of Arthur Seaton, they are content with 'the conventional ending'. The voluntary reintegration into the traditional code of behaviour of the class on the private level appears as the only guarantee left to protect the young from loneliness and confusion created by the modern world.

It would be wrong, though, to let the impression grow that these novels are basically acquiescent. The very resignation is mostly voiced with such bitterness and sometimes fury, that the criticism is obvious. It is certainly true that the novels do not paint lofty images of collective political actions, but some of them seem to take up a tradition of literary protest certainly much older than the socialist novel, perhaps even dating as far back as Thomas Nashe's *The Unfortunate Traveller*: they tell stories of individual rebellion, and they tell them in a very impressive way, even if defeat may be the outcome. One need only call to mind Sillitoe's *The Loneliness of the Long-Distance Runner*.

The writing techniques of these authors are on the whole more varied than those of the CP novelists, though the course of action usually follows along similarly simple lines. As narrative perspective mostly the first person method or at least the personal point of view is chosen, as a logical consequence of the interest focusing on a single individual. But unlike in the bourgeois novel this perspective is not used for the illustration of subtle mental processes, but the hero's thoughts are for the most part determined by his experiences in the outside world, thus providing a small slice of social reality, seen from the inside, so to speak. The section of society mirrored in this way is admittedly smaller than even that represented in the CP novels, but the restriction is made up for by a greater authenticity of representation and the conveyance of a particular atmosphere. This is not so much achieved by longish direct descriptions (though some authors like, for instance, Sillitoe, have a taste for them), but by drawing on social facts in constructing the narration itself. Sometimes they are actually the prime cause of events as when, for instance, the love between Machin and Mrs Hammond in Storey's *This Sporting Life* springs from the prosaic circumstance of her being forced to let rooms.

Of course, these authors, showing their greater individual ambition as artists for one thing in sometimes abundant use of metaphors, do also make use of dialect, usually the vernacular of their northern home districts, though they are careful not to overdo it. Most strongly used in dialogue, the dialect effectfully helps to intensify the feeling of a certain atmosphere. That the writers all make such free use of it seems a sure sign of their self-assurance and symptomatic of the new pride of their class in general: they trusted it to be no hindrance to a wider audience's interest and to publication.

But the very fact that they stick to their traditional home dialect and make only very slight attempts at an individual language, seems on the other hand a symptom of their still strong bonds with their origin and class. For it denotes the wish to communicate, communicativeness being one of the main characteristics ascribed by sociologists to the working class, even though the circle addressed is no longer only the class itself, but has widened to include anybody who might be interested in its affairs. The embourgeoisement has not yet gone so far that the worker-writers write merely for the sake of self-expression regardless of the possibilities to be understood as some experimental bourgeois writers have done like Joyce, for instance, in *Finnegans Wake*. The authors of the descriptive working-class novels clearly wished to communicate, and about a subject of common social interest, thereby showing a social responsibility comparable to that of the bourgeois novelists of the eighteenth and nineteenth centuries.

I want to end with the hypothesis that the descriptive novels, which picture a small slice of social reality, but with fresh observation and a great amount of authenticity in the representation, probably prompted more critical thinking, though they may seem more harmless on the surface, than the CP novels, precisely because they avoid to talk their readers into a certain fixed political belief.

NOTES

1 P. J. Keating, *The Working Classes in Victorian Fiction* (London, 1971), p. 124.
2 For a full list of publications see my study *Der Weg nach oben: englische Arbeiterromane 1945–1978* (Frankfurt, 1980), pp. 447–9.
3 Gudrun Schütz-Güth, Helmut Schütz, *Typen des britischen Arbeiterromans* (Grossen-Linden, 1979), p. 367.
4 Herbert Smith's two novels sold under one thousand copies each: *A Field of Folk*, 630; *A Morning to Remember*, 607. The books by

Doherty, Lambert and Bonnar sold between 1,160 and 1,810 copies. The most successful novel was Doherty's *A Miner's Sons* with 3,080 copies sold. (Information given by Nan Green, reader of Lawrence & Wishart, in a letter of 14 June 1972.)

5 Georg Friedrich Wilhelm Hegel, in Rüdiger Bubner (ed.), *Vorlesungen über die Ästhetik, Dritter Teil: die Poesie* (Stuttgart, 1971) (1842), p. 177.

6 Alan Sillitoe in James Vinson (ed.), *Contemporary Novelists* (London, 1972), p. 1132.

7 E. J. Hobsbawm, *Industry and Empire* (Harmondsworth, 1970) (1968), p. 281. See also Richard Hoggart, *The Uses of Literacy* (Harmondsworth, 1973) (1957). Hoggart's book was an attempt to describe traditional working-class culture in the historical moment of its impending decline.

8 For a discussion of Raymond Williams' novels see my study mentioned above.

9 See the two collections of essays and speeches published by the party: *Britain's Cultural Heritage* (1952) and *Essays on Socialist Realism and the British Cultural Tradition* (1953).

10 Len Doherty, *A Miner's Sons* (London, 1955), p. 6.

11 Herbert Smith, *A Field of Folk* (London, 1957), p. 228.

12 *Ibid.*, p. 248.

13 Herbert Smith, *A Morning to Remember* (Berlin, 1964) (London, 1962), p. 41.

14 *Ibid.*, p. 7.

15 Smith, *A Field of Folk*, p. 59.

16 Doherty, *op. cit.*, p. 135.

17 *Ibid.*, p. 134.

18 Bernard Bergonzi, *The Situation of the Novel* (London, 1970), p. 20.

19 David Lambert, *No Time for Sleeping* (London, 1958), p. 6.

20 These connotations are studied in detail by Peter Nusser in his book *Romane für die Unterschicht. Groschenhefte und ihre Leser* (Stuttgart, 1973).

21 John Sommerfield, *North-West Five* (London, 1960), pp. 153–4.

22 Alan Sillitoe, *Saturday Night and Sunday Morning* (London, 1968) (1958), p. 20.

23 Hugh Munro, *Tribal Town* (London, 1964), p. 42.

24 Hoggart, *op. cit.*, p. 176.

Chapter 9

SOCIALIST FICTION AND THE EDUCATION OF DESIRE: MERVYN JONES, RAYMOND WILLIAMS AND JOHN BERGER

Kiernan Ryan

Do not demand a Socialist Art. . . . Demand Socialist propaganda when it is needed and encourage art. Then artists will suddenly realize that they have created Socialist works, whilst only thinking about the truth.

John Berger[1]

One must not write for the people in the language in which they speak, but in the language in which they desire.

Alexander Ostrovsky[2]

Over the last twenty years or so in Britain the most sustained and significant contributions to the socialist novel by committed intellectuals have been made by Mervyn Jones, Raymond Williams and John Berger. This essay endeavours to salience the central concerns of their fiction so far and to give some idea of its scope, variety and value as a body of work. The fact that the writing of all three men is still evolving and very far from concluded makes it impossible, of course, to provide more than an introductory and provisional survey.

It is already clear, however, that Jones, Williams and Berger share in their novels a deep common purpose. To put it in the most general terms, they are all implicitly concerned in their imaginative writing to contribute as effectively as possible to the emancipative transformation of the prevailing social relations into a more truly human socialist society. Which does not and must not mean, as Berger's vital injunction above reminds us, the mere fictional reproduction of some ready-made, finalised version of socialist ideology. On the contrary: the essential function and value of fiction as such, and of a *consciously* materialist and dialectical fiction above all, reside in its relentless, uncompromising interrogation of the received in the light of an ever-changing reality, its restless explorations beyond the given horizon of experience and knowledge—including, where truth and need demand, beyond the hitherto accepted formulations and prescriptions of socialism. And it's within this general emphasis that the more specific common task on which these three novelists are engaged—and the task to which socialist fiction must increasingly dedicate itself—can perhaps best be understood in terms of what E. P. Thompson has recently highlighted as 'the education of desire'.

In the postscript to the revised edition of his book on Morris, Thompson speaks of the need to restore and develop the repressed utopian dimension within historical materialism, since a true Communist society is

unobtainable without the prior education of desire or 'need'. And science cannot tell us what to desire or how to desire. Morris saw it as the task of Socialists . . . to help people find out their wants, to encourage them to want more, to challenge them to want differently, and to envisage a society of the future in which people, freed at last of necessity, might choose between different wants.[3]

In a full account of the matter one would want to argue that historically this education of desire has always—certainly since the Renaissance—been one of the central functions fulfilled by literature (and, of course, art in general). The main point here, however, is that now, as a fully socialist society looms increasingly within the bounds of historical possibility and the struggle to suppress it correspondingly intensifies, literature and art need to fulfil this function more urgently and deliberately than ever before.

The recognition of the need both to educate desire and equally, indeed, to create the preconditions for that education, is clearly reflected in the novels of the three socialist writers considered here. For all of them strive, in varying ways and degrees, to engineer the critical cognition of the actual reduced terms of our reality in such a way as to rouse and develop our awareness of the human potentiality and need to live otherwise. They are all involved in compelling, from one angle or another, the more-or-less explicit confrontation of the possible and desirable with the divisive, oppressive and contradictory social relations frustrating their realisation. And at their best these novels not only bring the reader's enhanced desire into that acute tension with the constraining given which incites towards transformative praxis, but they project convincing, exemplary experiences of achieved understanding, endurance and renewal which invigorate the will to fight on in hope.

I

The prolific imagination of Mervyn Jones (born 1922) has produced to date some nineteen novels which between them map an
impressively wide and varied fictional territory, embracing both
the immensely public and the intensely private, the sweepingly
historical and the vividly contemporary. Jones' first novel, *No
Time To Be Young*, appeared in 1952, but it was not until the
successfully filmed *John and Mary* (1966) that his fiction really
began to claim the wider attention and respect which it now
regularly commands.

John and Mary remains, indeed, one of the best novels Jones
has written. In his customary lean and lucid, often deceptively
simple prose, it narrates the superficially trite experience of a man
and a woman spending the day together, sealed off from the
everyday world, following a casual sexual encounter the night
before; a day in which they gradually learn to know each other
truly and in the end, 'under a silent pressure of unbroken time and
unchanging place',[4] fall authentically in love.

The achievement is in the penetration beneath the prosaic
surface of the incident to reveal the subtle psychological dynamics
and implications of this process of falling in love: all the wary
tactical manoeuvrings on both sides through impulsion and
restraint, overture and resistance; all the fraught subliminal conflicts of anticipation and inhibition before the final courageous
breakthrough into the vulnerable commitment of full and honest
mutuality. The narration proceeds in stereoscopic depth through
the alternating and independent first-person accounts of each
phase by John and Mary. For Jones is thus able to show how the
man and the woman alike must struggle out through their socialised
preconceptions of each other's character and motivation to a
genuine recognition and trust beyond the confines of conventional
assumptions. The novel pursues its hermeneutics of desire and
relationship with spare intensity, quietly dramatising and cel-
ebrating the power of men and women to surmount the acquired
illusions, fears and prejudices barring their way to mutual self-
realisation.

The same strategy of creating a deliberately insulated situation,
under whose special pressures an exemplary process of development can be magnified and accelerated, is deployed in *Mr
Armitage Isn't Back Yet* (1971), which concerns a much more
drastic emancipative shedding of internalised constraints and
presuppositions. A wealthy executive is kidnapped by four benign

hippies and 'imprisoned' with them over a long period on a deserted, inaccessible island. Their aim is to study and understand the capitalist species *homo economicus* under whose domination they will have to spend the rest of their lives. The fascination of the book lies in Armitage's account of what becomes for him an experience of radical transformation.

By the surreptitious force of circumstance and the irresistibly gentle, humane example of the two young couples, Armitage is gradually driven to overcome his initially traumatic symptoms of dislocation and withdrawal from bourgeois 'civilisation', and to question his most basic suppositions regarding property, money, work, time and sexuality; to completely revise his least-considered presumptions as to what is 'natural' and 'normal' and 'common sense', and what really constitutes happiness. In short, he is induced to dismantle the whole individualist and instrumentalist way of life hitherto deceiving and degrading him, and to edge his way towards an alternative way of living in equal community with others. To be sure, the novel fails to evolve a reciprocal interrogation of the hippies' naive and apolitical anti-authoritarianism; the objective fragility of their vision in the face of the everyday world being but hastily adumbrated at the end. And the abruptly bitten off closure and generally uneven narrative structure leave much to be desired. But, like *John and Mary*, the text does succeed in producing a genuinely illuminating collision of the social modes of containment with the human drive for release into more and better, which other Jones' novels, in spite of themselves, do not always manage to achieve.

Strangers (1974), for example, is (as the title might suggest) a comparative study in the many forms of our alienation, but one whose preoccupation with charting the negative effects of division and estrangement leaves little scope for projecting preferable versions of feeling and relationship. The novel is overcast by the sense of our living 'in the century of the refugee', in an age when 'everybody's leaving somewhere'; the liberal middle-class heroine Val learning on her pulse the bitter truth of 'how many prisoners and how few free people there [are] in the world'.[5]

The narrative shuttles between Val in London and her pacifist husband Andrew in Uganda in charge of a precarious settlement of tribal refugees from the Sudan. In London and Africa by turns Val's liberal complacencies are put increasingly to the test, and the awareness grows that the experience of oppressive estrangement is not restricted to the wretched tribe abandoned and despised in Uganda, but is shared in different degrees and forms (social,

political, sexual, racial, generational) by all the members of Val's
ill-assorted London household: the lonely American draft-dodger;
the pregnant girl evading her parents; the black student harassed
for his relationship with a white schoolgirl; the working-class
tenants in the basement flat, to whom Val feels bound by nothing
but her sense of class guilt. Through Val the categories of the
English and the African experiences cross-question and relativise
each other, and the novel does at least begin to shape a liberating
sense of the virtual common humanity existing across all these
arbitrary barriers provisionally dividing people. So that, despite
a closing feeling of blockage, uncertainty and dismay, what prevails overall is the recognition that 'there wasn't a battle to be
won or lost; there was en endless effort, never likely to be
wholly successful, yet never to be abandoned, always worth
while.'⁶

This scaled-down yet realistic and resilient appraisal of our
situation and our task likewise structures Jones' much more
ambitious novel *Today The Struggle* (1978), a panoramic social
and political chronicle of England over the last forty years. Here
Jones traces the closely intertwining fates of various families and
associated characters representative of the whole class spectrum of
English society during the period. Through their personal experiences he endeavours to lock in on the nation's history at three
specific moments: the intensely political 1930s, with the Spanish
Civil War and the growing menace of Fascism; the late 1950s and
early 1960s, centring on the exuberant rise but eventual subsidence
of the CND movement (of which Jones himself was a prominent
member); and finally, in stark contrast with these politically rich
moments of united commitment and aspiration, the apathetic
1970s, the decade in which 'what was missing . . . was the quality of
idealism. The striving to make a better world—the reaching for a
vision . . . they led their lives, all of them, without trying to change
the world.'⁷

Jones deliberately juxtaposes the promise generated in past
struggles with the conditions and attitudes blocking the continued
effort to realise that promise in the present. And although on the
one hand this leads to a deadening apprehension of stagnation and
impasse, it generates at the same time a correspondingly urgent
insistence on the stubborn need nevertheless to defend unflag-
gingly the ground already won, 'to offer the whole of oneself,
without calculation and even without hope: to resist'. For in the
end 'always something was gained, if only the awareness of greater
possibilities; but always the success was partial, the impetus melted

away. What mattered was to remember. What was vital was not to lose hope.'[8]

But the structure and the vision do not always come through as clearly and forcefully as this. In several novels Jones sets out to explore an initially arresting narrative situation, the terms of whose conflict seem bound to generate a whole spectrum of valuable recognitions. But somehow the drive to attain a full imaginative seizure of the subject flags and fades, and the embryonic, ideal parameters of the fiction dissolve in a blur of mere circumstantial anecdote, obliterating all but the vestiges of the really significant narrative the text might have become.

Lord Richard's Passion (1974) is a typical example of the Jones novel which never quite manages to grasp and articulate its own central concern, and whose interstices afford maddening glimpses of the other, unwritten novel which could not finally be lured to the surface. Set in the Victorian period, it describes how the passionate love of a young aristocrat for a beautiful woman of his own class is persistently thwarted by personal and social-historical forces which neither of them can fully understand, but which are focused in the submerged contradictions between her nascent feminist consciousness and his unconsciously domineering sexism. But because the author fails to characterise the protagonists in such a way as to invest their imputed hunger for fulfilment with a more fully human, oppositional authority capable of interrogating and indicting the social relations which defeat them, the novel never realises the representative tragic status to which it aspires but remains a merely particular, incidental case-study in sad misfortune. Unable to select and structure the kind of telling action and charged detail calculated to impart general symbolic force to the narrative, the compositional focus slithers promiscuously all over the place and the novel peters out in a stammer of structurally superfluous gossip.

Much the same critique, *mutatis mutandis*, could be made of *A Survivor* (1968) or even Jones' most recent, disappointing novels, *The Beautiful Words* (1979) and *A Short Time To Live* (1980). In all of these that nagging sense of the repressed true text, swelling insistently beneath the actual diffuse and uncentred surface novel, is inescapable. Each defaults on its implicit narrative contract to illuminate the tragic tension between what could be and what is: to expand our cognizance both of the socially produced circumstances severing people from their potential selves, and of the irrepressible latent power of humans to subdue those circumstances nevertheless to their will.

At times, moreover, there is a clear feeling that what's stifling the fully dynamic and subversive tragic vision at birth is a deep-lying, profoundly static notion of social reality, an informing world view bordering at moments on paralysed resignation and finding its aesthetic expression all too readily in the spare descriptive naturalism into which Jones' novels tendentially veer. The problem with this minimal, anecdotal style being that it hyposta-tises the in fact processive reality which it addresses, confirming and stabilising even where it would disrupt. In place of a conflic-tive drama of becoming, the evolving narration of human fates in volatile, contingent solution, such a naturalistic descriptive mode, as Lukács observes, 'transforms people into conditions, into components of still lives. . . . The result is a series of static pictures. . . . The so-called action is only a thread on which the still lives are disposed in a superficial, ineffective, fortuitous sequence of isolated, static pictures.'[9]

The problem is manifest in one of Jones' most popular books, *Holding On* (1973), which was serialised on television. This novel chronicles the working-class experience of this century through the particular history of the East End docker Charlie Wheelwright. It recounts his life and times from his birth at the turn of the century through to his bitterly lonely yet proud death as an old man at the start of the 1970s, taking in his experience of both World Wars, the General Strike and the Depression, and the dehumanising 'pro-gress' of an increasingly callous and sordid postwar Britain. The courage, human warmth and dignity of Charlie and his class under even the most appalling conditions are rightly stressed throughout. And yet the overall picture is finally just too acceptably rosy and contented with itself altogether. For under the pressure of the naturalistic style and vision the proletarian experience of the twentieth century is implicitly depicted not as a series of socially and historically produced tragedies made and changeable by men, but as having been a 'natural', ineluctably fixed and necessary condition of being to be simply endured—the wars being con-ceived as deadly plagues, the Depression as a vicious winter, through which the working class stoically 'held on'. History, thus naturalised and stunned, is deprived of its conditionality and optionality, and thereby robbed of its constant inherent potential, displayed both in the past and in the present, to produce worlds other than those which have prevailed.

The essence of this subtly immobilising perspective finds ex-pression in the all too aptly (though doubtless sardonically) titled novel *Nobody's Fault* (1977), which concludes with the central female figure still locked in the impossible impasse in which the book opened:

> I go from here to there in order to go from here to there again. I don't know why, but it's always necessary. Things have happened, not as I expected or wanted them to happen, but as they had to. . . . We have struggled with one another without victory, only to remain locked together. We did what we had to do. We are where we must be. I suppose it will always be like this.[10]

The problem being again that there's nothing about the way the novel is written to suggest that she's wrong: nothing to convey, as Jones at his best certainly can, the actual contingency and transience of the existing forms of social relationship; the sense that there is indeed more to life, that it could indeed be otherwise, and that it can and must be made better.

II

No such insinuation of historical inertia mars the strikingly consistent and closely defined vision informing the fiction of Raymond Williams (born 1921), whose relentless imaginative stress is precisely on the process and the means of change. As Williams has recently remarked of the now completed Welsh trilogy:

> thematically the shape of the trilogy was clear. They were interconnecting visions of a specific kind of change, across borders. *Border Country* was the present, including and trying to focus an immediate past; *Second Generation* a true present; *Fight For Manod* a present trying to include and focus a future. There was even a linkage through the successive means of mobility: *Border Country*'s railway; *Second Generation*'s car traffic and factory; *Manod*'s potential electronic technology. And in each of these, through these different situations, the decisive problem of the relation of learning to labour, taking different class and political aspects.[11]

The constant site of all Williams' novels, indeed, including *The Volunteers*, is an intensely liminal conjuncture of social, cultural, ideological and generational conflicts through which the protagonist must painfully work his way before at last emerging, charged with a deeper understanding of his whole personal and social situation and with the renewed political energy and committed will to transform it.

Border Country (1960) presents us with Williams' first (and still most admired) study of a character moving between two radically disparate worlds and compelled by the harsh perplexities of that dislocation to confront and re-examine the very purpose of his life. Matthew Price, a lecturer in economic history in London, returns to the Welsh village of Glynmawr when his father Harry suffers an eventually fatal stroke. The crisis forces Matthew's recently mounting sense of disorientation and stagnation to the surface as he strives to construe the present meaning of his own life in the past light of his father's, opening up 'a dialogue of anxiety and allegiance, of deep separation and deep love'.[12]

A series of flashback chapters takes us back to the time of Harry's first settling in Glynmawr with his wife in the early 1920s, and movingly unfolds the unflagging moral integrity and self-sufficiency, the quiet passion, and the hard and limited yet genuinely fulfilling quality of Harry's life both at work on the railway and at home. A central, carefully differentiated contrast, framing crucial tensions of desire within the working class, is made throughout with the fate of Harry's close friend Morgan Rosser, who becomes politically disillusioned after the failure of the General Strike and abandons his once active trade unionism and socialist idealism to become a commercially successful small dealer and the eventual owner of a local factory. Morgan diverts the energy of his thirst for more and better into these narrower and shallower satisfactions and thus, as he later perceives, essentially betrays himself in betraying his own deepest aspirations. Harry, intuitively comprehending the real limits of his moment and its possibilities, gently refuses to join him and remains within his class, committing himself wholly to living his immediate fate all the way through, and implicitly investing his transcendent dreams of otherness in his son, to whom he entrusts the development and completion of all that he himself could not hope to accomplish in his own life with his hands so full of the present.

In realising this continuity, the fact that 'a life lasts longer than the actual body through which it moves',[13] Matthew begins to possess the full meaning of his father's unspoken legacy to him. From the contrast between Harry's life and Morgan's, moreover, what becomes clear—as Morgan himself points out in the key exchange closing Chapter 9—is that authentic, fulfilling change must proceed from a real affirmative desire *for* the new way, not merely from a dissatisfied, negative recoil from the old. It's a lesson endorsed and consolidated throughout the trilogy as vital to the building of an alternative socialist society. And by appropriating his father's powerful affirmative impulsion to himself Matthew at last breaks through to a living sense of his common humanity, overcoming all the internalised, individualistic pressures towards isolation and division and recognising now, in a new access of transformative energy, how he henceforth must move with and for the community of the people.

The same conviction of essential human community barely manages to contain, within 'the movement and traffic of a single city',[14] the much more bitter and disillusioning conflicts agitating *Second Generation* (1964), whose narrative is set in a thinly disguised Oxford starkly polarised into the separate worlds of motor industry and university. Here an even more traumatic and bewildering rite of passage through to true perspective and political decision is undergone by the student Peter Owen, the interjacent figure in whom all the discords and antagonisms of the book—within and between classes and generations, within and between labour and learning—violently intersect. But the sensation of final affirmative breakthrough is here more muted because subdued to the text's overriding stress on the sheer cost of straining to live otherwise under the remorseless counterpressure of the status quo, within 'the familiar bleak muddle in which everybody seemed tired'.[15]

Through the disconcerting experiences endured by Peter and his equally restless and discontented mother Kate, the novel provides a grim initiation in the realities of blockage and containment encountered by the craving for another way. It exposes in particular the subtly enervating hegemonic strategies by which the currents of need can be channelled off and absorbed into spurious alternatives and pseudo-ideals, here most conspicuously in the narrowing displacement of a comprehensive political emancipation into a false bourgeois version of sexual liberation. But the hardest insights to come to terms with crystallise at the end of the book in the climactic confrontation between Kate and Peter, which underscores not only the overwhelming difficulty of changing an intractable world, but the still more daunting home truth of what that struggle for change does to those dedicated to sustain it. The exchange is worth quoting from at length because it brings to clear definition a persistent argument within Williams' fiction. Thus on the one hand we have Peter, rejecting a too facile and absolute utopianism and reasserting the wisdom evolved by *Border Country*, the need to weave the future continuously from the achieved realities of the present:

Because we've got this wrong, this contrast we make between potential and actual. In the end it breaks us, because it is no way to live. If we keep reducing the present, by some idea of the future, nothing good can happen. We have to take hold where we are, and know good from bad. We've lived in this break too long. All it's taught us is breaking away. But the change will only come when we've learned to confirm.

On the contrary, replies Kate, 'it's only the break that has ever changed things'. Then she goes on to spell out the disturbing realisation borne out by the whole novel: that though the system can and indeed will be changed

it will break those who do it. It will break them to pieces, even inside themselves. We used to say, be humane and tolerant, make a better life. But to be human now we can't be tolerant. We have to break and fight, and go dry and hard in the process. . . . And not just hardness: that can be learned. But being broken, yourself, while you try to change things. Not just broken in their terms, but finally in your own. . . . Not just the strain either, but that the effort is quite different from the life we're making the effort for. Have you ever really thought when we say fighting for peace? It's quite real, that contradiction. The feelings we learn from the fighting disqualify us from the peace, yet there's still no alternative, we still have to fight.[16]

The final volume of the trilogy, *The Fight For Manod* (1979), closes likewise in this clear-eyed resolution to go on fighting for the future despite what the novel reveals to be the harrowing personal costs of political opposition and the smothering weight of the past and present contradictions blocking the historical impulse towards regeneration. At the heart of the text is another version of the trilogy's continuous debate on the essential strategy by which the new order should be actualised: whether through sustained evolution out of the present or through an absolute, qualitative break with it. But in this case the debate is staged on the threshold of a much more specific and plausibly concrete instance of the desirable future: the projected building of a viable new kind of city in the country, capable of supporting more human and communally satisfying forms of living and working.

Matthew Price and Peter Owen reappear together from the earlier novels as the two academic consultants appointed by the government to study its proposal to build this model rural city in mid-Wales. Matthew, the now eminent industrial historian who grew up near the area, goes with his wife to live in Manod, the village at the heart of the scheme, to get the feel of what the proposal will really mean to the people who live there – the drained and thwarted yet somehow invincible quality of their everyday lives being vividly realised by the novel. Peter Owen, now a young radical sociologist not long out of prison following a Vietnam protest, likewise settles nearby. Caustically cynical from the start about the motives behind the project, Owen soon succeeds in discovering a web of corruption and land speculation spun round the whole enterprise. And from then on the crucial issues of the novel organise themselves round the two men's opposing reactions to this revelation.

Both Price and Owen are united, of course, in resisting the attempted corrupt deployment of public money for private interests. And both, in their different ways, pay the severe personal price exacted of those who actively withstand the local and international oppressions of capitalist rapacity and guile— Peter in that callous hardening of the heart, even (especially) against those most closely loved, which his mother predicted at the end of *Second Generation*; Matthew in the sheer mental and physical exhaustion, climaxing now in a heart attack, accumulated through a lifetime's dispiriting fight for a promise endlessly deferred. But whereas Owen's characteristic response to the Manod proposition is of course absolute hostility and unqualified rejection, Matthew clings tenaciously, despite everything, to the knowledge released through his experience of his father's death in *Border Country*, and insists on the need to work on through all the contradictions for that real possibility of an alternative existence secreted nevertheless within the squalid manipulations of capitalism. The growing-points of the future are the rooted hard realities of the actual; and the 'pure passion for a different world', the 'dream of a country' which Matthew shares with his people, can only be served 'by working for, always. And by working against only when I finally have to'.[17]

The Volunteers (1978) marks in many ways a new fictional direction for Williams, moving through as it does into the sphere of the future and at the same time into the radically different mode of the political thriller. Within this projection, however, we find the protagonist negotiating and finally crossing the familiar strife-torn border country between cynical resignation and political engagement: the narrative of cool detection becomes the ironic process by which the investigator himself is manoeuvred into discovering his own deepest allegiances.

The scene is an increasingly totalitarian Britain in the late 1980s. The Labour Party has disappeared and a National Government rules over a country in which organised working-class resistance to capitalism has dwindled to occasional regional strikes and local occupations, reducing the only viable alternatives to various modes of clandestine subversion either within or outside the State machine. Following a deliberately vicious army suppression of a power depot strike in Wales, in which one worker is killed and several injured, the minister responsible is shot and wounded by an unknown assailant in a calculated public act of revenge. The reporter Lewis Redfern, a former left-wing activist but now disillusioned enough to have become 'consultant analyst on the political underground' for the Insatel news agency, sets out to investigate. He becomes wholly absorbed in a lone hunt for the assailant which finally leads him to the discovery of something much bigger: the Volunteers, a secret left-wing network of sub-stitutionist 'sleepers', whose long-range strategy is the patient infiltration of the institutions of power.

It's a discovery which necessarily brings Redfern face to face with the political conscience and ideals he thought he had outgrown, or at least successfully repressed. With pace and economy Williams skilfully exploits and transforms the popular narrative structure, conventions and idiom of the reportorial thriller format to turn Redfern's initially hardboiled and sardonically detached pursuit of his 'story' into a simultaneous unravelling of the morally hollow and complacent leech he has become. And with this recognition the way is opened for him, in a tense and testing climax, to reawaken in himself that different order of being which can make no compact with the ruling social world, but must subvert that world or atrophy within it. Breaking out of the alienated cynicism and ironising self-disgust into which he had sealed himself, he rediscovers his moral rage at an inhuman system and, against all the inner fears and doubts, aligns himself publicly with the emancipative cause fought for by the Volunteers, the cause of the working class:

There was only, now, the deep need to connect . . . all the time, within this impossibility, were the inevitable commitments, the necessary commitments, the choosing of sides. Through the persistent uncertainty, within the overwhelming process, I had now chosen and been chosen, in what would be, in effect, a quite final way.[18]

In its direct exemplary bearing on the current dilemma of so many disaffected and disheartened left-wing intellectuals, *The Volunteers* constitutes an intensely relevant and uncompromising contribution to that imaginative education of our political desire to which Williams' fiction has been constantly devoted.

III

Of the three novelists considered here, John Berger (born 1926) is certainly the most aesthetically adventurous and experimental, the most self-conscious and theoretically deliberate in his continually innovative use of fiction to extend the range of the senses, understanding and imagination and reorient them towards altogether new horizons and norms of human living. For Berger 'the modern artist fights to contribute to human happiness, truth or justice. He works to improve the world.' And hence the success of his work 'must be judged in relation to the always different and always present struggle of men to realize their potentiality more fully', for above all else 'a true work of art communicates and so extends consciousness of what is possible'.[19]

The source of these quotations is Berger's first novel, *A Painter Of Our Time* (1958), a rich and probing meditation on the fraught situation of the committed socialist artist as cultivator of human aspiration and volition, as disciplined dreamer. The novel centres on the painter Janos Lavin, a Hungarian Communist emigré who has lived and worked in London, his talent largely unrecognised, since the 1930s, but who—just a week after at last receiving his first London exhibition—suddenly vanishes, compelled to return and engage himself immediately in the Hungarian crisis of 1956. The text consists essentially of Lavin's diaries covering the four years preceding his disappearance. These record with arresting precision the man's innermost hopes, memories, aches of guilt and speculations as he works through a series of painting projects, wrestling tirelessly over and over again with 'the difficulty of making the intangible tangible, of creating a cold form to contain our fervent content'.[20]

At the constant risk, it must be said, of tilting and turning completely from fiction into discursive theorising, the novel generates a plethora of brilliant insights into the process and social purpose of aesthetic production. Informing these throughout is the contrast between the arid, dehumanised solipsism and moral spinelessness of so much modern Western art and the unflinching artistic integrity of Lavin's engaged socialist humanism, his proud practice of his art 'in the name and the virtue and the potentiality of the life that the working class can gain for the world'.[21] Through Lavin the presupposed aims and ideals which should implicitly drive and organise authentic art find unambiguous expression:

I live, work, for a state where the more honest the son the less the mother
need fear; where every worker has a sense of responsibility, not because
he is appealed to but because he has responsibility; where the only *élite*
are the old; where every tragedy is admitted as such; where women are not
employed to use their sex to sell commodities—finally this is a much
greater degradation than prostitution; where the word freedom has
become unnecessary because every ability is wanted; where prejudice has
been so overcome that every man is able to judge another by his
eyes. . . .[22]

The ultimate proof of Lavin's allegiance to this vision being
precisely his readiness, under the extraordinary pressure of the
Hungarian turmoil, to surrender 'the dreadful obliqueness of art'
to the violent constraint of 'immediate objectives'[23] and take his
stand in the streets with the rest for the protection and furtherance
of his dreams.

   In the light of this constructive, exhilerating conception of art
energising *A Painter Of Our Time*, Berger's next two novels, while
interesting, are disappointingly cramped and negative in their
achievement. Both *The Foot Of Clive* (1962) and *Corker's Freedom*
(1964) are dedicated not so much to extending our consciousness
of the possible as to the complementary task of stripping away our
illusions as to the true nature of the prevailing bourgeois social
relations, escalating and sharpening our dissatisfaction with the
poverty of the available. But this indispensable negational process
proceeds deprived of any real dialectical counterdrive to disclose
the simultaneous emergence within the social order of alternative
new vitalities. And both novels thus remain instructive but essentially dry and one-dimensional exercises in the deconstruction of
the false, the optative, utopian dimension finding articulation at
best *ex negativo* in the salient completeness of its absence.

   The Foot Of Clive revolves round the world of the group of male
patients occupying the 'foot' end of a modern hospital ward named
after Clive of India. As that name confirms, what we are confronted with is a microcosm of a superseded imperialist society
grasped metaphorically as a place of sickness and death but also of
potential curing and survival. The six main characters are selected
to embody and evoke, through subtly differentiated metonymous
compression, the generational, class and ideological span of the
social ensemble, and thus provide a paradigmatic context within
which to probe and gauge the moral health of a whole society.

   The catalystic incident on which Berger's clinically dispassionate
diagnosis turns is the arrival in the ward of a seventh man, the

silent, screened-off figure of the bank robber and murderer Jack House. His disturbing and enigmatic presence triggers the release of the other men's repressed anxieties and guilts, forcing the contradictions in their most basic assumptions and allegiances into the open. The mentalities of the various characters are refracted through the prism of House's presence and revealingly split into their component preconceptions about work, status, property, justice, and the value and purpose of human life. Berger's elliptical, disjunctive structuring of the text, his subliminal surprises of elision and juxtaposition, and his recurrent qualitative shifts in narrative technique all work likewise to frame and defamiliarise the presupposed, and dislocate the reader into fresh critical penetrations of the rationale of his society. This process climaxes in a phantasmagoric sequence conveying the book's core exposition of the hypocritical guile with which the system highlights the individual 'official' criminal the better to distract from its own *institutionalised* criminal barbarity of wholesale exploitation and, indeed, mass murder through deliberate warfare and starvation: in the thief and the murderer, the novel suggests, society beholds not the deviant exception but the very embodiment and mirror image of its own inhuman rule.

Corker's Freedom undertakes to anatomise the painfully divided self produced by bourgeois society: the dreaming private subject striving ceaselessly to pierce the reified shell of public identity. The novel pursues Corker, the pathetic owner of a drab employment agency in Clapham, through the long bathetic day in which his inarticulate yearnings press irresistibly at last up into the light, and he makes his frustrated fleeting dash for an anyway trite and factitious version of liberty.

Berger certainly succeeds in baring the mutilating contradictions between the romantic dreams of the exotic and the inescapably tawdry reality, between the desired and the socially permissible. The text itself is visually laid out and sub-headlined in such a way as to display graphically the gulf dividing what Corker really knows from what he lets himself think, and what he actually says and does from what he would like to say and do. But these critical juxtapositions of the subjunctive and the indicative, proceeding through the full anticlimactic length of the narrative without relief or significant modulation, swiftly become stultifyingly routine and mechanical. They exhaust their impact long before the cryptically whimsical closure of the book, which leaves one merely stranded and dejected, wryly smothering as it does any nascent faith one might have had in the dynamic human capacity to burst through

after all into a new universe of selfhood and relationship beyond
the accustomed definitions and accommodations.

Berger's next and best-known novel, *G.* (1972), undertakes a
much more powerful, epic investigation of the process whereby a
qualitatively different order of being evolves and erupts within the
ossified dominant structure of social relations. It is a strikingly
original though difficult text, an experimentally transfigured
historical novel of extreme intellectual and imaginative virtuosity,
vibrant with illuminations. What it seeks to project is nothing less
than the first great liberating surge of energy towards social and
sexual renewal galvanising Europe at the dawn of this century, as
the history of class society entered its final, irrevocable phase of
'vast historical changes . . . changes which would transform social
and private life and death in Europe', convulsing it in what has
indeed become 'the struggle unto death against what is'.[24]

This revolutionising moment in which the twentieth century first
drew breath is figured through the enigmatic protagonist G.,
whose brief life spans the period from the late 1880s to World
War I. G. is the bastard love-child of a wealthy Livornese
merchant and his emancipated Anglo-American mistress, and
throughout the book he serves above all as the intense embodiment of absolute sexual desire, the modern incarnation of
Don Juan, of the libidinal principle itself. As such he is susceptible
of strategic amplification into a paradigm of desire in general,
becoming in fact the symbolically condensed essence of all the
interrelated forms of awakened appetency electrifying Europe.
Recurrently encountered at various exemplary scenes and instances—amidst the insurgent populace at Milan or Trieste; with
working-class and bourgeois women on the threshold of emancipation; at Chavez's first flight over the Alps—G. acquires increasingly profound resonance as the mobile internal index of all
the tumescent propensities and as yet unstructured aspirations—
social, political, sexual and technological—forcing their way out
through the old, superseded formations.

This scenario forms the matrix for the text's essentially twofold
mode of composition. On the one hand there is the flow of
characteristically incisive, discursive passages expounding the
meaning of madness, the situation of women, the nature of time;
theorising on the significance of the sex act, of crowds, of aging
and of writing itself. But at the same time the text is equally
disposed throughout to disperse and compact itself into suggestive
but opaque sensuous immediacies, mesmerised by the intracta-
bility of the irreducibly particular. And in fact it's precisely this

constitutional fragmentation of itself into typographically discrete passages of *either* expository abstraction *or* intensely particular concretion—its refusal of the special task of fiction: to seize the general process in and through the flux of the particular—that suggests something deeply problematic about the novel, about the undialectical nature of Berger's vision and fictive method, which a full account would have to consider. Here there is only space to underline Berger's own awareness of expressing in *G.* 'little sense of unfolding time. The relations which I perceive between things— and these often include casual and historical relations—tend to form in my mind a complex synchronic pattern. I see fields where others see chapters. . . . I write in the spirit of a geometrician.'[25] Fine, we may say; but there's a price to pay for sacrificing the powers of realist narration to these more oblique and elliptical strategies of aesthetic cognition. *G.* thus shatters and finally freezes reality into a static mosaic configuration of discontiguous *aperçus*, isolated tableaux and scattered, internally vibrating epiphanies, evacuating in the process all real historical sense of continuous human becoming, of the ceaseless momentum of change.

This whole hypostatising tendency is superbly transcended, however, in *Pig Earth* (1979), which dynamically reintegrates the general and the particular to generate an outstanding collection of stories achieving full fictive communication through just that sensuously immediate 'controlled liberation of intuition' advocated in *A Painter Of Our Time*.[26] *Pig Earth* is the first in a three-volume project entitled *Into Their Labours*, which aims to trace in both fiction and essay form the meaning of the threat of historical elimination faced by the peasantries of the world.

Inspired by the life and history of the small French peasant community in which he has recently been living and working, Berger narrates a haunting series of 'mystery stories' which, like the villagers' own vital gossip and anecdote, 'testify to the always slightly surprising range of the possible' concealed within everyday village experience, and which themselves seek to contribute to that 'continuous communal portrait'[27] of itself on which the peasant community is continually engaged in the endeavour to define its own changing identity and purpose. Through the tales Berger renders articulate the rich subjectivity of the labouring peasantry, whose perspective and experience, despite their still constituting the mass of the world's population, have hitherto been confined almost wholly to the mere exotic margins and background 'local colour' of mainstream bourgeois fiction.

To restore that perspective and experience effectively to the foreground Berger, in a significant new departure in his writing, turns to reappropriate and yet wonderfully transform the possibilities of popular realist narrative, the whole sequence culminating indeed in the remarkable long story 'The Three Lives of Lucie Cabrol', which exploits and extends in its own unique way that utopian vein of 'magic realism' so memorably mined by the novels of García Márquez. Not the least virtue of this redevelopment of popular realism, moreover, is the way it enables Berger to grasp the dialectic of unremitting labour and tenacious desire at the heart of peasant life with a sensuous depth and penetrative immediacy scarcely equalled in English since Hardy. And what finally crystallises out of these stories, as with Hardy, is a bracing vision of the collective strength and endurance in work and love of people living together, and of the communal impulse to push through and on beyond all the particular divisions, frustrations and defeats: to survive.

Survival, in fact, in Berger's view, is the essential wisdom which the peasant experience can, and perhaps must, teach us in our struggle to defend and develop socialism. As he observes in the afterword to the volume:

The forces which in most parts of the world are today eliminating or destroying the peasantry, represent the contradiction of most of the hopes once contained in the principle of historical progress . . . if one looks at the likely future course of world history, envisaging either the further extension and consolidation of corporate capitalism in all its brutalism, or a prolonged, uneven struggle waged against it, a struggle whose victory is not certain, the peasant experience of survival may well be better adapted to this long and harsh perspective than the continually reformed, disappointed, impatient progressive hope of an ultimate victory.[28]

It is then a grimly realistic, though in the end tough and resilient vision which the narratives of *Pig Earth* extend. But it is precisely this kind of impassioned imaginative counselling in the hard truths and real options of our condition, and just such a revival of our faith in the intransigent desire and power of the human community finally to realize itself in history—despite everything; however long it takes—that we now more than ever need socialist fiction to provide.

NOTES

1 John Berger, *A Painter Of Our Time* (London, 1958), p. 182.
2 Quoted by Viktor Schklowsky, *Von der Ungleichheit des Ähnlichen in der Kunst* (Munich, 1973), p. 172 (my translation).
3 E. P. Thompson, *William Morris: Romantic to Revolutionary*, second revised edition (London, 1977), p. 806.
4 *John and Mary* (London, 1966), p. 191.
5 *Strangers* (London, 1974), pp. 107, 125.
6 *Ibid*, p. 31.
7 *Today The Struggle* (London, 1978), pp. 390–1.
8 *Ibid.*, p. 490.
9 Georg Lukács, 'Narrate or Describe?', in *Writer and Critic* (London, 1978), pp. 139, 144.
10 *Nobody's Fault* (London, 1977), p. 198.
11 Raymond Williams, *Politics and Letters. Interviews with New Left Review* (London, 1979), pp. 292–3.
12 *Border Country* (London, 1960), p. 22.
13 *Ibid.*, p. 225.
14 *Second Generation* (London, 1964), p. 9.
15 *Ibid.*, p. 38.
16 *Ibid.*, pp. 338–40.
17 *The Fight For Manod* (London, 1979), pp. 98–9, 186.
18 *The Volunteers* (London, 1978), p. 207.
19 Berger, *op. cit.* pp. 178, 75, 180.
20 *Ibid.*, p. 78.
21 *Ibid.*, p. 109.
22 *Ibid.*, p. 144.
23 *Ibid.*, p. 93.
24 *G.* (London, 1972), pp. 239, 80.
25 *Ibid.*, p. 137.
26 *A Painter Of Our Time*, p. 151.
27 *Pig Earth* (London, 1979), pp. 8, 11.
28 *Ibid.*, pp. 212–13.

INDEX